MARTI

APOSTLE OF FREEDOM

MARTI

APOSTLE OF FREEDOM

By JORGE MAÑACH

Translated from the Spanish
By COLEY TAYLOR

With a Preface by GABRIELA MISTRAL

THE DEVIN-ADAIR CO.
NEW YORK · 1950

The title-page drawing, probably the first sketch of Cuba published, is taken from Columbus's EPISTOLA, *1494. Courtesy of the Hispanic Society of America.*

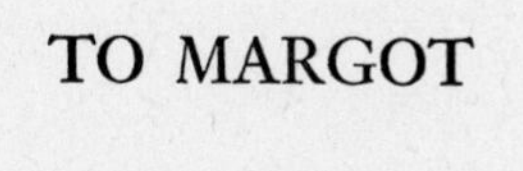

TO MARGOT

ACKNOWLEDGMENTS

MANY are the people to whom I owe a debt of gratitude—one I am most happy to acknowledge—for helping me in one way or another with this book. First is Señora Amelia Martí, sister of the Apostle of Freedom, who generously supplied me with a good part of the unpublished data which form the basis for my portrayal of Martí's family life in childhood and youth in Mexico. I have likewise enjoyed the coöperation of many others who have been very helpful, among them don Federico Edelmann, for whom I cherish the fondest memory; don Juan Gualberto Gómez; Dr. José R. Álvarez; Señora Blanca Z. de Baralt and the widows of the Revolutionary leaders Carillo, Peláez, Trujillo and Guerra. I am grateful for the help given me by Generals Loynaz del Castillo, Eusebio Hernández and Pedro Betancourt, and to don Ruperto Pedroso.

In matters of documentation I wish to acknowledge the assistance of Dr. Francisco de Paula Coronado, Director of the Biblioteca Nacional de Cuba; of Camilo Carrancá y Trujillo, of Mexico, and of Drs. Benigno Sousa, Emilio Roig de Leuchsenring and Carlos Azcárate for access to important documents either unpublished or all but forgotten. And for their more general assistance I wish to thank don Arturo R. de Carricarte and don Félix Lizaso, without whose scholarly edition of the *Letters of Martí* (Havana, 1930) this biographical work of mine would have been almost impossibly more difficult to do. I want to thank don José Sicre for permitting me to use as a frontispiece a reproduction of his bust of Martí, so deservedly famous a portrait of Cuba's liberating genius.

And, last but by no means least, I want to express my appreciation and thanks to our great American poet, Gabriela Mistral, for her gracious Preface to this work. She has done me an honor I could scarcely hope to deserve or to expect.

J.M.

Table of Contents

List of Illustrations

The Frederic Remington drawings are from CUBA IN WAR TIME, *by Richard Harding Davis, New York, 1897. The Grover Flint drawings are from* MARCHING WITH GÓMEZ, *by Grover Flint, Boston, 1898. The drawings of Generals Gómez and Maceo are from* THE STORY OF CUBA, *by Murat Halstead, New York, 1897.*

ON JORGE MAÑACH

JORGE MAÑACH belongs to the highest order of literary knighthood, and I like to refer to him as one of three who, having been born in the Caribbean region of the extinct Spanish empire, resemble the *caballeros* painted by El Greco. It is both his spiritual and his physical mien that I think of—for I presume the soul, too, has its substance.

There is in him the restraint we imagine in the living model portrayed by the Greek-Italian-Iberian painter: no dramatic overflow, but rather a serenity laid over his figure in a hand which is sensitive yet devoid of nervousness. Only in the very center of the eyes—where no one can feign—can one see the fervor of every grandchild of Spain.

Jorge Mañach's friends always find great pleasure in those two kinds of pulchritude that run through his person and his words. "Mañach's instrument of expression"—writes the essayist Concha Meléndez—"is manly, elegant, and possessed of a certain Castilian austerity." The Castilian quality in this Cuban is tempered, however, by a Catalonian strain, and this admixture is fairly evident both in his behavior and his writing, which are never feverish.

There is still another complication in Mañach's personality: he is Harvard bred. I suspect that, too, accounts for a certain coolness which assists him in any bad tropical emergency and helps him against any temptation to overheat his texts.

Like every Cuban, Mañach could only be a shield-bearer for Martí. Both a great honor and a trying responsibility arise therefrom, for ten or more biographies of the Cuban Liberator have now been written. Mañach's was the first in time;

and it was quite a test to handle the life of a beloved man on whom so much eulogy had already been written. But Mañach's *Martí* continues to be the outstanding choice of the best critics and the public as well—a fact which explains why it is now in its fourth Spanish printing.

The scholar from Harvard is possessed of certain graces which are far from common amongst romantic biographers. Never wordy, Mañach seeks *the* word. He belongs to the small family of those who are masculinely temperate in expression. On the other hand, while his prose preserves the constant objectivity which the historical genre requires, it is not wanting in that subjective warmth which can always be expected from subtle biographers. And he is careful not to omit anything essential in a life so replete with travail and so complex, both inwardly and outwardly, as Martí's was.

We are happy that the North American reader, usually indifferent toward Latin American letters, and even frigid toward the neighbors with whom he shares the Caribbean, should now be given this opportunity to know us through a hero-interpreter who is a subtle essayist also and a journalist of high rank. The United States is in debt to Martí. It owes him, as a matter of justice, a celebration of his deeds; for in *El Apóstol* there was a conciliator of peoples; he wrote the best papers on American life that have ever been written in our South, both in literary quality and in his concern for uniting what is disunited and opposed. And what chronicles they were! Whether it be a cattle exhibition in New York or Whitman the patriarch, Martí enjoys them and portrays them in the most beautifully descriptive language we have yet encountered.

Martí is a bewitcher of souls. He delights the child in his books for children; he inflames youth and strengthens the aged. This is why he lives, never losing an inch of the territory of his kingdom.

There have always been militant writers in our literature who fought, at first, for independence; later on, against despotism; nowadays, in the bitter struggle for social justice. But such battling is apt to be of the safer kind—one's pen, not one's life, is risked. Because that was not the case with José Martí, he commands an admiration warmed with genuine love. This man, in his own time the foremost prose-writer in Latin America, sprang into combat like any soldier, not realizing the quality of his own substance, or, if he was aware of it, giving it as if it were merely powder, fit only to make an additional cartridge for the battle.

In this book, not at all ponderous, but charged with the kind of electricity we call "action," you will find the achievements of the Antillean who divided himself like a pomegranate into two uneven halves—the literary and the civic. In both, Martí reveals himself in that pure crimson of strength and blood—a fruit fully matured and, therefore, incarnadine.

In the Yosemite Valley, which I have recently visited, there is a small body of water which feigns calmness but contains a certain slight shimmer. Some call it "the mirror"; others, "the perfect reflection." Both names adequately describe the short watery expanse, which neither deforms nor exaggerates the image of its master—a rock called "half dome"—which the filial water tirelessly receives and reflects.

So with our Jorge Mañach. His eye—which can be traced back to the Mediterranean, a dispassionate sea—delivers the image of his mother-stone as faithfully as the California lake. He too, like the water, is a sensitive skin; he feels his subject, is enamored of his creation, but does not change it—rather, he reflects it with a calm fervor which again reminds me of El Greco's Castilian gentleman.

This contemporary historian has an advantage over his dead-cold professional grandfathers in that he can, through his own personality, evoke characters who really live and breathe; he does not create literary stuffed owls. Which is as it should be. One must treat living matter *livingly* or let it alone.

Out of this biographer's understanding mind the subject issues without interference into writing, and the result of this technique is a style of delicate, transparent and throbbing nerve tissue, like the one you see in X-ray photographs. "Mañach seizes the most hidden vibration, the undiscovered flavor, the unsuspected reason," says Díez Canedo, the late Spanish critic, about our historian. As a journalist, his essays educate the reader into his way—so unusual in Spanish America—of being "human" without distortion and without saccharine romanticism.

In the noble persons and writers who are Alfonso Reyes, Sanín Cano, Vaz Ferreira, Henríquez Ureña, and Jorge Mañach—and in others who are not so well known—a new Latin-American classicism is rising, to our good fortune. The nineteenth century classicism of Montalvo, Bello and Ricardo Palma was something different. Between the two there is a cut as deep-hewn as those the stone-cutter makes in the granite blocks for his stairway. To each age its own: the something we call Time has changed, and the new artisans bring to their tasks such different strengths and ways of working that they seem to come from another planet.

Gabriela Mistral

Los Angeles, California

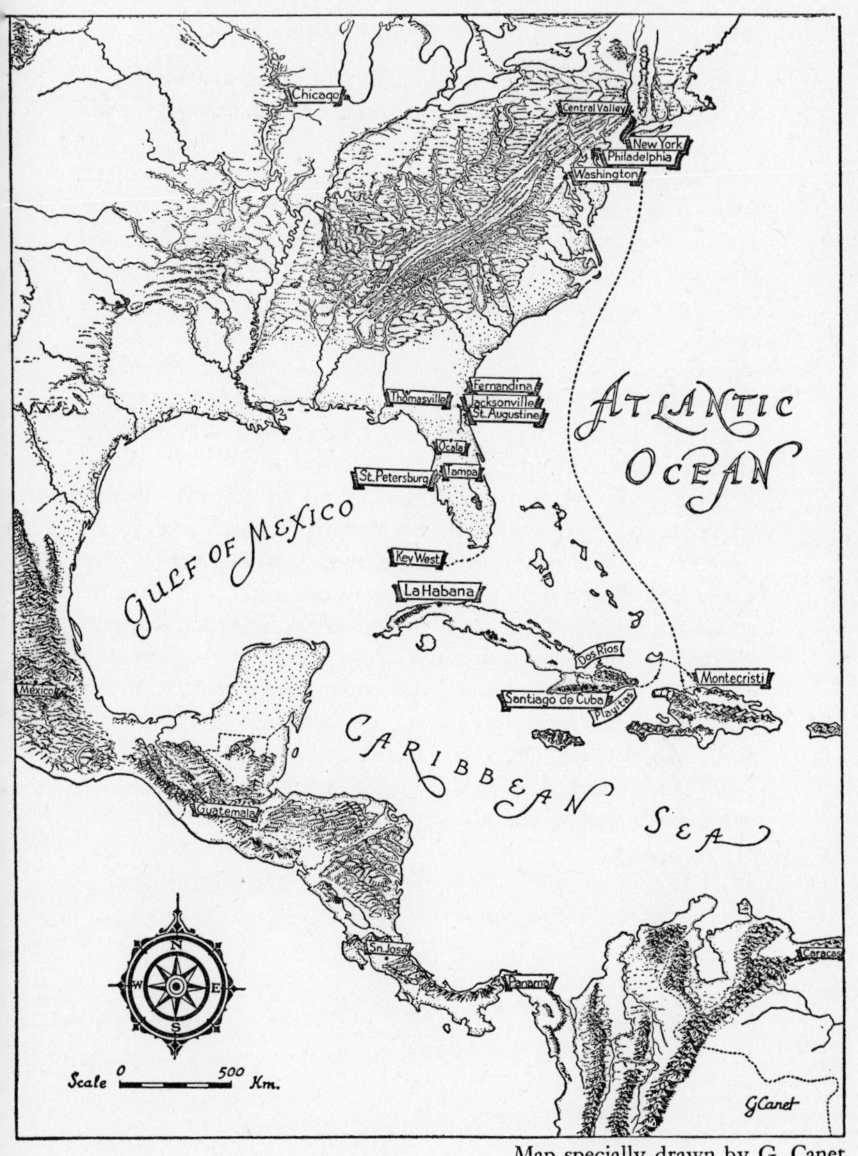

Map specially drawn by G. Canet

MARTÍ'S JOURNEYINGS IN THE AMERICAS

MARTI

APOSTLE OF FREEDOM

Chapter One

PARENTS

IN THOSE DAYS—half-way through the Nineteenth Century—Spain found it necessary to maintain a strong garrison in her "ever most loyal" island of Cuba. Yellow fever, fairly harmless to natives of the tropics, attacked Spanish flesh with obvious partiality, decimating the healthiest of battalions. Other enemies, however, worried the Home Government far more: Geography and a watchful colonial policy had not been able to keep Cuba entirely out of the libertarian currents of the time. Following the pattern of victorious revolutions on the Continent, signs of turbulence had long been noticeable in the Island. Lodges and other secret societies, boiling with revolutionary passions and quotations from Bolívar, had already forged several conspiracies, one of them, at least, designed to tempt the great Liberator himself. Native Cubans had been particularly bitter ever since Spain had excluded the Island from constitutional representation in the Cortes, in 1836. Some of them—from exile—had even gone so far as to talk of independence.

As if this were not enough, Spain was also aware that her colony's neighbor to the North harbored covetous designs on the Island. The enormous chunk recently torn out of Mexico had whetted the Yankee appetite for territory. Cuba looked like a strong addition to the slave-holding southern states, and some of the brashest politicians had already intimated that sooner or later the Island would pass to the United States. Now that the Revolution of '48 had emancipated the slaves in the French colonies, a like gesture was to be expected from quixotic Spain—and in Cuba many Creole slaveholders—and Spaniards, even—were considering annexation to the United States as a way of fending off this possible contamination of liberalism. Some Cubans considered annexation as the only practical way of winning freedom from Spain; or as bait to attract the Yankee and thus, by a shrewd move, to further the cause of independence. The fact is that while these ideas were maturing no objection was made in the United States when enthusiastically patriotic Cubans were plotting conspiracies in New York and planning invasions from New Orleans. One such, composed of Cuban troops with North American officers under the command of the "traitor" Narciso López, had invaded the Island in May. It was defeated; but the invaders had enjoyed the thrill of seeing their barred flag with a single star wave for a few hours over Cárdenas.

When, at the close of 1850, General Concha took charge of the Island government, "with powers of a siege commander," he did not conceal his fears from Madrid and ordered Spain to send out four battalions of infantry, four cavalry squadrons and one battery of artillery.

With this artillery battery came Sergeant Mariano Martí, a robust Valencian of no mean stature, his somewhat stern features set off by a small goatee. As a boy he had become hardened under the hot sun of the countryside, carrying bales of hemp for his father's cordage shop. The army draft took him away from the rope-braiding bench, and his experience with coarse fibers eased him into an apprenticeship to the barracks tailor—an assignment much too tame, doubtless, for a young man rough in manner and with a commanding air. When his company was about to be transferred to Cuba, these traits natural to the Valencian had already made him a corporal. The actual transfer gave him a promotion to the next higher grade as compensation for the dangers of America.

In less than two years after his arrival Sergeant Martí had progressed so far with his "naturalization" that he spent his Sundays enjoying the dances at the Escauriza and the Café de la Bola. In his spotless dress uniform of white drill, and with his military bearing, he did not cut a bad figure among the sedately moving crinolines. These dances were attended by the respectable young women of business and artisan families, and a keen observer would have noticed in the color schemes of the girls' dresses and finery a certain preference for blue and deep scarlet, the colors of the flag of Narciso López.

At these dances the Sergeant met a rather pretty, slender, "wasp-waisted" girl of twenty with jet-black curls and a charm vaguely Chinese in her high cheekbones and gently slanting eyes—one of which, alas, was slightly clouded. But to the soldier this must have seemed like a sweet spring cloud, for during the grand promenades, do-se-do's, and swing-your-partners a romance was budding that bloomed in marriage a few months later. Leonor Pérez was not a bad match. Although her family had been fairly well to do in Santa Cruz de Tenerife, her father had resolved to come to Cuba to better his fortune—which he had done by winning the lottery promptly on his arrival.

The newlyweds installed themselves in a modest little house in Paula Street, overlooking the harbor. There, in the early morning of January 28, 1853, a son was born. The chaplain of the sergeant's regiment christened the boy José Julián.

Parade-ground soldiers were not needed in Cuba; only men of fiber could cope with the restless Creoles. Mariano Martí was of this breed. Although not overburdened with intelligence or education—he and his nine brothers and sisters had scarcely known any other school than their father's cordage shop—he was well endowed with certain elementary military qualities: loyalty, energy, presence, and an almost chip-on-the-shoulder aggressiveness. So, it was not surprising that in February, 1855, when Cuba was declared in a state of siege and blockade, and volunteer militia were being raised, Martí was breveted to the rank of second lieutenant.

In reality, however, his wishes were quite otherwise. The rough soldier had his soft side, like any young man, and he would have preferred to stay at home quietly with his wife and youngsters. To General Concha, however, "fingers were legions"; as if the expeditionary preparations constantly being made by Cubans in the United States were not troubles enough, the General had just had to quench with blood a local uprising in which one of his cronies was most surprisingly implicated—the wealthy Catalan, don Ramón Pintó, an almost daily visitor in the General's circle. Such things had made Concha very suspicious. All the precautions and readying of forces seemed to him all too little. And as the enlistment of volunteers for the defense of the cities increased enough for him to dispose his regulars more freely, he submitted them to ceaseless drill and practice maneuvers, much to the disgust of Lieutenant Martí, in whom the satisfactions of promotion had not outweighed the desire for a sedentary life—a desire all the more cherished with his added years and children. To the first-born had been added a girl, Leonor, who had promptly become her father's darling, as such sprigs of femininity usually do.

A day came when the lieutenant had had enough. On getting back, worn out, from tactical maneuvers in the Matanzas country, he announced to his wife that he was asking for his discharge from the army.

This was a bold step. Months of lean living—almost poverty—followed. After a year of liberty, somewhat cured of his hearthstone longings, Martí applied for a good berth in the Carabineer Corps, doubtless because this militia group would permit something of domestic life. When his application was turned down, he looked around for some other job more or less military and not too demanding. It occurred to him that joining the police might not be a bad idea. The captain-general had just brought about a reform of the Corps, providing for a decent wage to members of the force so they would not have to live, as they formerly had, from graft squeezed out of shopkeepers, freed slaves and prostitutes. When the commissioner was informed that Mariano Martí y Navarro "enjoyed" good conduct and was physically fit and that "there was nothing against him," he appointed him warden of the Templete quarter.

What winds of good fortune blew upon the warden that winter of '56-'57? In May he asked for a leave of absence, alleging that he "was ill and desirous of going to the Peninsula to seek a cure." A voyage to Spain in those days was no casual undertaking, especially for a police warden burdened with a wife and three children. Perhaps a lottery prize had fallen to the family again, or perhaps his ailing father-in-law had died. We know only that Martí had no better use for his money than to spend it on a trip to Valencia, his wife and family with him, to visit his aged father, who had just married again.

The sojourn in Spain was brief. Doña Leonor had a hard time there. She suffered from chilblains in her hands, gave birth to another girl, and it is possible that she did not find her husband's family congenial. All in all, she was homesick for the comforts of Havana. As soon as they returned don Mariano asked to be reinstated on the police force. His "six years, six months and ten days' active service in the honorable career of His Majesty's Army" must have weighed heavily, for his request was again favorably received and he was appointed warden of the Santa Clara district.

Don Mariano liked this old, walled part of town. It did not have the snobbish, palatial atmosphere of the Templete section, but was lively, pleasant and "neighborly." Commerce and shipping had not yet entirely displaced gentility. In many cases an archway piled high with sacks partly concealed the entrance to a fine house. Traders did not blush for their wealth: The newly-rich wholesaler might boast of a title of nobility, a box at the Tacón Theatre and a Creole son—who would, like as not, grow up to be a rebel. The district had the delightful tang of the ocean and exotic goods from overseas. Its streets were thronged with sailors, Negro women with headdresses of shrieking colors, horse-and-buggy turnouts, and lawyers in top-hats and alpaca frock coats—and it boasted of a public school to which don Mariano was already thinking of sending his son; the boy was now going on seven and insatiably curious about everything.

Soon, however, the Valencian's star began to cloud over, and so did his disposition. He had passed forty. Asthma had not yet kept him from his regular, tough patrol duty, armed with nightstick and a brace of pistols, through the narrow, awning-shaded streets; but when he had to stop a market brawl or chase a trouble-maker, don Mariano grew short-winded and took things a little too easy.

Moreover, as an ex-soldier he had a speedy way of settling things which was not always in line with the refinements of legal procedure. The commissioner called him down one day for having too casually prepared a complaint, and for not having secured the evidence on an occasion when a freed slave had stolen some champagne—six cases of it, no less. Another time, when the coachman of a rich family was poisoned, he had neglected to take down the man's deposition, and the chief of police felt it necessary to inform the governor that "while the records of this department contain no evidence to impeach the conduct of the aforementioned Warden of Santa Clara, it is nonetheless true that his limited capacity and small aptitude are shown in the present instance and in previous ones."

His greatest mistake, however—because of the rank of the injured party—was made by the unhappy policeman a month later on the occasion of a traffic snarl involving a truckman's cart and the carriage of a lady of quality. The warden, required to decide who had the right of way, acted—according to the lady's complaint—"in a manner not at all befitting his office and Spanish courtesy" and, further: "realizing that it was impossible to carry out the truckman's idea, which was to back up the horse and carriage of the plaintiff, he fell upon it savagely, club in hand, and rained upon the poor animal such furious blows that, at last terrified by the force of this kind of persuasion, the horse did back up, but to the great risk of bystanders, to the plaintiff herself, and not without damaging the box of the carriage."

The dispute involved such serious social considerations and "principles of justice and morality" that the governor could not help looking into it, especially since the complaint was signed by one who subscribed herself Doña Adelaide de Villalonga, and who—to judge by the quarrelsome and high-flown tenor of the complaint—must be the touchiest sort of Creole aristocrat. Several months earlier, General Concha had been relieved of his command and had been succeeded by General Serrano, whose wife was a Creole; he had initiated a policy of catering to the sensitive aristocracy of the country. Don Mariano was relieved of duty, and his subsequent hope for a precinct captaincy was frustrated by official memory of this mischance and "other shortcomings no less to be considered . . . which appear not to have been intentional, but rather the result of limited capacities and a lack of good manners. . . . Otherwise," the report piously added, Martí "enjoys a reputation as an honorable man, and the undersigned considers him such."

His retirement aggravated don Mariano's testiness considerably, as well as it did the condition of his family, which had barely begun to recover from the extravagance of the trip to Spain. The Valencian as a matter of habit had always kept himself well-groomed, and now it shamed and irritated him to come home at the end of the day with his clothes constantly a little more the worse for wear as he tramped all over Havana looking for work. The little house rang with impassioned soliloquies relieving his pent-up feelings over insults and affronts, and if prying neighbors had been able to look as well as listen, they would have seen doña Leonor roughly dandling the baby while her husband stormily strode up and down the dining-room unaware of the flies and the dancing, rainbow-colored patches of light reflected by the crystal prisms of the hanging lamp.

At such times, if the boy had returned from school, he would go to his mother and caress her with a shy seriousness. José was barely seven, delicate and thin, his head a little large for the rest of him. Without saying anything, he would go over and sit down in the patio doorway, under the lovely fanlight, and pretend to write on his slate.

These scenes repeated themselves for weeks—months. There were days when the atmosphere cleared somewhat. Don Mariano, who was using all the means of influence he had, would come home with a promise of work or some hope given him by his friend Arazoza. On occasion there was something more concrete: a commission earned at a sale of cloth in the Old Quarter, or at a slave auction.

During the sugar-harvest, at least, things were bound to pick up. The father took trips to the interior of the Island—to the eastern tobacco region of Vuelta de Abajo, to Las Villas, in central Cuba. Scorning the idea of school, he frequently took his son with him so that he would learn something useful. On the slow train journeys or, more frequently, "riding the horse's tail" behind his father on some old nag, the boy would ask endless questions about everything he saw. Sometimes don Mariano was curt; at other times he would pinch the boy's chin with rough affection.

One spring afternoon Pepe[1] came home, completely drenched by a heavy May shower, afraid of the inevitable scolding. As he came in he saw his father, shoulders filling the patio doorway, watching the raindrops splashing in mad brilliance on the flagstones. Doña Leonor was very busy picking things up and packing them in bundles. His father's voice was gaily greeting the rain: "*Agua! Agua! que se quema la fragua!* (Water! Water! the forge is on fire!)"

Doña Leonor informed the boy, in a low voice scarcely audible, that his father had just been appointed circuit captain out in Hanábana. "And you have to go help him, sonny, now that it's vacation."

The circuit captain did not have much to do in Hanábana—a stretch of sugarcane country in the jurisdiction of Matanzas, not exactly a setting for dramatic police work: a zone of small cattle farms, plantations and peaceable folk. His work boiled down to making the presence of armed authority obvious, in attending the Sunday cockfights as a hint to keep hotheads from starting any arguments, and in stopping brawls born of *guateque*, or rural dances, and rot-gut liquor.

However, there was plenty of paperwork for the captain. Since Concha's time the keeping of complete and detailed official reports had been the rule in Cuba, in line with the most illustrious Peninsular tradition. Although don Mariano was, as we know, not addicted to such formalities, he had learned his lesson—and Pepe had an excellent handwriting.

He had, as a matter of fact, just completed his elementary schooling. In the little district school his punishments had never been more than a box on the ear—a real immunity given to reward his precocious gift for reciting odes for May

[1] Spanish for "Joe."

2nd, the Spanish resistance against Napoleon, poems by Tula Avellaneda in the days when the Cuban poet was honored at the Tacón and quatrains lauding her were the fashion. Pepe was the student the teacher always called upon, in a casual way, to recite whenever some inspecting member of the Economic Society dropped in the classroom unexpectedly. There was nothing more for him to learn at that school, and doña Leonor hoped that in the fall, God willing, the boy would go to San Anacleto, the private school so highly recommended.

Vacation, however, came to an end and the captain showed no sign of giving up his secretary. Doña Leonor, who had stayed on in Havana, wrote long letters, badly spelled, on the necessity of education. Don Mariano cared little for the opinions of women: somebody had to take care of *him*, alone there in the savannah, when he had his attacks of asthma, or in case he met with an accident, like that time he fell during the flood, a fall that left him with a lame leg.

Pepe was neutral, and it must be admitted that he did not appear to be very homesick for the city. He wrote to his mother:

> ". . . all my time is spent taking care of my horse and he is getting as fat as a pig; today I am breaking him to the bridle so that he will drive nicely. Every afternoon I mount and ride him a while. He grows more spirited every day. I also have something else to amuse me and help pass the time—a game cock that Don Lucas de Sotolongo gave me. He is very handsome and Papa takes a lot of care of him. Papa is looking for someone to cut his comb and train him for me for the cockfights this year, and says that he is a cock worth his weight in gold."

On his fat horse Pepe frequently rode all over the countryside with his father. At night on the veranda at police headquarters, while his father silently smoked a home-made cigar of rolled tobacco leaf, the lad, stretched out on his bench, studied the brilliant, shimmering beauty of the starry skies. The palm trees kept watch over the dark landscape, gently nodding their fronds. Sometimes at night the rough, rhythmic *psst* of the crickets in the savannah excited him to a high pitch: it was almost an ecstasy, almost like a call—a call from the land.

At Christmas time the captain obtained a furlough to spend Christmas Eve in Havana. He and Pepe arrived laden with rum and raw sugar. Doña Leonor played upon the good-natured spirit of the holiday season to persuade her husband to leave Pepe behind in the capital and register him at San Anacleto. He would soon be ten years old.

The months spent in the wild country, far from his mother's apron strings and given to manly tasks and men's ways, had greatly stimulated his natural independence. The headmaster of San Anacleto, don Rafael Sixto Casado, was surprised by the frank steady gaze and forthright attitude of the poorly-dressed boy who stood before his desk, supplementing in well-chosen words the mother's nervous, halting introduction, so confident that he could make up for the three months lost.

As it turned out, in barely a month José Julián Martí had outdistanced the leading pupils in each of his classes. At first such speed earned for him the hostility of his classmates, but he gradually acquired the art of winning them over. In class he found subtle ways of atoning for his excellences: among them, that of being very generous with secret promptings. At recess he displayed a real extravagance of initiative in games. Little by little the antagonism of his schoolfellows wore off.

The boy who was most attached to him was Fermín Valdés, a lad approximately his own age, tall and pop-eyed. Since Fermín came of a rich family, Pepe, always a little self-conscious about his shabby clothes, had kept away from him. But Fermín had openly showed his desire to break down that aloofness. He had done many little favors for Pepe, and over and over again offered him tidbits from his lunch. In the end they became fast friends.

Every afternoon they left school together, squired by the Negro slave who called for Fermín. They went to play on the flat roof of Fermín's house, or to the Campo de Marte where they could watch the soldiers drill and sometimes they strolled to the docks to look at the latest Confederate ships to get through the Union blockade. The ups and downs of the Civil War in the United States stirred them with intense excitement, especially since Fermín was a Confederate and Pepe—won over by *Uncle Tom's Cabin*—was an Abolitionist, and one so devoted that he was struck dumb with grief when the news of Lincoln's assassination came, and wept bitterly.

In the autumn don Mariano insisted that his son, judging by the fuss his teachers made over him, already knew enough and did not need to return to San Anacleto. Doña Leonor protested in vain although she pointed out that the boy's godfather, Arazoza, was paying the tuition fees. The captain arrived suddenly in Havana one day to take Pepe off with him to the country. The boy secretly put some books in his travelling bag.

But even don Mariano's harshness had in it an open integrity that was of service to the boy. Because the captain refused to overlook the secret smuggling of Negroes, a matter in which the lieutenant governor was interested, that worthy asked for Martí's dismissal and got it instantly, replacing him with don Mariano's predecessor, a more pliable fellow. Don Mariano was footloose again. One of his wandering jaunts looking for work took him to British Honduras, and Pepe with him.

Years later, on revisiting that country, José Martí was to

Grover Flint

CUBAN PLANTATION BEFORE AND AFTER A VISITATION BY SPANISH TROOPS AND VOLUNTEERS discover that reality differed from his memory of that first contact with a foreign land and strange customs: imaginative impressions of forests, of Indians silent and barefoot, of a patriarchal colony in which work was a sacrament. Recollections, indeed, of a sinless world.

Chapter Two

MENTOR

UPON RETURNING from that trip, don Mariano agreed to allow Arazoza, his crony and the lad's conscientious godfather, to advance Pepe's well-being by presenting him to don Rafael María Mendive, Arazoza's kinsman, who had just been appointed director of the Municipal High School for Boys.

Mendive was a generous man, with a poet's sensitivity of spirit. Contemporary Spanish letters did not have—according to the critic Martínez Villergas—another who could surpass him "in melody of feeling." Nevertheless, it had been necessary for Count de Pozos Dulces—who was then shaping reformist opinion in *El Siglo* [The Century]—to defend Mendive from the attacks of various jealous hack writers who seemed to think it was scandalous to turn over to a poet the administration of a school. The count had opposed them by pointing out that "in all stages of teaching, but particularly with early adolescents, the teacher needs to draw upon many qualities, among them sensitivity, which plays the greatest part."

At twelve years of age, Pepe was susceptible to such qualities. He was of a thoughtful nature, impressionable and extremely sensitive. At the school he was in the rather equivocal position of the poor but worthy scholarship student who was at once pupil, monitor and chore-boy. Don Rafael soon came to have a fatherly affection for the pale youngster who blushed whenever he made a mistake and was helplessly confused by a disapproving glance or harsh word. There were, however, very few of these, for Mendive had learned the delicate art of developing the child mind from his model, the unforgettable José de la Luz.[1] His seriousness was tender; his firmness, kindly. Teaching at his school was friendly and informal. His daughters whispered to each other and did their embroidery under the salon chandelier while don Rafael, dressed in white drill, lectured on history, underlining emphatically the great moments of civic integrity in the world's past eras, from the Gracchi to Bolívar.

Although publicly an advocate of reform, Mendive, like all the Cuban intellectuals of the day, was devoted to ideas of independence. There was no one unaware of the fact that from his pen had come certain satirical, patriotically Creole sonnets which were secretly passed around from one to another. Years later, one of his favorite pupils preferred to remember him "alone, walking up and down the long veranda, weaving poetry out of the moonlight and the rustle of the leaves, long after silence had fallen over the house. Or while speaking of those who had died on Cuban scaffolds, rising from his chair in wrath, with his beard trembling."

But, at the time, this disciple of Mendive's—José Martí—was only thirteen, and was learning to imitate his master. He had already read half way through Mendive's library. At night he was taking down by dictation a drama, scene by scene. Afternoons, at the round-table discussions, learned young men gathered at the school to talk avidly with Mendive about the verse technique of Espronceda, articles by Frías, and General Dulce's notions. The master had already

[1] José de la Luz y Caballero: 1800-1862. W. Rex Crawford, in his *A Century of Latin-American Thought,* calls him "a great educator and trainer of teachers." We consider him one of the three forefathers of Cuban national consciousness–the other two being Varela and Saco. A philosopher of positivistic tendencies, he carried on Varela's fight against scholasticism and in favor of scientific training. He was above all a builder of ethical principles. Despite the oppressive atmosphere in which he lived, he reared a generation of Cuban patriots, most of whom attended his famous school, "El Salvador."

published his translations of Moore's *Irish Melodies.* One day Pepe surprised him by producing a translation of his own—made with the help of *The American Popular Lessons*—of Byron's poem, *A Mystery*. Don Rafael could not conceal his astonishment. Pepe blushed, thinking he was being reproached for having selected this poem on incest. He stammered an excuse: To be truthful, his first intention had been to translate some scenes from *Hamlet*, but after starting with the gravediggers, he had given it up because it seemed unworthy to him for a great genius like Shakespeare to be so vulgar.

New family hardships threatened to take these advantages away from Pepe. Until the older Martí "found something" and doña Leonor and the girls could get more sewing to do from outside, Pepe would have to help a little. Was it don Mariano's fault if he could find nothing better for the boy than a job as a clerk in a store, keeping the books and looking after the merchandise? The best he could do was to arrange with the shopkeeper to let Pepe off early in the afternoon so that his classes with Mendive need not be interrupted.

And so, for several months, the student had to alternate the conjugation of verbs with debits and credits. His exercises in rhetoric and even some original compositions were set down on brown wrapping paper. However, his life was not barren of other pleasures. By chance he had struck up a friendship with an old wig-maker who supplied the vaudeville actors. Pepe very gladly made himself useful in delivering wigs and make-up to the comedians, for this gave him the unchallenged right to go to the theatre, via the stage entrance, at any time he pleased. When there was no lesson to be done at night—and at times even when there was—he would take himself off to the Tacón or the Albisu. The theatre fascinated him and made up for his daily round as a clerk.

Eventually don Mariano "found something." Mendive then laid siege to his vanity and his sense of fatherly responsibility: It would be a "crime" to deprive Pepe of definite opportunities. If don Mariano was not able to give the boy a chance at higher studies, he, Mendive, would. This generosity was decisive. In August, 1866, don Rafael applied on Pepe's behalf, for entrance examinations to the Institute:

> "desiring . . . to reward in some way his notable application and good conduct, I have thought it fitting, with the previous consent of don Mariano Martí, to assume all expenses for his studies up to and including his baccalaureate degree."

Mendive's protégé did not cheat him: He completed his first year at the Institute with honors and prizes. And, too, he had rubbed elbows with youths who, like himself, had had to prove their blood, although they came from the two most completely different orbits of Colonial society. One group, usually robust and with hair closely cropped, wore rough half-boots and spoke with a strong Spanish accent. Sons of military stock, these "Sparrows" were definitely in the minority although they had the constituted authority behind them; they were arrogant at times, echoing the Volunteer[1] battalions. The others, the majority, were slight of build, sallow and small-footed, and were apt to be fussy

[1] Volunteers: In 1811, upon the growing rivalry in Cuba between Spaniards and Creoles, partly as an expression of the liberal movements of the time, and of the mood for independence which characterized the continental Spanish colonies, Governor Someruelos established for the first time a militia of volunteers as reënforcement to the regular troops in case of emergency. These militia forces consisted chiefly of Spanish business men. In this way the tragic practice of arming the civilian Spaniard against the civilian Creole or native began. The tendency grew apace with the years, resulting in increased tension and antagonism between the two groups. After 1868, the volunteers became so numerous and aggressively powerful that they virtually dominated the internal politics of the Island and could even force Captains Gen-

about their appearance. The swaggering Spaniards contemptuously called them "humming-birds" because they stuck together with an instinct for solidarity and treated the rival faction with a sort of humorous disdain.

Although he was obviously the son of a Spanish veteran, Pepe Martí from the first day sided with the humming-birds. He was exactly their type: rather frail, rather pallid, quick and nervous in movement—hereditary characteristics derived from the *Guanches*, the ancient Canary Islanders, his mother's people. He was, in fact, a little surprised at the fervor with which he talked of his Cubanism in hallway arguments.

His consciousness of country was still quite recent, and he owed it to don Rafael. At home there had been other things to worry about. The only time he had heard his father talk on politics he had expressed himself with a certain indifference, as if Cuban points of view as opposed to those of Spain were matters of very little importance whatever. Nor had Pepe had much of a chance to learn of the smothered and remote native problems. Very confused rumors of "trouble," had reached his ears, and as for the lengthy and solemn articles in *El Siglo*—the organ of the moderates—they had always bored him a little. He had not been able to understand those subtle distinctions between "assimilation" and "autonomy"—so much talked about everywhere.

Don Rafael, however, undertook to dispel these fogs, once for all. The point at issue was whether it was to Cuba's advantage and Spain's pleasure to put the Island on the same footing as the provinces of Spain, or to give it a régime of relative independence, like that of Canada. Both, to Mendive, were only ways of compromising, in short, only illu-

---

eral to bow to their will. They were notably intransigent and violent in their activities. In a word, they were the forerunners of such groups as Ku Klux, and the nazi, fascist and communist party-troops of our time.

sions, "ways of wasting time." "The truth is, my son, we Cubans have now become mature enough to govern our own country."

Pepe from that time on began to follow the course of events. When, in 1866, the easy-going General Dulce—called "Taffy" by those who distrusted him, poking fun of his name [Sweet]—was replaced by the sour Lersundi as Commander of the Island, the campaign for reform seemed to have been won. At the instance of her Prime Minister, Cánovas, the Queen ordered the formation of a "Committee of Inquiry for Reform"—a minority of the members were to be chosen by the people of the Island—and the local elections of the delegates held all over the Island, in a very heated atmosphere, had resulted in a clear victory for the reform party.

Don Rafael went on shaking his massive head skeptically. He did not believe in Spain's good faith. In his office at the Colegio de San Pablo, of which he was then the director, he reminded Pepe Martí and Fermín Valdés Domínguez of the famous rebuff of 1836. Then, too, Spain had promised reforms to the only colonies she had left, and a party actually calling itself "Progressist" had rudely—don Rafael underlined the adverb heavily—driven out the delegates of Cuba, Puerto Rico and the Philippines. Since that time there had been nothing but promises, delays and new aggravations.

The boys listened, wide-eyed, to Mendive's doubts. The note of secrecy that don Rafael communicated with his words accented their dramatic meaning. "These things, my boys, you can't discuss with everyone." When they left the Colegio, the two friends gazed at each other proudly and a little scared, feeling themselves to be the sharers of a tremendous secret. But, the following morning, at the Institute, several of the more radical humming-birds gathered around Pepe and he relayed to them in conspiratorial style the revolutionary skepticism of the poet-professor.

Events soon proved Mendive right. Lersundi demonstrated that he did not consider himself "another Cuban" as Dulce had fawningly called himself on leaving the Island. Lersundi was decidedly for the status quo. He knew that he could count on all the "good Spaniards" generally, and especially on the Volunteers, who were publicly boasting that they would prevent any reforms, by bloodshed if necessary. The twenty-two members of the Committee of Inquiry chosen by the Spanish Government to collaborate with the elected Cuban delegates were among the most notorious enemies of reform. And when at last the Committee did meet, under oath of secrecy in an isolated, guarded room of the Overseas Ministry in Madrid, Morales Lemus, the scholarly Cuban economist, had difficulty in holding an amused attention while he set forth a complete plan for insular autonomy. The Committee was promptly dissolved, and with it vanished the last hope of keeping the "ever most loyal" Island Spanish.

1868: Pepe Martí and Fermín Valdés were taking their sophomore year of study at San Pablo, Mendive's private academy in his own house on the Prado. Don Rafael was not especially devout; he had given this name to the college "because Don Pepe had named his school El Salvador" and every Cuban teacher revered the memory of the great José de la Luz, who had moulded patriotic consciousness in his classrooms. Mendive, too, wanted to make his school a civic seminary, a place warm and friendly in spirit, in which every student would be like a son.

No one could be more grateful for this than Pepe Martí was, in days to come. At fifteen, he had been awakened to a life more noble in vistas than those prevailing in his own family's home on Peñalver Street, where doña Leonor and the girls talked about their sewing and don Mariano, increasingly bitter with the years and his money troubles, kept his ex-sergeant's profanity ready for action. In Pepe's relationship to his father, affectionate filial respect had given way to a more conscious tenderness—yet tinged with bitterness because of an inevitable feeling of difference between them. Don Mariano had not again openly interfered with his son's studious vocation since Mendive had taken him under his wing; on the contrary, he boasted about the honors won by "the kid" in his first year at the Institute. But whenever money troubles grew more aggravated, oblique hints on the help Pepe "might give," and on the vanity of intellectual aspirations, revealed to the lad how precariously his father's consent was balanced. Don Mariano was at these times rude and contemptuous and his outbursts drove Pepe to Mendive, his spiritual father, for refuge.

How different from home was that rambling house at 88 Prado! There he was like another son who repaid affection with spontaneity and eager thoughtfulness in helping with the work.

> "The whole school is clean. I have had Salvador dust everything and give it one sponging; but all the benches, carpets and blackboards were so dirty that they needed another washing, and I told Salvador to do them over again."

On the day Pepe wrote this note to his teacher, don Mariano had come in person to call for him at school, compelling him to go with him, because "he doesn't want anyone to see me looking like a pig and is going to buy me a hat and some shirts before we come back." Don Mariano looked out for Pepe's outward grooming; Mendive cared for the cleanliness and refinement of spirit—a rivalry in fatherhood.

"Command your pupil who loves you like a son," the note ended. And another time, when don Rafael—"whose temper had been tarnished by adversity"—had rebuked him, Pepe wrote, heartsick and solemn:

"Señor Mendive: I did not know that a generous father had to remind a loving son of his duties. Your reprimand surprised me so much, since at any time I would give my life for you, for it is yours, yours only, and a thousand lives if I had them to give for you."

This eager substitution, this necessity to seek a spiritual haven and authority outside his family and blood cast the first shadows over Martí's nature. The suppression of his intellectual talents in his parents' home engendered in him a melancholy resentment from which he tried to escape by writing poetry. Naturally it was poetry on the theme of family affection and in it he was already able to express his tenderness with a rather protective maturity.

In the summer of 1868 the atmosphere of San Pablo became increasingly political and less and less literary. Pepe Martí and Pancho Sellén[1] both composed elegiac poems on the death of one of don Rafael's sons. In Sellén's poem the official censor struck out the line:

The glory of Bolívar and Washington.

Mendive substituted for it another line, a bit too long, but less vulnerable to the censor's fund of knowledge, and no less pointed:

The glory of Harmodius and Aristogeiton.

Such classic allusions were hailed with delight just then. The leading delegates of the Committee of Inquiry had returned to Havana, and between the sarcastic jibes of the Spanish faction and the acrimonious threats of the Creoles, the city was in a ferment. Throughout the Island, recently scourged by cholera, an intense feeling of uneasiness prevailed, daily growing worse through the crushing taxes and

[1] Francisco Sellén, who was to become one of the most delicate Cuban poets of the post-romantic school.

the obnoxious way they were being collected. Impassioned editorials appeared in the press, but the censor cut every liberal insinuation; Volunteers were committing provocative excesses, and drumhead trials were being held by the military, supplanting the civil courts on any pretext; barracks-room justice was being administered to all and sundry. Secret meetings and anonymous publications angrily proclaimed that the Madrid Government and the Spanish in Cuba were forcing the Island into rebellion.

Lersundi and his followers, a breed fanatically loyal to the Bourbons, paid little attention, however; they were too much worried over news from Spain itself. Isabel II, although she had put the reins of power in the hands of the "muckraker" who had formerly exposed her "libidinous carnalities," could sense coming to a head all around her, under the hand of General Prim, the liberal revolution which was to drive her from the throne.

On the 17th of September the exiled *espadones* entered Cádiz, rousing the fleet and the city to rebellion with the cry: "For Spain and Honor!" And not by design, yet not by chance, a few days later came Lares' fruitless rising in Puerto Rico, and on the dawn of October 10th, a lawyer of Bayamo, Carlos Manuel de Céspedes, struck an armed blow for Cuban independence from his plantation near Yara.[1]

[1] Carlos Manuel de Céspedes is Cuba's Washington. We call him "el fundador," the father of Cuban independence, for although the Ten Years War which he ignited in 1868 did not bring about separation from Spain—frustrated as it was by the Zanjón Agreement in 1878—it did lay the foundation for Cuban liberties, by proclaiming the emancipation of slaves and holding the first Cuban Constitutional Assembly. Céspedes himself, however, did not fare very well at the hands of Cuban revolutionists. Accused by them of dictatorial tendencies, he was deposed from the Presidency of the Republic-in-Arms and forced to retire to the country-place of San Lorenzo, where the Spaniards besieged and finally killed him in 1874.

Chapter Three

INITIATION

A FULL and immediate extension to Cuba of the gains of the Spanish revolution—purely political though it was—would immediately have snuffed out the flame of revolt just lighted at Yara. But General Lersundi was a moderate of the old school. From Pau the exiled Isabel had gone to the trouble of cabling him: "Tell me whether that country is quiet; if not, count always on my affection."

Lersundi would have preferred at the moment to rely on something a little more substantial—for example, a few more battalions of regulars. Lacking them, he decided to send Valmaseda, his second in command, to the savannahs of Oriente to harass the "traitor" Céspedes, who had just taken Bayamo. Meanwhile Lersundi rattled the sabre in Havana, dispatching unceremoniously the Spanish and Cuban notables who came to him to petition for liberalization of the insular government in tune with the reforms in Spain.

Over there, the brand new government brought out a new edition of promises to the colonies in the circumspect prose of don Adelardo López de Ayala, a poet who had been appointed to the Overseas Ministry. But Lersundi was not recalled. The famous *omnimodas*—the security decrees giving the military governor "unlimited" power—were carried out to extreme lengths under the pretext of war emergency; military commissions were nothing but so many "committees of public safety" and the new corps of Volunteers, strengthened by the enthusiastic enrollment of men from Spain who had grown rich in business and the slave trade, spurred the

governmental zeal against everything Cuban with a new fury.

Naturally, the desire for independence grew by leaps and bounds. While Céspedes in the Eastern region[1] was rejecting the bribes offered him by Lersundi's agents, Camagüey joined the uprising, and the young men of Occidente sought ways of joining the ranks of the insurrectos. Secret societies were organized to aid the revolutionaries and to take reprisals against the Volunteers.

Pepe called together the most important humming-birds at the Institute in a secret meeting. He harangued them passionately and quoted lines from a sonnet he had written: "The Tenth of October":

From wide Rio Cauto to the distant peaks
The cannons roar, and to the martial bursts . . .

They ended by forming a club of junior revolutionaries, repeating the name of Carlos Manuel de Céspedes with reverence and wondering how they could get to the savannahs to help him. But that was next to impossible. All exits from the city were guarded. Soldiers summarily disposed of Cubans caught without a pass. The police were unusually vigilant, and the Volunteers distrusted everybody's looks and could scent the "underground worker" at almost any distance. Mendive had had to hide young José de Armas in his own room because he had shown signs of "disloyalty."

As luck would have it, the post of warden that had at last been given to don Mariano was in Batabanó, and involved the inspection of ships. Even so, Pepe felt a little ashamed of his father's connection with the government, and was more

[1] Cuba was then divided into three main "departments"—Occidente, or West, comprising the present-day provinces of Piñar del Rio, Havana and Matanzas; the Central or Las Villas provinces, Santa Clara and Camagüey; and Oriente, the Eastern region whose main city is Santiago de Cuba.

and more "away" from home, and more regularly to be found at Fermín's or at San Pablo. His friend's parents were sympathetic to The Cause, and at the rambling school on the Prado each night a group of enthusiasts "leaned on the grand piano, tracing Céspedes' movements on the map of Cuba."

Finally Lersundi succeeded in getting the Spanish government to let him drop his red-hot coal. In the first few days of 1869 General Dulce returned to Cuba to resume command. He was coming, according to Madrid, "authorized to modify taxation and to govern by liberal standards." The tamer Cubans still had illusions and received him with joy. But the Spanish faction fêted Lersundi and did not hide their dislike for his successor: If he were going to try to compromise with the *mambises*—as the Cuban rebels were called—they, the Volunteers, would take charge of defending the true honor of Spain, somewhat sullied by this so-called "Glorious Revolution."

Dulce actually did everything possible to mollify the Cubans with formal promises and by granting a certain amount of real freedom. To begin with, he granted freedom of the press and of assembly. Eagerness—so long suppressed—to clarify the issues in print where everyone could read them, now broke out with a tropical luxuriance: No less than seventy-seven flaming periodicals were issued between the 10th and 28th of January. Many of them were from the pens of the same writers—the important thing was to make a good showing and thus demonstrate beyond any doubt the desire and the right to express opinions freely. The Sparrow faction was furious.

Young Martí did not pass up this chance. He, too, had something to say, and after the publication of his sonnet, "The Tenth of October," in *El Siglo*, an underground student paper, his desire to break into print had grown quite feverish. He gave Fermín, who was getting out his own paper, *El Diablo Cojuelo* [The Crippled Devil], some commentaries on events, epigrams, and jokes a little forced, for Pepe's nature was incurably grave and lyrical. Among his *bon mots* on the freedom of the press he coined a provocative slogan: "YARA OR MADRID?"

The Crippled Devil came out on the 19th of January. It was an amateurish sheet of only four pages. Pepe aspired to something better and applied for governmental permission to publish, with the help of Mendive and his planter friend, don Cristóbal Madan, a "democratic, cosmopolitan weekly" which would be called *La Patria Libre* [The Free Nation]. He would have liked to call it simply *La Patria*, but Madan had already published a paper with that name, and if the new name were sensationally daring, so much the better.

Doña Leonor guessed something of the intrigues in which Pepe was involved, and a compelling intuition filled her with sudden dread and foreboding in the absence of don Mariano, who had just been transferred to Guanabacoa. The police officer was not unaware of his son's sympathies for the rebel cause. At first he had tried to impress upon him, through sheer regard for tradition, a strict loyalty to Spain. But he soon learned that it was part of the fate of Spaniards in America—as a current popular song had it—to be fathers of Creole rebels; and since in his own heart he could not help but recognize that they had "some right" on their side, he had chosen to wink at Pepe's first patriotic adventures, now growing more and more contagious "through that rebel Mendive." Once, to the lad's surprise, he had even gone so far as to admit that he would not wonder if he were to see Pepe fighting for the freedom of Cuba someday.

But shortly after that a great many changes took place. Cubans had actually "taken the field" and, above all, don Mariano had again become a police officer. This rejuvenated his patriotism. Pepe, ordered, at doña Leonor's suggestion, to explain his constant absences from home until late every night, confessed to his father that he was getting a magazine ready for press. Don Mariano exploded. A rebel paper! How could a man entrusted to keep public order allow his son to make such a show of himself? He thundered a command to stop such dangerous nonsense at once. Pepe received the command with absolute silence.

That same night, however, doña Leonor had to take every precaution to prevent her husband from finding out that the boy, as usual, had not come home until around midnight.

The policeman's fears were not in reality exaggerated. Havana was going through a time of violence only slightly under control. Dulce's liberal decrees had not won the Cubans over, and had, on the other hand, infuriated the Volunteers. There were sporadic brawls and riots. All the liberals agreed that passions were being inflamed by the irresponsibility of the press.

On the 22nd of January all Havana talked about what had happened the night before at the Villanueva Theatre. The story went that one of the comedians had dared to sing from the stage a certain rebel refrain and the audience, almost all Creoles, applauded wildly with vivas for Cuba and Carlos Manuel. The comedian had been fined, but the Volunteers were smoldering with rage because the governor, upon the promise of the actors not to repeat the offense, was going to allow another performance of the show as a "benefit for the poor"—and one could be certain that "the poor" were none other than Carlos Manuel de Céspedes and his gang.

That night the theatre was packed: Dandies from the Louvre, students, old line reformers, ladies with blue and scarlet ribbons over their white headdresses. . . . At the entrance, in the bar, a group of Volunteers watched everything grimly, out of the corners of their eyes. The governor, at the last moment, doubled the guard around the theatre. The show, *El Perro Huevero* [The Egg-eating Dog], was given without incident. Then, just as the curtain was about to fall, one of comedians shouted the line: "Long live the land of sugarcane!" From the top balcony came another shout: "Long live Cuba!" Immediately a loud "Long live Spain!" came in response. People began to run from the theatre. In the bar could be heard sounds of breaking glass and chairs being thrown around; the guards rushed in and soon two revolver shots rang out. While the audience in panic crowded to the doors, a volley of shots came from the street. The air was filled with shouts, the smell of gunpowder, the noise of galloping horses and the clatter of carriage wheels. When the civil authorities arrived it was with difficulty that they restrained the Volunteers, who were ready to burn the theatre to the ground.

The disturbance spread out over the neighborhood. Near the theatre was Mendive's house. The Volunteers knew it to be a "nest of humming-birds" and a victim for their wrath was essential. They crossed the Prado and gathered as a mob in front of his house.

Mendive had been at home all evening with his wife, who was recovering from childbirth. Pepe had asked to spend the evening with them. The reading of the first issue of *La Patria Libre*, ready for distribution the next day, was suddenly interrupted by the sound of shots and yells. Master and disciple went to the windows and watched through the venetian blinds while the militia rode down the Prado, shooting at coaches, dispersing with drawn sabres the curious throngs attracted by the uproar. A group, not in Volunteer uniform, started a fire alongside Mendive's doorway . . . From the patio, where some of the girls were crying and praying, bullets could be heard hitting the wall. Finally the shouting died down and the fickle mob moved on to try its luck elsewhere, although from time to time a bullet buried itself in the massive door. . . . At last all was quiet. Suddenly there came four loud knocks. Pepe could stand it no longer. He opened the door and fell into his mother's arms.

A few years later some of his *Versos Sencillos* recalled that moment:

And after we had kissed
Like lunatics, she said:
Let's go now, let's go, boy,
Baby is alone at home in bed! [1]

It was on this dramatic stage that the new journalist made his first entrance. On Saturday morning many of Havana's citizens, terrified, turned from reading Dulce's proclamation announcing that "there will be justice, and prompt justice" to look over a new weekly called *La Patria Libre* which everyone said was backed by Mendive.

The new sheet did not set out "to preach immediate independence" but it grew more radical on every page. As if the praise of Dulce with which it began were not enough to irritate the intransigents, another article, well thought out, rejected assimilation and proposed that Cuba should have the kind of government that Cubans themselves decided upon. A third essay justified the right of revolution. But the most ardent contribution came at the end: a long, dramatic epic, a poem entitled *Abdala*. "Written especially for *La Patria*" was the subtitle—in capital letters—a clear indication of the poem's political significance. Nor was there anyone too stupid to see the clear allusion to the rebels of Yara in the exalted stanzas praising the heroic defense of Nubia—a "far-off land" whose name was a conveniently none too subtle disguise for Cuba.

Espirta, mother of the young hero warrior Abdala, tried

[1] Y después que nos besamos
como dos locos, me dijo:
"Vamos pronto, vamos hijo;
la niña esta' sola; ¡vamos!"

to keep him from going off to fight, but Abdala rejected her counsel with the most ardent persuasion:

> *It is a rancor eternal for those who attack us*[1] . . .
> *Is not the mere love of earth*
> *Nor of the grass we tread under our feet.*
> *It is the invincible hate of the oppressor;*
> *It is a rancor eternal for those who attack us* í.....

Such eloquence did not win any Spartan approval of Pepe's underground activity from doña Leonor. Did not the poem itself recount how the young Nubian warrior had paid for his patriotism with his life? When her husband, alarmed by news of the Villanueva riot, arrived hurriedly from Guanabacoa, doña Leonor told him her fears for Pepe. The warden read *Abdala* and understood all its implications at a glance. When Pepe came home, his eyes shining with excitement from his first brush with danger and his first taste of fame, his father received him with a storm of anger; and that afternoon Pepe learned—also for the first time—how badly you can be hurt by loving hands.

Part of the captain-general's "prompt justice" consisted in ordering Mendive's arrest. The Volunteers insisted that he was the man behind the scenes of the Yara revolt and one of of the instigators of the provocation at the Villanueva. These charges were based on nothing more tangible than the fact that Mendive's mother-in-law was the owner of the theatre, and that, in making a search of his house, a rebel cockade was found in the desk of doña Micaela, his wife. But something had to be done to placate the Volunteers, whose dis-

[1] El amor, madre, a la patria
no es el amor ridículo a la tierra,
ni la yerba qui pisan nuestras plantas:
es el odio invencible a quien la oprime,
es el rancor eterno a quien la ataca . . .

SPANISH VOLUNTEER

turbances were becoming more and more violent. Mendive was jailed in the Castillo del Principe.

Against all advice and warnings, Pepe succeeded in obtaining a pass from the governor to visit his teacher. He wanted to mobilize all his friends, or protest all alone, against the injustice of putting a man behind bars for the crime of teaching love of country. But everything weighed too heavily against him—the difficulty of establishing connections, the prevailing terrorism, the extreme aspects of vigilance, the voices of common sense and of love—pleading or angry—which beseiged him from morning till night.

With doña Micaela he went every day to see Mendive. Through the bars under the sour scrutiny of the guard, he confided to his teacher the struggle going on in his mind: his sudden enthusiasms and the depths of frustration, his shame at not being already out with the Cuban soldiers.

Mendive consoled him like a father, making him realize that he was still too young, that he would have other ways of serving Cuba, and that in any case it would hardly be possible to get to the revolutionary camps from Havana. . . . From one of these visits Pepe emerged, very grave, escorting doña Micaela. He carried in his pocket the manuscript of a fine sonnet, "By the Light of the Moon," which don Rafael had written in prison.

At the end of five months Mendive embarked for Spain to serve out the sentence of exile imposed by a Council of War.

Chapter Four

PRISON

HIS TEACHER'S DEPARTURE left Pepe like a bird without a tree for shelter. He was at that age of mysterious urgencies when life must reveal for the adolescent some meaning if it is not to oppress him with emptiness. Mendive had provided the first mainstays for Pepe's spirit by imbuing him with his own honest patriotism and appreciation of beauty. This had offset the blunt parental authority, substituting for it an ideal at the moment when the mind needs examples and a boy like Pepe needs a hero to worship.

Now all that sense of security had vanished. Pepe was left to his own restlessness at the precise moment when he began to experience the most ardent curiosity and a dramatic sense of responsibility. He tried in vain to make contacts with the revolutionaries: The more prominent ones were already far from Cuba, exiles or emigrants; those who remained behind were almost inaccessible; thanks to a necessary caution —they did not trust the excitable, talkative boy, who was the son of a police official. . . . The students? San Pablo was closed, and don Mariano refused to let Pepe go to the Institute, "fearful," as he explained a long time afterward, "that the excessive freedom resulting from upset schedules of classes might distract his son from the studies to which he had formerly dedicated himself with such marked success."

Don Mariano had resolved to keep the boy on short rein. Before sunset every day Pepe had to be home, at the big house in Guanabacoa, where the family were now living.

The villagers called Mariano "Blackmouth" because of the notable big black mustache the police warden of Cruz Verde wore, and possibly also because of his abundant flow of profanity. Ever since the *Abdala* incident, Pepe had had to endure this violence of language, and a great deal more than that; the constant suspicion, vigilance and admonishings of his father became intolerable.

> "I have been so deeply hurt," he wrote to don Rafael in October, "that I confess to you with all the brutal frankness you know I believe in that only the hope of seeing you has kept me from committing suicide. Your letter yesterday was my salvation. Some day you will see my diary and realize that this was not a childish gesture, but a resolve carefully weighed and measured."

Doña Leonor made up a little for her husband's harsh regimen with her tenderness. But Pepe needed a more understanding consolation. He found it in Fermín—who, later, kept in his room a photograph on which Pepe's rhymed inscription alluded to the "hours of sorrow" in which Fermín had been "best friend, good brother."

The Valdés Domínguez house on Industria Street had, as a matter of fact, accepted him as another son. The Guatemalan gentleman and his wife were fond of the poor boy whose speech and manners were those of one born to wealth and luxury. And from the well-bred refinement and Creole stateliness of their home Pepe in turn derived a serious pleasure. . . . He went there every afternoon to attend the French lesson given to all the children of the house by a M. Fortier. And there, too, at the table in Fermín's study, he read his friend's books, discussed the insurrection with him, and made elaborate plans for getting to the war in the Savannahs.

Eventually don Mariano decided that while there were difficulties in the way of Pepe's continuing with his studies, it would be better for him "to turn his hand to something." Accordingly, Pepe worked in Don Cristóbal Madan's office "from six in the morning until eight at night, earning four and a half *onzas*,[1] which he turned over to his father."

He was not, therefore, at the Valdés Domínguez house that afternoon of October 4th at the time of the Volunteers' disturbance.

M. Fortier was standing just inside the iron grille that opened on the street, watching for Fermín to come home, talking with Fermín's brother Eusebio and his friend Sellén. Since the pretty girl across the street had just come to her window to look out, attracted by the brassy music of a parade of Volunteers on the point of breaking up at the Campo de Marte near by, there began an exchange of pleasantries and jokes from window to window. The men were laughing; the girl was laughing. Just then a squad of the First Battalion of Light Infantry came marching past. They were very conceited about their improvised military bearing, and observing the suddenly stifled laughter at the windows, they became annoyed. The menacing looks that ran through the ranks of the soldiers prophesied reprisals to come. Sellén and M. Fortier left the window.

When Fermín—who had come from seeing Martí at the office—entered the house a little later, there was scarcely time to tell him what had happened before a group of Volunteers swarmed into the entrance hall, shouting, and seized the boy. By night, Fortier and Sellén were caught and imprisoned also, and a search had been made through the Valdés Domínguez house. In the drawer of Fermín's study table they found a letter written that very day, addressed to a certain Carlos de Castro y Castro. The letter ran as follows:

[1] About 72 pesos.

Comrade:

Have you ever thought upon the glory of the Apostates? Do you remember how apostasy was punished in ancient times? We hope that a pupil of Rafael María de Mendive will not let this letter go without answer.

José Martí
Fermín Valdés Domínguez

It took the Volunteers some time to puzzle out the meaning of that note. The mention of Mendive was suspicious, but—what apostasy was it they were referring to? At last the slow military intelligence discovered that the Carlos de Castro addressed was a Cuban youth who had joined a Spanish regiment. He had formerly been a pupil of Mendive's, and the letter writers inferred that they considered the honor of being a Spanish soldier was a disgrace. Pepe was arrested, and the indictment, started against his friends, "for insulting a pioneer squad of the First Battalion of Volunteers," was broadened to include don José Martí and don Fermín Valdés Domínguez "under suspicion of disloyalty" —a crime of considerable flexibility in those days.

Months and months in a stinking prison where all kinds were herded together, months of brotherly protectiveness between the two friends, of finally winning the good will of the hardened jailor by their friendly spontaneity.

One day, at last, the jailor read to them in a trembling voice the writ of the military prosecutor, in which the death penalty was suggested. The boys smiled nervously. On October 4th, the first anniversary of the "crime" of the prisoners, they appeared before the Council. The guilt of all was, apparently, firmly accepted by the court; the only thing that needed clarification, a matter concerning Martí and Valdés Domínguez, was: Which of the two had written the compromising letter? Experts had not been able to decide, since Fermín and Pepe wrote very similar hands—the old "San Anacleto script."

Asked to testify, Fermín confessed authorship of the letter. In his turn, Martí protested that he had written it. The army officers looked at each other in dazed surprise. The prosecutor warned them that the one most responsible would incur risk of the death penalty. The two prisoners maintained their ground. They were ordered to confront each other, and when Fermín stepped forward to speak, Pepe cut him off by walking in front of him and interrupting what he was trying to say. Pepe approached the bench and fervently repeated his confession. The fluent phrases, smooth, distinctly spoken, charged the atmosphere of the room with a clear rhythm that cut through the stuffy obscurity of officialdom. Fermín and his comrades were hypnotized. Counsel assigned to the defense forgot his gold braid for a moment and smiled. The battalion's witnesses nervously fingered their mustaches. Pepe continued, undaunted, unhesitating—enraptured himself, as if he felt within him a secret spring gushing up and overflowing—until the presiding colonel came to, banged the table with his fist, declared the trial over and passed sentence: Fermín Valdés Domínguez—six months in jail; José Martí—six years at hard labor at the Presidio.

I go to a big house in which they tell me
Life itself wears out.
My country sends me there. For one's country
To die is sweet enough.[1]

Pepe had written these lines a few hours before he was sent to the provincial penitentiary. In jail they told him of the chain gangs; actually he had seen them himself, many

[1] Voy a una casa inmensa en que me han dicho
que es la vida expirar.
La patria allí me lleva. Por la patria
morir, es gozar más.

times, passing in front of his house at sunset, groups of bent, weary men, with jackets thrown over their shoulders, their clothes mere rags, dirty with lime and red clay, each with a chain linking waist and ankle. At the cafés, noisy with dominoes and political talk, the passing of the chain gangs produced a sudden silence that made the clanking of the chains, the heavy pounding of feet, and the short, harsh commands of the guards even louder.

Pepe had witnessed this scene many times, trembling with an ague of pity and anger. But he did not as yet know, in all its horror, the black hole of the Presidio, where the Colony segregated its dregs of humanity, where injustice would show itself, not a mere political act, or as civic wastefulness, but as a calculated blow to all that was human in each man.

On the 5th of April they brought him from the jail, cropped his hair short, gave him a crude basket and a palm sleeping-mat. He became No. 113, first tier, Whites. He was immediately put to work pushing the rusty handle of the pump up and down. He was all alone. The other prisoners had left for the quarries at dawn and would not return until dark. . . . From the curb of the cistern, under the ironic gaze of the guard, he watched the bright stripe of sunlight slowly diminish on the high wall of the prison yard until the eaves were lost in shadow, the sparrows were done chirping, and a lonely, melancholy quiet fell on everything. At last muffled voices were heard, oaths, and the dull clank of men in irons. The prisoners were returning from the quarries. Pepe saw them fall to the ground, shoulders propped against the wall, their ghastly white faces bent down over their knees, or perhaps gazing longingly at the arched entrance of the cell block—waiting for the time to stretch out in sleep.

Martí saw an old man suddenly fall down as if someone had pulled his only support from under him. He ran over to help him. The old man looked like a ghost: his head was white with snowy hair; from head to foot he was white with lime dust; his face was without color.

"What is the matter?"

The old man looked at him wonderingly; he considered his youth, his naïve innocence, and muttered tonelessly, "Poor kid!"

When Pepe insisted on helping him, the man turned, lifted up his ragged shirt and showed him his back, zebra-striped from flogging, each wide wheal a festering wound.

"But—did they do this to you here? Why did they do it?"

The old man shrugged his shoulders and murmured: "You wouldn't believe me, son. Anybody can tell you why."

When Martí, the next day, saw the quarries for himself he hardly needed anyone to tell him. The quarries were about a league away from the Presidio fortress, in an irregular hollow, hewn out of massive walls of lime rock. Above the quarry floor and its high piles of *cocó*—broken rock and limestone— the sun's fierce heat brought the atmosphere to a boil; the rays of reflected light playing on the lime-whiteness were blinding. The prisoners' work was to dig out and break up the rock with picks and sledge hammers and cart it to the dump trucks or to the lime kilns on top of the cliffs.

Bent double over the stone and carting the crushed lime in boxes or large chunks of it on their shoulders, they tried to dodge the rock slides that came without warning, and to keep out of reach of the whip of the overseer who drove them without mercy. The prisoners were whites, Negroes, Chinese; old men were there, and boys; all were shackled by triple strands of chain which hobbled their feet and made them stagger among the ruts filled with stagnant water and rotting filth. As they clambered over the heaps of stone, the quicklime burned their feet and the fine white powdery dust choked their breathing. Air, men and all manner of objects were covered with that pervading, unmerciful whiteness which inflamed eyes and tortured the nerves, converting every figure into a ghost and the whole landscape into a kind of torrid winter.

That very first morning they told Pepe the story of the old man, don Nicolás Castillo. Two days ago his legs had refused to bear him up any longer. They collapsed under him, and he was unable to get up. Two prisoners carried him, half dead, to a cart. At the infirmary the doctor looked at him with indifference and suggested that he could be cured by "more baths in the quarry." Stretched out on the cart, his head hitting the floor boards with every bump, he was brought back to the rock piles again. Not even beating him with the hard *yaya*-wood stick could bring him to his feet. They left him stretched out, all day, in the sun and stagnant water.

When young Martí asked the reason for such savagery, Cubans and Spaniards both explained that the Volunteers thought Castillo was a rebel brigadier, and the Volunteers had to be appeased.

It was all incredible. Pepe would not have believed it had he not seen, for instance, what they did to the boy Lino Figueredo—a political prisoner at the age of twelve. Lino, a little country boy, was the son of a "neutral" family, but of neutrals who had taken the name Figueredo after the hero-author of the patriot song.[1] Nobody knew what had become of his parents. Lino had been sentenced to the Presidio. He carted stone like everyone else; they flogged him as they did the others. One day he was overcome by a violent nausea and the other symptoms of smallpox, but he had to continue carting rock until the fever felled him and had made of him another shadow of misery. . . . Then, too, there were the cases, no less horrible, of Ramón Rodríguez, and that of Juan de Dios, the old Negro idiot, jailed for

[1] Not long before, in Bayamo, Pedro or "Perucho" Figueredo had composed the rebel song which was to become the Cuban national anthem.

"treason"; and that of the little colored boy, Tomás, a mere terrified boy of eleven. And there was another example still —that of the strapping, gloomy youth obsessed by the dazzling whiteness who had tried to commit suicide by jumping off the highest quarry cliff. The guards had picked him up and took care of him because it was the Captain General's saint's day, and they did not want the news to spread. One morning he returned to work, and when he took off the prisoner's black hat—called "the mark of death" —his head displayed three wide hairless stripes shining in the burning sunlight.

The young Martí saw all this. He himself felt the brutal sting of quicklime, sun and whip. He worked in water up to his waist. He dragged chains that gnawed at his ankles. His eyes were inflamed, burned by the blinding whiteness. . . . He hoped that his family would not find out what was happening to him. But don Mariano arranged one day to see him during the brief breathing spell. Doña Leonor had made little pads to protect the boy from his iron shackles, and don Mariano fitted them under Pepe's irons. He told the boy that his mother and the girls were going the rounds of influential officers asking for clemency. Pepe did not venture to protest; he expected nothing and did not wish to destroy his father's hope. When they called him back to work, and the whip of the guard hurried Pepe to the stone-carts, the father remained on his knees, staring in the broiling sun, anger blazing in his face.

Pepe's keenest pain, however, was for the suffering of others. He was himself sustained and tempered by a kind of pride. "A slave of his age and its teachings," he described himself to his mother in a dedicatory rhyme on the back of his photograph as a prisoner. And he asks a friend to see in that likeness "the robust picture of his soul and the beautiful page of his life's story." Rather than any enjoyment of martyrdom, his spirit experienced a bitter compassion for all misery. Don Nicolás and Lino and all the others appreciated the ministry of his encouraging words and the generous hands that helped them lift up their boxes of lime or fixed their bandages or treated their bruises and abrasions. One afternoon one of the Chinese prisoners was seized with a convulsion, his face greenish in pallor. Although he was helpless and foaming at the mouth the guards tried to get him up by flogging him, their invariable custom. One of the other Chinese rushed to his defense with angry monosyllables. The guards did not understand him, did not want to understand. It was not until a vein was cut and a spurt of black blood gushed forth that they knew what was the matter—it was cholera. . . . After that, many others likewise fell among the rocks. Martí ran to help them always, raising them up, chafing their arms and legs. The guards, according to mood, would either let him help the stricken or would shove him away with a push: "Keep on with this doctoring business, Little Humming-bird, and the plague will get you, too . . ."

Martí, even after all he had experienced, through some vague feeling of loyalty to Spanish blood, felt that these things were done in the name of Spain without Spain's knowledge of them. It was unthinkable that the liberal politicians of Spain could know and permit them. Perhaps even the fanatical supporters of "integrity" in Havana did not know the real truth. Such brutality just *could not* be planned and designed. It was a terrible secret of the Colony, a hidden festering that the good Spaniards of the Island were utterly unaware of . . . and yet, and yet, this white hell was open to public gaze. Was it possible that hatred had so thoroughly pulverized conscience that even the best people could tolerate such things in the name of political expediency? Was it possible, for instance, that such a man as José María Sardá, the wealthy owner of the quarries, did

Grover Flint

A PLANTATION SUGAR-MILL

not know at what price in crimes against humanity his revenues were derived?

Yet Sardá seemed to be a good man at heart.

One afternoon as he passed by the quarry called "La Criolla," he called Martí over to him. He noted the lad's sunken cheeks and inflamed eyes. He put his hand on Martí's shoulder and later called the guard to one side. After that Pepe was treated with a certain amount of deference.

A week later he was transferred to the Cabaña Fortress. A friend of the Captain General, the rich Catalan, had been able—perhaps prodded by don Mariano—to do all that the imploring of doña Leonor had been unable to achieve. Pepe was freed from the Presidio and temporarily exiled to the Isle of Pines in the custody of Sardá himself while the authorities discussed the possibility of deporting him to Spain.

He had been "at hard labor" for six months. He had come out half blind and with a hernia caused by a blow from a chain; he was much thinner, much more pale, and his smile was gentler. He was seventeen.

Three months later he wrote to Mendive:

> "I have suffered much, but I am convinced that I have learned how to suffer. And if I had the strength for it all, and if I have the qualities to be really a man, I owe it to you alone, and from you and only you I have come to have whatever there is of virtue and kindness in me."

Chapter Five

THE OATH

MADRID WAS BLEAK and gray those early months of 1871. The strong north wind from the Guadarrama mountains, with every tree already bare of leaves before it, amused itself with abandon along the sidewalks and streets, blowing torn fragments of the *Gaceta* [the official newspaper] about and snatching up the little clouds of frosty breath as soon as they appeared from the depths of coat collars and mufflers. And there was another coldness in the atmosphere: Amadeo I [1] had begun his reign, but the people of Madrid were not at all reconciled to the intruder whom the Septembrists and their "Spain with honor" slogan had imported from Italy after Prim's[2] scandalous hawking of the Spanish crown through all the courts of Europe. With Kingmaker Prim now dead, how would *Macarronini I* conduct himself on the throne abandoned by Bourbon Isabel?

But the thin young man who walked the windy streets of Madrid like a ghost, bundled up in a heavy overcoat, was thinking of other things, more personal and less immediate. Madrid! . . . This was Madrid, the city Cubans loved in vain. From here the captains-general and royal decrees went

[1] Amadeo: Fernando María, Duke of Aosta, born in Turin, 1845. He accepted the crown of Spain in 1871. It was first offered to a prince of the House of Hohenzollern. France objected. The "Spanish Succession" was one of the causes of the war between France and Prussia in 1870, resulting in the defeat of Napoleon III and the organization of the German Empire under the Prussian Hohenzollerns.

[2] Prim: the Spanish general, Juan Prim y Prats (1814-1870), a military and political leader. Took part in the liberal revolution of 1868 in Spain, which overthrew Isabel II. Prim was killed by unknown assailants in Madrid.

forth to Cuba. Why was it that Madrid was not hated, this exploiting, subjugating capital? He remembered how he himself had always associated Madrid in imagination with an idea of irresponsible grace, a way of political frivolity not in the least like the hard fanaticism of the Spaniards who came to Cuba. . . . Creoles who visited Spain always returned talking of the captivating smile of Madrid. It was true: he had perceived it, even in the fierce winter weather; and in spite of the fact that don Rafael, drawn to Paris, had not been there to welcome him, he scarcely felt the loneliness of a strange city. It was like a relative one had come to know.

It was also true that Pepe was favorably predisposed by his literary inclinations. The feelings of rage and exasperation with which he had at first entertained the idea of exile to the Peninsula had been calmed somewhat by the thought that Spain was the home of a beautiful and famous literature. During the last three months he had spent on the Isle of Pines he had been able to consider this prospect and to examine himself. What a perfect solitude, broken by the kindnesses of Señora Sardá and her daughters! He had been able to read the Bible through, no less—and *Les Misérables*. In the airy little cottage, "El Abra," at the foot of a little slope white with marble outcroppings, or along the narrow cartpath to Nueva Gerona, bordered by young pine groves, Pepe had many times experienced an inner sensation of creative readiness and of growing clarity. He had felt a strong, confident need for self-expression.

Now, in Madrid, upon his first contact with a way of life older and richer, his hopes were replacing his memories and dreams. For him, a Cuban, Spain was still the pattern and mould of culture. On the Island, French influence had not flourished, not even through liberal reading. Mendive, who had been host to Lamartine's literary representative, had remained loyal to his own tradition despite the persuasive message of gratitude sent to him by the French poet with its flattery of the culture of "the beautiful land that has produced the poetess Avellaneda and the poet Heredia." And it was only when Mendive's circle discussed literary topics that Pepe had heard Madrid mentioned with respect, and even Martínez de la Rosa.[1]

Well and good; all this—orators, Atheneums, poets, magnificent paintings—was now at his whim's elbow. Exile had its compensations for a youth made spiritually hungry by a lean, provincial diet.

Supplied with a great deal of advice and the little money that his father had been able to give him on the dock at parting, Pepe planned to enter the Central University at once and to extract from Madrid all the advantages it offered.

Young Carlos Sauvalle—whom he had known slightly in Havana—put an end to his initial loneliness and introduced him to the city and its people. Sauvalle had been obliged to leave Cuba after the Villanueva Theatre episode, in which he had played a rôle no more significant than that of leaving his coat in the clutches of the Volunteer who had grappled with him at the theatre exit. He had arrived in Madrid just a year before young Martí. Pepe wrote in his friend's album:

Cuba unites us under strangers' skies;
We long for her calm airs from fragrant sea.
Cuba is your heart, Cuba my paradise;
My word, in your book, can only Cuba be.[2]

[1] Martínez de la Rosa: Francisco Martínez de la Rosa (1789-1862), a Spanish poet and politician. As a poet, he was one of the first to introduce in Spain the romantic ideas, especially in the drama; as a politician, he was a leader of the liberal movement against Fernando VII, but later became rather moderate and was always indifferent to Cuban travails.

[2] Cuba nos une en extranjero suelo;
auras de Cuba nuestro amor desea;
Cuba es tu corazón; Cuba es mi cielo;
Cuba, en tu libro, mi palabra sea.

Cuba was, likewise, the word caressed in every conversation: it was the charm against sorrow and cold weather. But in evoking it, sweet recollections now prevailed—images of far-off childhood, of landscape, of avenues of palms, and the mysterious whisperings in the leaves. . . .

The winter, with its quiet, was a healing season, providing temporary forgetfulness.

Spring quickened the Creole blood and brought the past to vivid memory, and Pepe was confined to bed: the hernia injury of quarry days was again painful. Only Carlos Sauvalle came to his lonely bedside—Sauvalle, tall, fair-skinned, with the blue of his Norman lineage in his large, expressive eyes. He secretly fattened Pepe's lean purse; he brought the doctors who were to operate on him.

In his feverish visions Pepe met the ghost of old Nicolás Castillo, with his white hair and his wounds. . . . The sheets of his bed seemed to be the lime-white brilliance of the quarries. . . . When at last he was able to get up, all the past was a torturing memory. The city greeted him more enticingly than ever with its smiles of springtime, but the familiar glance people gave each other on passing, as if in mutual congratulation on the returning sunshine, the very fraternity of men and things, aroused in him a bitter memory and a need to blame someone. He had sudden impulses to stop strangers on the street and surprise them with his tremendous secret.

Along the slope of Atocha he saw Manuel Fraga, another exiled Cuban, coming towards him. He was accompanied by a young man Martí did not know. Fraga introduced him: Zeno Gandía, a South American. Martí was so rapt in his memory-misery that he could not go through with the usual conventional civility, and when the lad held out his hand, Martí said strangely:

"You do not know me. Before shaking hands with me you ought to consider whether it is fitting to be friendly with a man who has been outraged and whose honor has not yet received the satisfaction it requires."

Fraga burst out laughing. But Pepe, terribly solemn, led the astonished young man aside to a doorway and, opening his shirt, showed him the scars of his prison floggings.

His memory was "a basket of flames," as he would later write. He had to set them down on paper to see if they might burn official consciences for whom "the Colonies" were only a rich treasure chest open for plundering, or a chronic cause of parliamentary dispute.

Upon reaching his room in the boarding house on Desengaño Street, Martí sat down to write out his experiences: *El Presidio Político en Cuba.* Without hatred—because he "did not know how to hate"—and reticent about his own suffering—"Why should I speak of myself when I talk of suffering, since others have borne far more than I have"—his pure anger was transferred to fifty pages vibrant with sorrow and pity and dramatic realism, colored by apostrophe and antithesis in the style of Victor Hugo. Through all these pages, in tragic rhythm, stalked all the terrifying scenes of his imprisonment—and that of the Island itself in its secular Stations of the Cross.

This printed accusation reached the desk of Labra[1] in the Cortes, and reminded him that there was in Cuba another type of slavery even blacker than that which he had condemned in his great speech of April 3rd. It reached don Francisco Díaz Quintero, publisher of the newspaper *El Jurado Federal* [*The Federal Juror*], and excited the repub-

[1] Rafael Maria de Labra (1840-1918): Cuban lawyer and journalist who became prominent in Spain's political life. A good orator, he was one of the champions of the abolition of slavery and the granting of self-rule to Cuba.

lican bloc to high indignation. Cánovas,[1] having a fallow season politically, deplored the fact that "an agitator" was endowed with so great a pamphleteering vigor. López de Ayala frowned sarcastically in the Overseas Ministry and noted down the new name: José Martí. And from the pages of the pamphlet, which Carlos Sauvalle had taken pains to get into the hands of every Cuban in Madrid, doña Barbarita, Creole widow of General Ravenet, wiped off more than one tear while she was reading. Old and illustrious don Calixto Bernal,[2] idol of the expatriate Cubans, gave Martí a great hug.

Pepe's illness and the cost of printing the pamphlet exhausted the last reserves of the money don Mariano had given him. Further help from his father, who was probably living from hand to mouth on the impoverished Island, was unthinkable. Sauvalle, too, was in Spain through necessity, but his father was rich and he received a generous allowance punctually every month; he did his best to make Pepe share it. But Pepe was proud and stubborn: Carlos could contribute the amount he would ordinarily spend on trifles and gay dinners to patriotic causes if he wished. But for personal expenses, Pepe would manage on his own, somehow.

He burned his boats by entering the Central University. The exceptional flexibility of the curriculum permitted one, among other things, to pursue his graduate studies along with those required for the baccalaureate degree. Pepe, like

[1] Cánovas: Antonio Cánovas del Castillo, Spanish statesman (1828-1897). The conservative boss who alternated with Práxedes Sagasta, the "liberal" boss, for the control of Spanish politics during many years. They had a nice game of "you-first-then-me." Cánovas was premier at the time of the Spanish-American War. Was killed by an Italian anarchist in 1897.

[2] Bernal: Calixto Bernal y Soto (1804-1886), a Cuban jurist and liberal thinker. Lived most of his life in Spain, helping and sometimes representing the cause of Cuban autonomy or self-rule.

every Cuban youth who could speak with assurance, naturally had to be a lawyer, although the practice of law did not appeal to him. Soon he was studying *res mancipi*—and ways and means of paying for next week's board.

Fortunately, doña Barbarita Echevarría, who had been so deeply moved when she read Martí's prison experiences, perceived his situation and once when Pepe came to call, seeking the warmth of Cuban hospitality, the widow "with the soul of an angel" asked him if he could possibly undertake to teach her children.

Why not? So, in the morning, he was a law student; afternoons, a teacher who had to rely on seriousness and affection for the little authority his eighteen years represented to doña Barbarita's children. They learned more quickly than they ever had before, and the Cuban lady spread the news of the gift Pepe Martí had in winning the love and stimulating the intelligence of children. Her praises of the tutor reached the ears of don Leandro Álvarez Torrijos, who thereupon entrusted the education of his children to the Cuban youth.

And so he was able to support himself. Not too well, perhaps, but well enough to pay his board regularly and to go occasionally to the theatre—the Español or the Teatro Real. Now and then something unusual came his way, for instance, the translation of a certain English contract "full of technical and unusual words." This windfall came at the right time, since Pepe's shoes were worn out. He earned eight *duros* by this tiresome work; he did not spend the duros on shoes, however, but on photographs of fine paintings.

At the University the students did not neglect, either in friendship or in their pranks, the pale Creole youth who was so extremely generous in spite of his poverty. In respectful silence they listened more than once to his reporting on the Presidio quarries, and from their lips he heard honest indignation and professions of faith in the imminent arrival of a

Spanish republic. The students were of all shades of political opinion—from radicals to partisans of Bourbon Alfonso, Isabel's sixteen-year-old son, and there were even a few Carlists, advocates of the cause of don Carlos, another claimant to the throne. The majority, however, were Republican followers of Figueras[1] and Pi y Margall;[2] they formed a noisy claque at the political meetings in the Alhambra Theatre.

From gossip at school, and through editorials and articles in some of the small, liberal periodicals, Pepe familiarized himself with the ins and outs of Spanish politics. The neutrality of the foreigner king, Amadeo, had not succeeded in reëstablishing harmony in the Spanish family. Sagasta and Ruiz Zorrilla,[3] political leaders, were at each other's throats. Carlism had broken out again strongly in the North, and while the most new-fangled monarchists were tenderly grooming their young Bourbon princeling Alfonso for the crown, the Republicans were noisily working for their hour. From the press box in the Cortes Pepe heard oratorical battles of eloquence and brilliance. Listening to Manterola's polished dialectics, to the ornate Castelar,[4] to Cánovas, to

[1] Figueras: Estanislao Figueras (1819-1882), a Spanish political leader. Fought Amadeo I and, when he abdicated, was put in charge of the executive power in the new-born republic.

[2] Pi y Margall (1824-1901): a Spanish (or rather, Catalonian!) statesman and thinker, leader of the Republican movement in Spain and first president of the "First Republic," established in 1873. Was in favor of granting Cuba home-rule and, later, even independence. A fine character, a courageous leader, a radical thinker. Revered by Cubans.

[3] Ruiz Zorrilla: Manuel Ruiz Zorrilla (1834-1895), a Spanish politician, member of the Republican party.

[4] Castelar: Emilio Castelar (1832-1899), famous Spanish orator and republican leader. Took part in the 1868 "glorious" revolution against Isabel II. Opposed Prim's monarchical policies. When the Republic was first established in 1870, Castelar was its first premier. After the restoration of the monarchy in 1874, Castelar–a professor in the

Moret,[1] Pepe was awed at times by the wealth of language. At others, he was amused—or disgusted—by the cunning wit of Sagasta and the quick, beak-like thrusts of the "Chicken of Antequera." [2]

The whole spectacle—and was it, actually, more than a spectacle?—always left him with a sad impression of futility. Spain was divided by walls of words and petty jealousies. Everything in political life was here reduced to quarrelsome personal factions like the everlasting feud between the two irreconcilable schools on the art of bull-fighting—the disciples of Frascuelo and those of Lagartijo.[3] In all this constant discord—which frustrated the best good-will—parasitism, inertia, and rhetoric flourished like the green bay tree. Martí began to see clearly that the problem of Cuba derived from the problem of Spain herself; and he realized that Cuba's dilemma would be settled only when the Spanish difficulties were settled—unless, in the meantime a Cuban revolution should cause a parting of the ways.

Don Calixto Bernal, in whom he confided these impressions, agreed with him to a great extent. Some of the young man's opinions seemed to him excessively mystical, especially those touching the colonies: Pepe was a poet. While, on the other hand, the old Camagüeyan, who had been fighting for the dignity of Cuba since the days of Tacón, was of a logi-

---

Madrid University–devoted himself mainly to writing. His reputation as an orator in the grand style was European. Despite his republicanism, he looked askance upon Cuban efforts for freedom.

[1] Moret: Segismundo Moret (1838-1913), a Spanish statesman, often a collaborator of Sagasta. A lesser orator than Castelar.

[2] This reference is to the Spanish politician Francisco Romero y Robledo (1832-1906), born in Antequera, hence the popular nickname "Chicken of Antequera," chicken having the slang connotation of "young fellow." Was a biting orator, a member of the conservative party.

[3] Frascuelo and Lagartijo: the two most famous *matadores* or bullfighters of the time. There was a perennial rivalry between them.

cal, legal, positivist nature. On the Commission of Inquiry his clear charges of outrages had made whiplash impressions; he advocated a straightforward régime looking to dominion status for the colonies. In spite of this moderate point of view for Cuban affairs, he nevertheless championed daring and original ideas in politics. He frequently discussed with Martí the vices of parliamentary government and the necessity of reëstablishing "pure democracy" through the direct government by the people, and other themes from his books. And he perplexed the young student a little with more soaring theories: the inevitability of a future Society of Nations, the certain imminent rise of a "fourth power," the proletariat, after great revolutions that would surpass any in history. . . .

Pepe enjoyed talking with no one more than he did with that old "practical theorist," as don Calixto described himself. They were often seen together, the white-haired old man somewhat stooped with age; Pepe, skinny, nervous and talkative. Don Calixto coached the youth in his apprenticeship in democratic doctrine. He was, for political education, a little of what Mendive had been to him in the world of letters.

In all things pertaining to Cuba, however, the old lawyer's ideas disturbed the young author of *El Presidio Político*. Autonomist "through conviction and through law," Bernal considered any aspiration to independence premature. He considered annexation to the United States preferable to independence; it would assure Cuba internal peace and prosperity until the time came for union with the other West Indies into a separate country when the United States split up, as was inevitable, into smaller republics.

These daring prophecies obliged Pepe to exercise his imagination a good deal and forced him to project his thinking in political matters much farther than the current problems. He hesitated in accepting Bernal's autonomy program for Cuba; he always found himself caught by his own question: Yara or Madrid? The memories and enthusiasms of his boyhood drew him to the Yara ideal of independence. But the other also weighed heavily—with the secret voice of hereditary ties, the feeling of affinity with a beguiling culture which appealed to him in its Spanish setting. If the Republic were to come into being! If Spain, worthily governed, would only at last herself redeem Cuba!

Many times other expatriates shared in the talks of the Cuban ancient and the Cuban youth, forming lively groups around a table at a café or in some friendly editor's office. Conversation at such times grew more and more heated over the latest news from the Island—the progress of the Revolution, as given in some letter from Havana, the news of the shooting of the poet Zenea,[1] the terrible reprisals Valmaseda took against the Oriente rebels—or perhaps the discussions were over the details of colonial politics in Madrid itself.

Malicious echoes of these discussions reached the editors of *La Prensa*, a newspaper supporting Sagasta which boasted of its liberalism, and which was probably financed through the colonial fortune of Manuel Calvo.[2] *La Prensa*, which had already alluded guardedly to the "filibusterism" hidden "behind the screen of advanced theories and radical principles" of Bernal, decided to make a sensation and scandal of these gatherings and warned the government that the Cubans living in Madrid were nothing but "sneaking filibusterers, hypocrites, and spurious sons of Spain."

These, and similar remarks, made Martí and Sauvalle determine to publish in the more genuine liberal paper, *El Jurado Federal*, a strong denial and they signed it "Various Cubans." The awkward reply was not from Martí's pen;

[1] Juan Clemente Zenea, a romantic Cuban poet who, having sided with the patriots, was seized and shot in Havana.

[2] Manuel Calvo: a rich Spanish merchant with interests in Cuba, an indefatigable lobbyist against the abolition of slavery and against liberal measures for the Island.

but the conditions for revolutionary action were suggested, adding the insinuation that if any Cuban in Madrid harbored the idea of starting a Cuban revolution, he should know that Spain was not, and could not be, the best place in which to work for it.

La Prensa, galled by its own lie, insisted on repeating the accusation and called the signers of the denial a "secret society." The controversy became involved with the usual exchanges of vituperation between the two papers, and when, finally, the *Prensa*, claiming public opinion in support of its position, challenged "Various Cubans" who were hiding behind a nom de plume, Martí openly entered the arena to close "a question which insults prevent bringing to further public discussion." Sauvalle also signed this last communication to *El Jurado*, but the vivid words and the clear dignified tone of it recalled the pages of Martí's pamphlet. Although *La Prensa* threatened a civil suit—and even hinted at a duel for the satisfaction of honor—no blood flowed in the streets.

At the end of November Martí again became ill, undergoing another operation for the removal of the tumor formed during his imprisonment. Sauvalle insisted on having Martí brought to his lodgings so that he could give him better care. There, Cuban and Spanish friends came to chat at his bedside. They discussed, first and foremost, certain fresh news from Cuba in dispatches to the newspapers—first year medical students at the University of Havana had "desecrated the tomb" of Castañón, the fanatic spokesman of the Volunteers, who had been killed a year previously by a Cuban in Key West. According to the terse dispatches, feeling was at fever pitch.

Castañón . . . Volunteers . . . students. . . . The mixture could not have been more explosive. The youthful gathering in Pepe's bedroom wondered fearfully about the

AMATEUR SURGERY IN CUBA

turn of events, and talked of the past. Pepe, pale as a ghost, tried to curb his imagination, which was running wild in his feverish state. There must be something very serious going on in Cuba. . . . From the 28th on, there had been no news at all. And Fermín Valdés Domínguez was one of those medical students!

"Do the papers have anything to say, Fraga?" he always asked.

One day his friend went out to get a paper. He came back shortly with a sombre face, a copy of *El Jurado* in his hand.

"They have shot eight!"

Making a violent effort, Martí sat up, snatched the paper and read the meagre details which the editors had not dared to expand: Eight executed; thirty-five condemned to the Presidio. There was a stunned silence in the room. Pepe fell back on the pillow. The others remained grim and silent.

All that afternoon Pepe chose to be left alone. From the adjoining room, Carlos heard him speak Fermín's name again and again. What could not be heard was the silent oath that destroyed forever all that had remained of Martí's ancestral loyalty to Spain; in its place a decision crystallized for life-long action.

Chapter Six

"CUBA WEEPS"

THE HORRIBLE NEWS was presently reported in clear detail. Fermín, however, was not among those executed: he had been sentenced to the Presidio. The Volunteers in a spasm of collective fury had forced the shooting of eight innocent youths; they were satisfied. This frightful vengeance was followed by a tidal wave of indignation and embarrassment. The foreign press played up the event and likened it to the times of Alba and Torquemada; in Spain itself even the press supporting the government did not dare endorse such barbaric violence.

Martí, still ill and feverish, went to the dingy office of *El Jurado Federal* in San Mateo Street to show Díaz Quintero and his associate editor, don Eduardo Benot,[1] letters from Havana which narrated the tragic events of November 23rd through the 27th. These sincere Republicans joined him in his anger. So that was what the Volunteers were like —the heroes in whose honor the Sagasta government had struck a medal as a testimonial of a grateful country!

The matter became the center of political combat, and the *Jurado* began to publish daily on its front page a demand for the release of the imprisoned students and for a parliamentary investigation of the execution of those slain. At the opening of the Cortes of 1872, Benot delivered an impassioned and noble speech.

[1] Benot: Eduardo Benot (1822-1907) a minor politician and political journalist, as well as a rather noted philologist, was at this time a member of the Cortes.

Martí became a tireless mobilizer of opinion. Into Spanish ears, sympathetic or not, he poured an account of the tragedy described with all the powers of his imagination and the vivid memories of his own experience. He wrote unsigned articles, attended sessions of the Cortes to gauge the possibilities of a pardon for the students, took part in Republican gatherings at the Café Oriental, and kept the zeal of exiled Cubans at white heat. He had become an agitator—on however small a scale—now that his own doubts were resolved, and his own course charted. On the 2nd of May there were military parades and patriotic exercises in the streets to celebrate the resistance of Spain to Napoleon in 1808. Pepe hung a Cuban flag from the balcony of the boarding house to the great alarm of Sauvalle and the scandalized curiosity of the populace.

All this activity and feverish excitement kept him from regaining his health. He was, of course, still earning his living by teaching and writing articles for the radical papers. And he had to study, besides. How could he apply himself to those dry-as-dust assignments in law, at odd times in his cold garret, with his mind in a turmoil over Havana, the Presidio quarries, and Fermín?

At long last, on May 10, the *Gaceta* announced the students' pardon. Pepe could relax. He passed his examinations in Roman, political and administrative law, but failed in political economy. A better record would have been too much to ask.

In July, just when Madrid was in a ferment over the attempted assassination of King Amadeo, Fermín arrived, with Pedro de la Torre, a fellow-student who had also been released from the Presidio. Their pardon was a conditional one, entailing exile in Spain. They too had been sent to the quarries, and on the afternoon when they were released, they had been marched out with a group of a hundred regular prisoners so that news of their transfer might not reach the Volunteers. For nineteen days they had been held aboard the frigate *Saragoza* until they could be transferred to the regular steamship. As their ship had passed before the Valdés Fort, crowds celebrating the feast of Corpus Christi had shouted insulting remarks.

When Martí had heard the whole tremendous story in full detail, he could study Fermín with affectionate care: Fermín had grown a great deal, and his face showed the maturity that comes from deep suffering.

The murder of the students gave to patriotic Cubans the unique value of symbol and precedent which martyrdom always gives to a cause. The circumstances of that sacrifice —the youth of the victims, the fact that they were students, the monstrous disparity between the alleged offense and the punishment meted out, the violent and fanatical conduct of the Volunteers and the spineless complicity of the Insular government—made November 27th the sacred symbol of Cuba. The fact that in Spain the men of good-will had nobly condemned the deed did not matter. Memory pricked consciousness too deeply, and the symbol was to be nurtured, not with hatred as a motive, but as a witness for liberty.

On the first anniversary of the execution of the students, the principal street corners of the city and court broke out with posters reminding passers-by of the "terrible day on which eight sons were stolen from the earth and a people wept at the graves of eight martyrs." Behind this virile lament the less sentimental reader could detect significant reticences in the sentence: "There is a limit to weeping over the graves of the slain, and it is an oath of infinite love of country and of glory that is sworn over their bodies." This solemn broadside was signed by Pedro J. de la Torre and Fermín Valdés Domínguez, the two survivors who were then in Madrid; but it was the work of Martí, the youthful pamphleteer of the exiles.

In the Caballero de Gracia church a memorial mass for the students was celebrated that morning. When they had distributed printed handbills at the door after the services, the group of young Cuban students in mourning went to Carlos Sauvalle's. They had decided to profit by the occasion to form a permanent organization and to discuss its objectives. One of them, with the fun-loving psychology of the Cuban, tactlessly suggested that they form a sort of club, with social gatherings as well as patriotic meetings and program. To Pepe Martí, the times seemed too out of joint for fun.

After an exchange of ideas and suggestions, he went up to the improvised platform above which Carlos had hung a map of Cuba on the wall to serve as their device or standard. Pepe was still convalescent from a third operation, which had been done under Fermín's brotherly watchfulness, and he seemed, in his black coat, weaker and paler than ever. As he stood there on the platform, under the map, his curly chestnut hair blotted out the Isle of Pines.[1]

He began to speak in a soft and pleasant tone, touching lightly on the frivolous aspects of the proposed idea. A master of contrasts, he quietly pointed out the opposition between the festive club idea and the tragic occasion which had brought them together. He described the martyrdom of the boys. The smiling faces grew serious. He portrayed, in perfect detail, as if he had been an eye-witness, the events of the three incredible days of fury and anguish. Tears came to the eyes of his hearers; Sauvalle leaned forward breathlessly in his chair. Martí went on, speaking of the tragedy of those lives cut off, the loneliness of friendships severed so brutally, of the endless sorrow of the mothers despoiled of their sons. . . . It was so still one could hear a fly on the wing and Fraga's slight nervous cough. . . .

"And, like this sorrow of mothers, much greater indeed,

[1] A small island situated just below the southern coast of Cuba.

is the sorrow of the great mother of all, Cuba. Cuba weeps, brothers, and . . ."

The ironic imp that lies in wait to trip up orators staged a really good prank at that moment: The map of Cuba fell from the wall and draped itself over Pepe Martí's head. How could anyone expect seriousness from such a youthful audience? The tears changed spontaneously to laughter, and Martí saw himself plunged into the ridiculous.

But he saved the situation, adding his laughter to that of the others and, pulling together a net of apt phrases, treating the fallen map as a symbol of Cuba's anxiety over her sons, he brought his listeners back to a serious mood. Little by little his words created anew a dramatic intensity and when he began once more to repeat his peroration, "Cuba is weeping, brothers, and we must . . ." there was no comic jester to disrupt his eloquence. All his listeners embraced him, and when a vote was taken the idea of a club was voted down.

From that day on, to the Cuban exiles—always alive to humor—Pepe's nickname was "Cuba Weeps." It was one, however, thoroughly endowed with affection and respect: Love for the modest comrade who was always helpful and generous, and respect for his greatness of soul and the intelligence which was so obvious. And for his gifts as an orator.

The Republicans of *El Jurado Federal* had already persuaded him to join the Masons, thinking perhaps that such a step would in time lead him to work for the Spanish Republican cause. But Martí probably thought his own thoughts. In the Harmony Lodge, of which he was a member, other Cubans fraternized simply with Spaniards of various ranks and means. Martí brought to the lodge, in his romantic dissertations on Universal Love, a veiled protest against the hatred and injustice that stubborn blindness maintained in Cuba. His lodge brothers occasionally frowned on hearing a fiery paragraph on politics, which lodge rules prohibited, and which, moreover, painted such a picture of Cuban misrule as to make autonomy, even within a future Spanish federal Republic, seem irreconcilable. While the musician Max Marchal listened raptly to the rhythmic flow of Pepe's argument, General Perrat had to pound his gavel frequently, recommending discretion to Brother Martí.

But, for the most part, the Cuban knew how to promote his immediate objectives, seeing at least that his lodge rendered aid to some destitute Cuban, sending help to compatriots who were political prisoners in Ceuta,[1] or to ask their secret support for the abolition of slavery, about to be proposed in the Cortes.

"Cuba Weeps" moved behind the scenes with singular effectiveness. And the nickname did not offend him: In spite of all, it was true. Cuba, all Cuba's wrongs, cried out in him. A bitter baptism of tears had sealed his oath of consecration to work for the liberty of his people. One night in the winter of '73, while Fermín was finishing his book on the executions, handing each page to Pepe as he made the final editing touches, they both cried over the "tale of woes"—as Fermín's brother called it. With the suffering they had prematurely witnessed and undergone and carried in their minds, they had in them also all the outmoded romanticism of their race. Fermín summed it up in his invitation to poetry: "A book which was born in martyrdom must end in poetry." And Pepe added the poem: "To My Brothers Slain on the 27th of November."

But all was not patriotic tragedy. Madrid, hospitable and gay, offered the exiles many pleasures, and, after all, they were only twenty years old.

When there was no gathering at doña Barbarita's, they were welcome at the rather formal Villaurrutias' or at the

[1] A Spanish possession on the northern coast of Africa.

home of the Marqués de San Gregorio or the Marquesa de la Vega de Armijo, in whose stately drawing-rooms Pepe perfected his instinctive good manners. Even more regularly the young political exiles formed a part of the lively bohemian group at the Café de los Artistas, or at the English Alehouse, where one could almost always count on the ready wit and brilliance of Marcos Zapata.[1]

In the beguiling atmosphere of Madrid, Pepe's love for the theatre increased. He was often in the balcony of the Teatro Real. Examinations had to be very close at hand, or his health or finances at a low ebb, for him to miss an opening night at the Español, where he was almost as much at home as a member of the cast. In the green room back stage he could enjoy the breezy sallies of the actress Teodora Lamadrid, and could leave by the stage door in the company of don José Echegaray, who in the Cortes would deliver speeches which were the cool, dispassionate essays of an engineer, and in the theatre the impassioned drama of the orator. Stimulated by these contacts, Pepe began to write a Utopian play in which he hoped to portray "men not as they are" but "as they ought to be."

Painting interested him almost as much as the theatre. He spent Sunday mornings alone in the Prado museum, with its creaking floors and its waxy-smelling silence. Here he was especially captivated by the easy grace and dramatic idiom of Goya. Returning from these visits, he wrote down his impressions in thoughtful notes, apparent exercises in criticism seeking to explore the reasons for his tastes. On the *Maja Desnuda*, for instance, he noted down the mysterious beauty of the legs, "separated and at the same time united by a fold of fine gauze," praising in it "the delicacy of the painter: voluptuousness without eroticism."

That formula was to become expressive of his own tem-

[1] Marcos Zapata (1844-1913), a minor Aragonese poet, rather popular in his time.

perament. For he, also, was voluptuous without "eroticism," without professionalism. . . . There were certain happy-go-lucky damsels of the Fuente de la Teja,[1] certain waitresses at the Lavapies and Vistillas taverns who also had their Goyesque charm, the very archetypes of the serving-maid of song and story who succumb to the romantic blandishments of students. Pepe liked the girls, and his way with them did not remind friends of his weepy nick-name, although there was a trace of melancholy always blended with his gaiety which made him all the more interesting to the girls.

He did not run away from ardent adventures that came along. But when he encountered purity he conducted himself with the most chivalrous restraint. "If I had wished, I could have plucked these lilies," he wrote, "but if I had done so, afterwards they could have said of me what the flowers say of the hurricane; and people on seeing the needless havoc would curse me as the hurricane is cursed."

Besides, he was too poor for frivolities. When he and Fermín went out together for a good time, Fermín provided the means. He had managed, once for all, to silence his "brother's" scruples: What he had belonged to them both. And as Pepe felt in himself an identical generosity, and never considered anything of his merely his own, he accepted Fermín's surplus and repaid him in brotherly affection. His generosity in helping others, with the little money he had, was little less than extravagant. He would calm an infuriated carter by giving him money to buy candy for his children. And he went at night to teach a school of poor children supported by the lodge, taking them sweets, books —and his great imaginative gift for story-telling.

[1] The Fuente de la Teja seems to have been a spring or fountain, probably provided with a "teja" or roof-tile to lead out the water, in the suburbs of Madrid. Near it a kind of spa or little café for more or less wild and popular parties was established.

Chapter Seven

THE REPUBLIC

ON THE DAY before Christmas, 1873, the Congress of Deputies, in a gesture of parliamentary sanctimoniousness, dedicated the entire holiday session, the final one of that Cortes, to passage of the bill through which Ruiz Zorrilla's administration would abolish slavery in Puerto Rico. Labra's forceful and eloquent campaign was beginning to bear its fruit, although a smaller harvest than had been expected. Pepe and Fermín, greatly hoping for generosity and justice after Castelar's impassioned speech during the previous session, felt defrauded when they heard that the Government regretted in its resolution that "the folly of a few stubborn rebels . . . prevented it from granting the same benefits to Cuba."

They left the palatial halls of the Cortes discussing the blind malice of this action. As opposed to such sickly liberalism, how heavily the interests of slaveholders counted, interests defended by Manuel Calvo and his henchmen in the Colonial Ministry!

Madrid was exhausted with the holiday preparations. People hurried through the streets, turning their shoulders against the icy wind. Many carried baskets or packages under their coats. Here and there were stalls where nougats and marchpane Christmas candies were displayed for sale with figurines of the Nativity. The air carried in it the muted sound of *zambombas*,[1] punctuated by shrieks and

[1] Zambomba: a noise-maker peculiar to Madrid and the Low Countries—small and drum-like in shape, with skins stretched over each end; in one end a stick is inserted and pulled back and forth to make a scraping sound.

shouts of excitement. For awhile the two friends walked along in silence, lost in the same reverie—memories of other Christmases, Christmases warmer and more expansive, smelling of pan sugar and suckling pigs roasting on banana leaves.

Fermín was the first to break the sombre mood and on a note of optimism he suggested that perhaps the abolition of slavery might not be too far off for Cuba. Estébanez, don Nicolás Estébanez,[1] to whom he had been introduced a few nights ago at the Café de Venecia, had assured him that the Republic was well on its way. Spain had already had enough of its foreign king.

Pepe took a deep breath. Yes: he too had high hopes in the birth of the Republic. The signs of a political turnover were becoming obvious. The attempted assassination of King Amadeo, the mutiny of the republican seamen at El Ferrol, and especially the frantic storm signals of crisis-politics—lobbying and secret meetings. Sooner or later the Republic was bound to come, with its idea of a new Spain, reborn, respecting regional integrity and values. Under the leadership of men like Pi y Margall, Salmerón,[2] Figueras, Estébanez, would not the Republic have the courage and conscience to recognize that Cuba had already made up her own mind in the battlefields and that her decision was to be respected?

The answer was not long in coming. The year 1874 was ushered in heavy with omens. Almost at the beginning an insignificant incident—an insubordinate gesture against the Government by the artillerymen of Vitoria—darkened the political sky. Amadeo thought it an opportune moment to favor the restless military and when his action was repudi-

[1] Nicolás Estébanez: A Spanish Republican journalist, noted for his courageous condemnation of the student massacre of 1871 in Cuba.

[2] Nicolás Salmerón (1838-1873), also a Republican statesman in Spain, and a philosopher. He, too, was president of the "First Republic."

ated by the Cortes, he decided to use the occasion to please his Queen, who was becoming day by day less fond of that turbulent country, where the Bourbon court ladies almost openly condemned her for nursing her newly-born child. Amadeo abdicated.

The Cortes met on February 11 in joint session and ushered the King out with all Castelar's florid rhetoric and proclaimed the Republic immediately thereafter. Pepe and Fermín, in the press box, were enthusiastic in their applause. But when the liberal deputy Martos, with the Republic just born, saluted the unity of Spain and Spanish Cuba, the two Cubans remained silent. Pepe would have liked to have stood up at that moment and shouted: "No! Long live Spanish Cuba if Cuba wants to be Spanish, but Hail Free Cuba, if Cuba wants to be free!"

But he thought it would be better to say it in writing and to give his reasons.

On the 15th of February, as a matter of fact, he sent an extensive essay entitled "The Spanish Republic and the Cuban Revolution" to don Estanislao Figueras, the head of the new Government. Before doing so he had read it to Bernal and his Cuban friends. Fermín knew many of its paragraphs by heart. Don Calixto nodded gravely in approval of the lyric opening designed to win the "generosity" of the victorious Republic; but when Bernal saw his own democratic doctrines carried to their logical application as regards Cuba—with freedom the only solution, since she had indicated her desire for freedom—the old lawyer was taken aback by the carefully worked out dialectic:

> ". . . and if Cuba declares her independence by the same right under which Spain declares herself a Republic, how can Spain deny Cuba the right to be free, which is the same right she used to achieve her own freedom? How can she deny this right to Cuba without denying it for her-

self? How can Spain settle the fate of a people by imposing on them a way of life in which their complete, free and obvious wish does not enter at all?"

Bernal admired the terseness of the reasoning, the nobility of thought and vigor of his style, incredible in such an inexperienced writer. But twenty-five years spent in observing Spanish politics made him shake his head skeptically. Pepe was trusting too much to man's consistency: he was forgetting that history had a logic of its own. When the reading was finished he embraced his young disciple and with his voice trembling with emotion, said only, "God grant it, my son!"

Figueras received his caller with some vague phrases of general agreement, but when the visitor had left his office, he put on his spectacles, glanced here and there through the lengthy manuscript, made a wry face and shoved the document away in a drawer.

The Government did not go into the matter any further, but Madrid did. Carlos Sauvalle and Fermín took good care that a copy of the essay went to a printer they already knew on San Mateo Street, who put it in pamphlet form for them to distribute to all the editors, discussion groups and official channels of public opinion. The first reactions to it commented at length on the brashness of the youth in "laying down the law" so presumptuously to the new Republic. His journalistic opponents at *La Prensa* struck the attitude: "We told you so!"—even more disturbed now by a fear that "subversive" shouts for freedom might be listened to.

But the Republic paid no attention whatsoever. It was still too preoccupied with its own problems. It had made its entry on the stage of history through the prompter's box and no one, not even the Republicans themselves, quite believed in that meek and tentative entrance as victorious drama. Many of the most astute thinkers held that the new régime would not establish itself without its "baptism of blood." Estébanez went to bed every night "with his boots on," expecting revolution, and the other leaders of the Republic—Salmerón, Pi and Figueras—were no less fearful.

By April Martí had lost all hope. Unofficially, the Cubans living in Madrid had been called together at a meeting in the Academy of Jurisprudence. The aim was to get from them an explicit declaration of support for the Republic, confiding the future of Cuba to the triumph of the federal idea, which would give her virtual autonomy. All the "official" Cubans of the city and the Court were there, of course, the majority favorable to the new régime; a little apart from the orthodox group, Bernal, and more noisy than numerous, the young men for independence, with Martí in their forefront, flanked by Fermín and his brother Eusebio, who had just arrived in Spain.

When the discussion began to lose itself in polite, diplomatic generalities, Martí asked for the floor. He maintained —agreeing with a question raised earlier—that the Cubans living in Madrid had no authority or right to compromise in any way the free determination of Cuba's will—which was being shown in her war for independence.

Shouts and catcalls, cries of "Be sensible!" hoots of derision from the Spaniardized Cubans greeted him. Unperturbed, however, Martí parried all the witticisms, refuted the serious objections to his point of view, and repeated with impassioned sincerity all the points he had brought out in the essay which he had presented to the Government. He held the floor for seven hours—a twenty-year-old, poorly dressed youth, vibrant in phrase and gesture, appealing to that assembly of frock-coated elders.

The hostile reception he encountered that night made him understand that his neglected appeal to the generosity of the Republic had received all the official attention that could be expected. Actually, he had never had much faith in its efficacy: He knew that in Spain political opinion was not moved by principles unless emotion carried them along. With his writing he had only hoped—as he explained in a letter to a Cuban in New York—to educate the Spaniards, who were "completely strangers, if not to the idea of the possibility of our independence, at least to the justice of it" . . . and he also wanted to make them understand "that Spain's war with Cuba, up to now shameful, had become since the advent of the Republic doubly a matter of brother killing brother."

This letter was sent to Néstor Ponce de León, secretary of the revolutionary committee in New York. Martí also sent him copies of his pamphlet to distribute on appropriate occasions. And he explained:

> "From these pages I have written, you can see that I hold myself ready, if there is any way in which you think I can be of service, to hear your suggestion on what you think most convenient for Cuba, or the things you believe need to be done to hasten our complete independence. To the accomplishment of this, alone, I shall dedicate without fear and without rest my humble talents and all the strength of my will power, which now regrets not having any real sphere of activity in which to work."

Chapter Eight

THE BRANCH OF FLOWERING ALMOND

For Aragón, in Spain,
I cherish in my heart—
Open, proud, true, free of pain—
All Aragón's, a place apart.[1]

NOR WAS THERE to be a "real sphere of activity" for his patriotic zeal in the very beautiful and ancient city of Saragossa to which Martí moved, a month later—in May, 1873—with Fermín, as soon as they had seen the ridiculous performance of a "revolution" that had done nothing but change the form of government into a republic. Not very well adjusted to the natural climate of Madrid, and deeply embittered already by its political temperature, the two Cubans decided to act upon the advice of a doctor that they go farther north. To Barcelona or Saragossa? Chance, more than anything else, made them choose the latter, the capital of Aragón. They had progressed rather haphazardly in their studies: perhaps in two years more they could complete them in the illustrious and gracious university of the city named for Caesar Augustus.

Actually, they were never able to discover any healthful advantages in the climate of Saragossa, which was as inclement and variable as it could possibly be. The sultriness of

[1] Para Aragón, en España,
tengo yo en mi corazón
un lugar todo Aragón,
franco, fiero, fiel, sin saña.

summer, however, did not prevent the Cuban lads from quickly coming to like the Aragonese city. It was very little frequented by foreign students and the fact that the two young Cubans had chosen to come there, even from Madrid itself, flattered local pride and people openly expressed their friendship and good will. As for the two friends, they found in that provincial quiet, after the nervous and transient life of Madrid, a tranquillity and sense of security almost home-like.

At Don Félix Sanz's, on Manifestation Street, there was offered them not the commercialized and somewhat sordid lodging-house environment of Madrid, but real hospitality in a family atmosphere. Don Félix had—more important than his large house and garden—two pretty and charming daughters, affectionately nicknamed "the little green legs" by the Sarogossians ever since they had taken part in a procession of the Virgin of Pilar wearing green stockings. Fermín and Pepe, by lucky chance, happened to pair off with the girls, their choices mutual, and this immediate solace to their strangeness in a new city was an added gift of Saragossa, which sweetened exile. And, to make things even more like home, there was a Negro servant, a Cuban—"a man of words and weapons" as Fermín described him. Simón had been deported to Ceuta by Lersundi, accused of black magic and worse. Having served his sentence, he had come to Saragossa to stay, and after working as a boot-black in the Arch of Sineja he had come to serve at the boarding house. Simón's happiness over the "insurrecto" guests, and the picturesque tales that the boys, hungry for Cuban memories, inspired him to tell, can only be imagined.

They were also delighted with their new academic affiliation. In the ancient university, which actually went back to the days of Caesar Augustus, the "centralization plan" of 1845 had not yet done away with all the independent tradition, nor the custom of intellectual fraternization between professors and students on a basis of equality. The Cubans were as welcome as gold. Their ideology as insurrectos was quickly revealed, but the reaction was more likely to be good-natured joking and intelligent discussion, in class and out, rather than the occasional sarcastic jibe. Pepe's extraordinary maturity, his gift of phrase and logic, and the ardent gentleness which was the special quality of his character, earned for him the esteem and affection of his teachers, and he was often to be seen of an afternoon leaving the university with them. Such circumstances, as one may imagine, did not hamper his law study or the work for his bachelor's degree, which he was doing at the same time.

This double course of study restricted his activity a great deal, but it left him time enough to lose himself in reading history, and with enough left over so that he could drop in on the discussions of the cafés and at the office of the *Diario de Avisos* or at the studio of the painter Gossalvo, who often went for a walk with Pepe at night through the winding, moon-drenched streets, to contemplate the mysterious silhouette of the Aljafería, or the gleaming scimitar of the silent river Ebro.

On holiday mornings he would submerge himself in the nave of the Cathedral, which stirred in him a gentle religious emotion. He was not very religious; his reading of atheist literature and the indifference of the "widow's sons"—as a scoffing Spain dubbed the Masons—had tended to let the religious flame started by doña Leonor burn down to a flicker. But he still believed in God, without a doubt, and at certain times when the Cathedral was not too full of pious women he experienced a feeling of awesome sublimity in the vast and silent church.

The ancient walls of Saragossa stimulated Martí to give free rein to his powers of evocation of the past, and he relived in imagination scenes from the history he had recently studied. A connoisseur of detail and niceties of style, he recorded his impressions carefully, greatly helped by Gossalvo's erudition on local matters. He filled a whole notebook with lavish accounts of his observations in the ancient capital.

During the winter passable acting companies from Madrid presented comedy and drama; Pepe and Fermín never failed to go to the *Teatro Principal*, occupying Box 13, boycotted by provincial superstition. The two Cubans were the cynosure of all eyes: Fermín, slender, with his sleepy-child expression, Pepe with his air of palely-loitering knight-at-arms, elegant in manners.

One night he surprised hazel-brown eyes glancing up at him from the orchestra parterre. Startled on discovery, the eyes quickly turned away. This happened a second time, and a third. On the fourth meeting of their glances, Pepe grew paler and the fair beholder, pink and white, blushed more rosily. During the last intermission he managed to meet her. Her name was Blanca: Blanca de Montalvo. And that night, Pepe, an engaging escort after the theatre, stood for a long time enchanted outside a manorial house on Platerías Street, until the light in a certain window went out.

The rest was a matter of a few days and a few formal calls. Love, which until then had only playfully tripped him up, tackled him this time and brought him down. He was kindling wood to love's fire: a bundle of sensitive Cuban nerves, a spirit filled with longing, and so constantly eager for tenderness that even friendship with him had in it a poignant, passionate quality. Fermín had often joked about the lover-like accent of Pepe's letters to his mother and sisters, to Ana particularly, who replied "in poetry." Pepe's youth, torn up by its roots and trembling with impatience, had been until now rather stark and dramatic. In his gaiety one always could detect a certain intensity and forcing which gave it a melancholy air. Now, Fermín noticed, with pleasure and yet with alarm, that Pepe laughed more easily than he had known him to laugh for several years. Literally, the almond tree in the garden was lifting "its flowery dark branch" up to the level of the window of the friends' room —and Pepe felt within himself that something springlike had entered his own life.

In the first rush of optimistic love the idea did not occur to him that such sudden rapture demanded prudence, that he would have to overcome the obstacles of fashionable convention, the plans of a family of distinction for their daughter, and his own status as a bird of passage. He threw himself into his first love affair with an intense finality of purpose and, indeed, not without some philosophy behind it. Imbued with the doctrines of German "harmonicism" which had been popular in Spain ever since Sanz del Rio had brought Krause's theories from Germany, Pepe had reasoned lyrically that "each being comes to earth only half a being."

And so it is of human life the goal
To seek, forever to seek, the kindred soul.

And he was certain of having found his in the sweet and golden Blanca de Montalvo. His thoughts played about his "perfect love" as innocent "as the grass on the bank of a river." And Fermín watched over him vigilantly.

Only the passing pressures of study, or a nostalgic letter from Havana disturbed the almost stylized romantic peace of this idyll. In August, as soon as Pepe had taken his examinations in seven law courses and ten for his baccalaureate, he enrolled for eight new ones in philosophy and literature. From Havana doña Leonor wrote about his father's asthma, their poverty, and the thinness of the girls as they were growing up. Don Mariano had just been retired again, and since economic despair was spreading all over the Island following the sugar crisis and the burning of the sugar mills by rebels in the field, the Valencian Micawber kept talking of going to Mexico and taking all his family to try to better their luck. Doña Leonor and Ana were enthusiastic about the venture, for then Pepe could rejoin them when he finished his course, in case he could not return to Cuba.

This news, and information gleaned from Carlos's letters and items that appeared in the newspapers about the revolution, each day more threatening in the Island, aroused in Pepe impulses which had been lulled to sleep in the pleasant provincial life of Saragossa. Blanca began to encounter silences in him, and had an impression that he was curbing a wild impatience. Love usually exerted its influence, however, and overcame his restlessness. Pepe justified himself before the bar of his conscience: He was forging his weapons in readiness for the day when he should find the "sphere of reality" in which to move. At other times the pleasant self-awareness of a man in love silenced all else.

Autumn came, with its feast of the Virgin of Pilar, a mixture of pageantry and worship, and in the same season the festivities of the grape harvest. The Christmas holidays soon followed, with their revelry, Nativity crêches, and special pastries and sweets. (How beautiful Blanca was, with her black lace mantilla a delicate web over the gold of her hair!) Icy snows, with all the force of real winter, came from the Pyrenees. But at Blanca's, it was sweet to talk of love, withdrawn from the family circle, over the charcoal braziers.

One night the talk was all concerned with the tumult at the Casino over the incredible news from Madrid that General Pavía had dissolved the Congress the morning before. Everyone was upset by this stab-in-the-back thrust at the Republic. To Pepe the new turn of affairs was not very surprising. He had followed with great interest the difficulties of the régime: the desertion of Figueras, the failure of Pi y Margall in his attempts to calm with philosophy the extremists of the provinces, who, irritated by the procrastination of the federal authorities, had gone so far in Cartagena as to raise the flag of separatism. Pepe had known privately about this farcical uprising through letters from Carlos, whose adventurous Spanish cousin, Alfredo Sauvalle, was mixed up in it—as Minister of the Interior of the secessionist government, no less! Salmerón, for libertarian reasons, had not wished to punish such a breach of discipline severely, although it had distracted the Government from concentrating its efforts to stamp out the Carlist war, now more violent than ever. Pavía's coup d'état had now cut down as with the single blow of a powerful sword the administration of Castelar, fourth president of the Republic in eight months' time.

Saragossa revolted the next day. During the night the streets were loud with shouts and shots. When Martí got up that morning and went to ask Simón what all was going on, the Negro replied, shivering: "It's so cold your words freeze in your mouth!"

But something more serious was going on: The Republicans had taken to the streets ready to repeat the riots of '69. Barricades were being thrown up hastily, in the grand and glorious tradition. Simón, who feared nothing but the cold, was constantly in and out, getting the latest news of the riots as they progressed: In the cellars of the Coso—the city's famed thoroughfare—arms were being distributed to enraged citizens and to militiamen wearing liberty caps. General Burgos, Captain General of the region, had already placed his troops at the principal street intersections.

Simón had hardly recovered his breath and warmed himself a little in the kitchen when he turned to go out again, saying he too was going to fight for his second country,

Spain. The "little green legs" were both praying to the Virgin of Pilar and stealing desperate glances at Pepe and Fermín. In the street outside gunfire increased and there was shouting and suddenly the galloping of horses. The Cubans had wanted to get out into it, but don Félix, the girls' father, remembering the tragic incidents of 1869, had argued them down: What did *they* owe to the Republic? And wasn't it their duty to reserve themselves for their own, more beloved, cause? That appeal had been decisive.

All morning and a good part of the afternoon the rattle of rifle fire continued, punctuated at intervals by the hoarse roar of the Krupp cannons which General Burgos had had installed, without any compunction, to blast out the barricades. Late in the afternoon the explosive noise of battle died down and a little later Simón returned, his sheepskin jacket in rags, and black with blood and gunpowder.

"Holy Virgin! Worse than Havana, boys," he shouted.

Everybody crowded around him and Simón, in an almost festively excited voice, with his Congo accent comically interspersed with badly placed Spanish Z's, told the events of the day. He had fought until the end, in the big barricade in the marketplace square. The soldiery shot to kill and had respected neither women nor children. Ten or twelve men had fallen by his side after fighting like wild animals. The same thing had happened at the San Ildefonso Gate, at the Tripería, and on the main thoroughfares. Cannon-fire had wrecked bridges and buildings. Now the soldiers had just about cut off the city and were shooting everyone caught bearing arms. "A miracle I escaped, boys—maybe it's because of my color . . ."

The next day Saragossa was quiet. Guards—in groups—were patrolling the streets. In the marketplace where once the heads of Lanuza and Padilla had fallen, Pepe and Fermín saw parts of the barricade still standing, and puddles of dried blood round about. The love-sick youth went to see for himself that no harm had befallen his loved one's house. Then he returned home at once in a raging, bitter sadness. In Saragossa, too, the Republic had died at the hands of a general greedy for decorations and promotion.

When, days later, Martí was asked to speak at the gathering at the Teatro Principal for the benefit of the widows and orphans of the fallen heroes of the massacre, he could not refuse. It was the first time Saragossa had asked him to do anything as a public service; perhaps it was felt that there was no voice like that of the young insurrecto—in spite of his modesty—to deliver an elegy on Liberty with just the right intonation.

Martí composed a philosophic-heroic poem which was to have been read by the actor Leopoldo Burón, a poetic essay on death, charity and love, written with the necessary discretion. But once on the stage, he forgot the prepared ode, and improvised a rhapsodic hymn to civic rebellion which made the Government representative squirm uneasily in his box. The theatre shook with applause and while Fermín ran excitedly backstage to embrace Pepe, Blanca, blushing more than ever, twisted her lace handkerchief to ribbons.

In May, Pepe had to make a flying visit to Madrid for "reasons of health." Although provincial life had greatly strengthened the two maltreated youths, Pepe had lately begun to feel ill and nervous from too much study and too intense an emotional life. His adoring love for the blonde damsel of Platerías Street took its natural toll from his sensitive, high-strung constitution. And the tumor of prison days began again to bother him.

Pepe found Madrid in a turmoil over politics, with don Calixto, as usual, making his daringly caustic and picturesque cracks. At every sort of gathering, wrathful comments were still being voiced over the "humiliation" the United States had inflicted on Castelar and on Spain over the capture of the expeditionary ship *Virginius.*[1]

The cause of Cuba lost adherents in Madrid. Even the most cautious Cubans mourned for Céspedes, who had fallen early in the new year; they found consolation in even the vaguest news reports of the victories of Máximo Gómez, now pushing the revolution to its climax. Martí missed the quiet enthusiasm of Carlos, no longer in Spain.

When he returned from his vacation in Madrid, the final examinations for his baccalaureate degree awaited him, and

[1] This was one of the most dramatic episodes of the Ten Years War for Cuban independence. The *Virginius* was a small ship purchased in the U.S. by revolutionists to send arms and munitions to the Island. At the time it was seized by a Spanish battleship it had already carried two "expeditions," as they were called by Cubans, consisting of men and weapons. When caught, in 1873, the *Virginius* was taken to Santiago de Cuba. The military governor of that port and province ordered that the crew and over a hundred enlisted men who were found aboard be immediately tried by a Spanish military court as *pirates,* notwithstanding the fact that the ship had been seized in English waters —near Jamaica—that it bore the flag of the United States, and that no implements of war had been found aboard—these had all been thrown into the sea during the ship's race from her attackers.

Of course the *pirates* were sentenced to death before a firing squad. They began to be shot in groups. Among the first ones to be executed were the Cuban General Bernabé Varona, called "Bembetta," famous for his years-long opposition to the Spaniards, Pedro de Céspedes, brother of Carlos Manuel, the leader of the Revolution and President of the Republic-in-Arms, and the American Colonel Washington O'Ryan. More than fifty patriots had already been executed, much to the distress and anger of Santiago's citizens, when the English frigate *Niobe* showed up in the harbor. The captain of the *Niobe,* Lampton Lorraine, threatened to bombard the city if the slaughter was not stopped. It was. Lorraine's humaneness and courage saved 102 lives.

The incident brought much vilification on the Spaniards, enhanced the prestige of the Cuban cause internationally, and caused some diplomatic tension with the English government, for Great Britain warned Madrid that she would not tolerate any seizure of her subjects on the high seas under suspicion of being engaged in activities against Spain. Later, the United States demanded from the Spanish Government the return of the *Virginius* (which was under U.S. registry) and of the survivors.

then, in quick sequence, the finals for his law degree. Pepe had not aspired to more than a passing grade in his law studies, and that is what he achieved. He had undertaken without enthusiasm the formal apprenticeship to this subject which was rather repugnant to him, since it rested upon the quarrels of mankind. In sharp contrast were his enthusiasm and intentness for philosophy and literature which he "loved spontaneously and craved with the hungry man's need." To pay his tuition for these subjects he had tried to find a job of some sort—"intellectual, translating, or menial" —at publishers' and booksellers', but he had not found one. His "hungry man's need" kept him going, however, and the tall young man was now an honors graduate in his favorite academic field. From a fortuitous list of subjects for degree theses he had naturally chosen the one entitled "Political and Forensic Oratory among the Romans." This had allowed him to discuss Cicero in paragraphs that must have seemed to the faculty examiners almost Ciceronian, except for a rather tropical lushness.

It was the 24th of October. It was raining. When he returned from the formal exercises the "little green legs" received him with a great to-do. They had prepared a saint's day feast with all his favorite dishes to celebrate his graduation. But Pepe's smile was a little sad. Fermín, alone, embracing him silently, understood. The "preparation" had come to an end: Now life, and a spartan duty, were awaiting him.

To the same editor who, months before, had turned down his application for a job, Pepe wrote a rather more unusual request. He had finished his studies—he related with modest pride—and would soon begin his career outside Spain. He needed to have Escriche's Dictionary and Gutiérrez's *Commentaries*. "And besides these, I should like to take with me Azcárate's works on philosophy." Lacking money to buy them, he could only offer in payment the article he enclosed and whatever other literary work the editor might require of him to pay for the books. He needed the books, he wrote, to help him in his profession, which he intended to pursue—he added in his involved style—not for his own interest, which would be satisfied with the sole career of being a man, but to help support his poor family.

He waited in vain. Responsibilities urged him to leave, but love kept presenting him with new excuses for delay. Fermín had not made up his mind either—and Christmas was again very close at hand. One night in November the inevitable decision was reached. Why had he had since childhood such a stern, commanding sense of duty? And what presentiment, what innermost vocation, was it that made him feel more obligated to an uncertain future than to the sweet reality of the present?

Blanca understood, or let him think that she did: All along she had loved him with the anguish of knowing it was only temporary, fatally temporary. They wept together that night and made promises to each other they both knew were false. Next day Saragossa witnessed the departure of the birds of passage. Springtime's flowering branch was now withered and leafless against a patch of gray sky. Sick at heart, Pepe left the land "where the only flower in his life had burst into bloom."

Chapter Nine

THE ROMANTIC

May the limitations of love not cast a spell
On the serious ambitions of my mind.
Martí: Sin Amores

FROM THE STERN of the English ship which was taking him from Southampton to Vera Cruz a pale young man, his hair flying in the wind, watched the foam of the ship's wake dissolve into the steel-gray sea.

How remote everything seemed! Even the past events in which he had been involved most intimately were already hazy, as if they had all been part of a dream. Only old impressions remained clear in the mind: a friend, a flowery land, a woman, another friend. In addition to these there was a kaleidoscope of recent impressions: a scanty and belated glimpse of Spain's antiquities, its other cities of centuries and stones . . . the flying trip to France, the restless Paris of the '70's, with its beautifully dressed women so attractively undressed in the paintings of Gérome and Jules Lefebvre . . . The farewell embrace of a friend at Havre . . . England, full of fog and the smell of pipe tobacco, and in Southampton, the temptation to an adventurous soul: a pretty English girl and "a memorable half-hour." . . .

Four years and a few weeks; how far away it all seemed. Now, heading for the old past and the uncertain future, here he was with his three diplomas and his knowledge of the wide world—in third class.

Fermín had insisted on his procuring passage more suited to his station, but Pepe was short of funds—and who knew what privations his parents in Mexico, recent arrivals in an alien land, and with Ana ill, were going through? The prevailing stench of dirty, wet canvas and slaughtered animals nauseated him. The wretched emigrants in search of fortune, crowded together for lack of space, bowed down by their troubles, distressed him. But who was he, after all, with his diplomas and patent-leather shoes, but another one of them: a poor, sick young lawyer also journeying into the unknown?

"Mr Martí?"

It was the ship's captain, no less, come to tell Martí that at Havre a tall young man with large eyes, who would not leave his name, had put up the difference for a first-class passage for Sr José Martí. With misty eyes and unsteady steps, Pepe followed the captain to a luxurious cabin. It seemed to him now that Fermín himself, "part of his own Cuba," was accompanying him on the long voyage home.

Victor Hugo's latest book, *Mes Fils,* also kept him company. It was the literary sensation of Paris during Pepe's stay there. The young traveller had had a brief moment of friendship with Hugo's friend, the poet Auguste Vacquerie. Martí had translated one of his "lovely songs" into Spanish and the poet had presented him with the copy of *Mes Fils.* How grateful he felt to the poet now in the silent solitudes of the Atlantic. The Olympian anger of the Guernsey exile alternated in these pages with the poignant memories of the disconsolate father, and messianic visions with the sorrows of a patriot for a humiliated France. Hugo's eloquent reflections on the bitter sorrows of the exile and the pleasures of sacrifice were as much a tonic to Martí as the very sea air.

Vera Cruz, at last. Blue sky, blue sea, and over the docks and the flat roofs and the isolated castle of San Juan de Ulúa, the violent sun of America once again!

An almost childish happiness suddenly dissipated his nostalgia for things past—and for Havana, which his ship had passed the day before in the sparkling noon. After all, Mexico, too, was native soil: the soil of a larger, extensive motherland. Such a thought, on which he had reflected so many times as an exile, now took on an emotional quality. The luminously clear distances, the intoxicating air, the dark-skinned men arguing on the docks with a volubility and accent which reminded one of Cuba, gave him a real feeling of homecoming. When, on the train, he began to notice, as they filed by, the coastal plain, the purple shadows cast by vultures, plantations of bristly *maguey*, a river silvery under the sun, the mysterious and distant Indian ruins among the *nopal* groves, the forests, finally, and the rose-tinted mountains, he felt that his imaginary impressions of America were materializing in contours almost recognizable.

From idea alone, the concept of kinship gained from reading was now becoming emotional reality—a matter of enthusiasm and pride. This land, also, was his native country!

There were two days of drinking in the landscape. When finally the restless expectancy of arrival spread among the passengers it was already midnight. On the platform Pepe spotted the wide shoulders and soldierly head of his father. A moment later he felt the familiar rough caress of his mustache on his cheeks.

A pale, melancholy young man with polished manners had come with his father. "This is Don Manuel Mercado, Pepe —our neighbor."

Martí offered his hand to the Mexican friend about whom he had heard much in his family's letters. He noticed that his father was dressed in black, and a sudden fear froze his soul. "And Ana, Father?"

Don Mariano's answer was so long in coming that the reply was unnecessary. This was the first toll to pay for absence. The carriage rattled along the cobble-stone road and wound through deserted streets whose darkness was pierced at intervals by gas lamps. Don Mariano uttered vague remarks now and then that Pepe did not listen to. His mind was fixed on the remembered image of his sister; he was recalling her blonde hair, her long, somewhat poetic letters which had often carried the warm breath of home to him in his cold solitude in Spain.

Inside their humble little home, after tears and the laughter of welcome, he heard the details. Ana had died a romantic death: The altitude of Mexico City had brought on a heart ailment which had been made worse by sorrow. Her fiancé, the painter Manuel Ocaranza, had had to go to Europe to complete his studies for the post he sought as director of the School of Painting. Then both he and Pepe had announced their homecoming. Ana looked for them every night. The painter had been delayed. Pepe's final travels also delayed him. And then one day Ana "took her departure" without waiting longer for either sweetheart or brother. She was barely eighteen.

Don Mariano broke the mournful quiet with forced joviality. The girls gazed bashfully and studiously at their brother who had returned to them a grown man: Leonor, "La Chata," in the bloom of her twenty years; Carmen, fifteen; Amelia, a riot of golden curls; and Antoñica, the dark, little one. He kissed them silently, and then referred to "inexpensive little gifts" he had brought them in his trunk. Then he allowed himself to be seated like a child in doña Leonor's lap. Her eyesight was very poor and she kept touching his hands and his face. . . .

The upper floor of their house was shared by Manuel Mercado and Manuel Ocaranza, who finally had arrived from Europe and who was now painting a portrait of his lost love. Pepe stood at long intervals before the beautiful likeness, his eyes shining with tears. The two Manuels initiated Pepe into knowledge of the spreading and picturesque city, with its churches whose façades were tumultuously rich with carving, its wealth of tree-shaded avenues and plazas, where under the awnings motionless Indian women could be seen offering their wares on their sleeping mats or disheveled men in huge hats, walking about with a slow, solemn gait.

Mercado, Governmental secretary for the Federal District, gave Pepe a good survey of current politics. Sebastián Lerdo de Tejada presided over the Republic which Benito Juárez[1] had recently freed from the ill-starred Maxmilian. In the cabinet of the venerated "Little Indian" don Sebastián had been Minister of Foreign Affairs. He inherited from don Benito the policy of separation of Church and State; the people loved him, but since he had become president he had made enemies, above all among the "mochos" or clerical-fanatics whose power he was daily whittling down. Now and then there was launched a local uprising among the Indians in distant Mexican states, "not for any good reason but because in Mexico it is the custom to attack those in power."

Martí paid close attention. Except for literature, nothing interested him so much as politics. The art of making a people and ruling them impressed him as something magical which must have its secret to reveal. And he surmised that after his experience in Spain, this spectacle of a people in the process of becoming, exploring its way with a re-acquired turbulence, would be for him a very rewarding study.

But there would be plenty of time for observation. Pepe had to be preoccupied at the moment with the pressing needs of his family. Don Mariano had been compelled to fall back upon his usual emergency means of earning a living—piece-work tailoring. He, doña Leonor and the girls untiringly cut and sewed for one Borrell, contractor for the army and other uniformed corps. The house was full of

[1] Benito Juárez (1806-1872): Mexican patriot and statesman who led the nationalistic movement against Emperor Maximilian in 1863. As president of the Republic, Juárez gave vigorous impulse to liberal policies, especially in his fight against the encroachments of the clericals—the so-called Reforma. He was a full-blood Indian.

scraps of cloth—and poverty. The day came when Pepe, even though he had just arrived, was compelled to go out with his pride in his pocket and take whatever work he could find to help supply the necessities—a need which doña Leonor tried in vain to hide from him.

His impoverished parents did not try to keep him within their bounds, as of old. Pepe was aware of the delighted pride with which his father listened to stories of his trips and his studies, turning his head at every instance to make certain of the admiration of the others who were listening, while doña Leonor's face shone with bliss. She already had had his diplomas hung in the place of honor. The top one, as if it were a silent invitation, was his diploma in Law. But the idea of practising law evoked in Pepe a real distaste and he persuaded himself that he did not yet know the customs and the people of the country well enough to enter an already overcrowded profession. For the present he would earn money by teaching or writing for the papers.

Mercado, who had great influence in the government press, obtained for him some beginner's assignments for *El Federalista.* When he later spoke to Colonel José Vicente Villada, friend of President Lerdo and publisher of the *Revista Universal*, he confirmed the recommendation made for Martí by his countryman, Antenor Lescano,[1] a distinguished contributor to the *Revista.* This periodical was strictly devoted to "politics, literature and business"—the three cardinal preoccupations of the time in order of local importance.

From the beginning of March, Martí began to have a hand in the anonymous work of the newspaper, and his name was signed to certain verses which revealed the poverty of his home and of his anguished inspiration. But the "favor of

[1] Antenor Lescano: Cuban journalist exiled in Mexico. There he published, with Nicolás Azcárate, *El Eco de Ambos Mundos*. He was also director of a school of farming. Died in Mexico.

literary circles" which the *Revista* had prophesied on publishing the verses was not to go out to the immature poet but to the astonishingly mature translator of *Mes Fils*. Villada had thought it a good idea to publish as a serial this latest work of Hugo, poetic oracle of America, and Martí felt a "boyish happiness" in having the opportunity to translate that "serious and beloved" book.

Nevertheless, he took all the warranted literary precautions. He was not a romanticist:

> "I do not live within the confines of any school of thought . . . Being is more than existence . . . There is neither romanticism nor classicism . . . I love nothing but this abstraction, this mysticism, this pride, which makes souls akin to each other. . . . All things follow a natural order; life unfolds in a plurality of lives, but everything is universal and powerful, everything is grave and majestic, everything is as simple as light and high and dazzling as the sun."

The novice did not suspect to what extent his own protest of independence was evidence of romantic adherence. But that very prologue declared his desire to "write with all the limpid clarity, elegance and graceful turns of the Spanish tongue" and his translation actually succeeded in carrying the turbulent Hugoesque tidal wave into a stream so limpid and pure that Mexican literati were loud in praise of his skill: Where had such a spirited writer been hiding? He should not be wasted in anonymity.

The *Revista* entrusted to Martí more subtle and informative tasks. Afternoons, the best minds of Mexico met in the editorial offices. Guillermo Prieto, veteran of literature and political battles, presided by common consent over these meetings with his skeptical mind and the bearing of the old newspaper man. At times his authority was challenged by the two illustrious Ignacios: Ramírez "The Magician,"[1] of vast knowledge and sharp wit, and Altamirano,[2] a Greek soul in an Indian body. Still rather self-conscious of his status as a foreigner, Pepe listened in silence to the long discussions on the politics of the country and the progress of "enlightenment." Now and then he took part in the conversation with self-confidence, but only when the older members had left would he chat for long intervals with Manuel Flores, inexhaustible poet of the erotic; with Justo Serra,[3] a budding Pindar; and above all, with Juan de Dios Peza,[4] who "always had a smile on his lips and his hat over his eyes." One of the veterans, however, often stayed on among the younger literati: the heretical Juan José Baz, scourge of the clergy, but "benevolent and cordial to one who, orphaned by his own country, had sought shelter in this new land."

Martí's status as a political exile, together with his ardent youthfulness, his great intelligence and genuine friendliness evident in word and action, soon conquered the cautious reserve of the Mexicans he met. They had soon begun to call him Pepe and to consider him one of themselves. They saw in his delicate and restless figure an embodiment of the

[1] Ignacio Ramírez (1818-1879) was one of the more aggressive members of the literary and liberal romantic movement in Mexico. His *nom de plume*, "The Magician," had no special implications. The articles so signed won for him a reputation as a Mexican Voltaire and he introduced the study of modern psychology to Mexico.

[2] Ignacio Manuel Altamirano (1834-1893) was another prominent liberal writer in Mexico at that time. He was a close friend of "the other Ignacio" and was a noted orator, poet and novelist.

[3] Justo Serra (1848-1912): One of the most prominent and beloved figures in Mexican letters. Poet and prose writer, orator, educator. Minister of Public Instruction under Porfirio Díaz, he did much to modernize higher education in Mexico. He was also Director of the Academia Mexicana and a corresponding member of the Spanish Academy.

[4] Peza was to become Mexico's most popular poet of sentimental themes.

wealth of sensitivity, rebelliousness and hope which was so much the ideal of the times.

Mexico was going through the ebb of romanticism. Feeling expressed in verse was still a matter of poetic *O*'s and *Alases*, and young women, naturally pale, had delicate madrigals inscribed on their fans.

There was even an actual romantic "muse"—one of those beauties more seductive than literary, who eventually will have a past and help make history. This Mexican Georges Sand was Rosario de la Peña, but known as Acuña's Rosario since—a year or so previously—the poet Acuña[1] had committed suicide after having written in her album a moving nocturne which declared for her a love as despairing as it was ardent and bade her eternal farewell in view of the deep abyss that separated them. Naturally, everyone in Mexico, knowing by heart the sad dedication of Manuel Acuña, held the woman he loved responsible. In the Liceo Hidalgo, the chief literary center, groups formed for and against the Señorita de la Peña. The matter became a national—and almost a continental—concern.

From that time on, "Acuña's" Rosario was wrapped in a fateful aura, an added reason for women to envy her and men to adore. She paraded her proud melancholy and splendid beauty under the *ahuehuete* trees in the Alameda and at night received in her salon the most brilliant of the literary world. Innumerable and competitive were the tributes written in her album, on the first page of which the illustrious Ramírez (smitten with Rosario in spite of his wife's recent death and his fifty or more years) had summoned the poets to "scatter incense and flowers at the feet of the goddess."

Immediately friends took Martí to consecrate him. He

[1] Manuel Acuña (1849-1873): Mexican romantic poet, one of the most popular of his generation in Spanish America. Noted for his skeptical attitudes. Committed suicide at the age of twenty-four.

found Rosario tall, dark, graceful, with large, unfathomable eyes; her black hair, wound around her head, created the appearance of a prophetess's crown. He was profoundly impressed.

The flowering branch of the almond tree was nothing now but a sweet memory. Impetuous twenty-two clamored for love. Pepe had arrived in Mexico "with the illness of a soul lost in emptiness"—the malady of his age. The news of Ana's death had depressed him, obliging him to unburden himself in mystic and poignant lyrics. But the bracing air of the table-land and the flattery of Mexican hospitality were beginning to act as a tonic. He was full of impatience and ready tenderness. Cuba was still a dream, implacably shut out by immediate responsibilities: At home were two elderly people, still hurt by his absences, and girls who were working too hard. But the very frustration of his patriotic idealism created in his spirit a need for intensity. It was necessary for him to express his emotions and his dreams—and Rosario was so beautiful!

He ventured at once in the promiscuous album the confession of an ardent dream:

Of you I was thinking, of your hair
Which the powers of Night might bemoan,
And I left a part of my life there,
Wishing to dream that you were my own.[1]

A part of his life and a wish to dream, nothing more. But Rosario smiled contentedly. She was very much taken with the ingratiating young Cuban whose eyes held "imprisoned all the sun of his native Isle." But Martí wished to move too rapidly. Within a few weeks he had filled another page of

[1] En ti pensaba, en tus cabellos,
que el mundo de la sombra envidiaría.
Y puse un punto de mi vida en ellos,
Y quise yo soñar que tú eras mía.

the album with phrases that were really a declaration. They ended by saying: "I am excessively poor; rich only in the strength and eagerness of love."

Wise in affairs of the heart, Rosario understood that the Cuban did not love her, but was in love with love. In spite of this awareness, or rather because of it, she decided to follow Pepe Martí's impetuous emotional tide. It was interesting to find herself courted by an exiled poet, and he had such a piquant way of dreaming about love. Pepe was welcomed almost every night at her informal salon with special attention.

The fictions of love did not succeed, however, in consuming all the energies of the young exile. Other instincts, of a more public character, had to find an outlet.

Seeking political "reality," Martí consoled himself with all that national affairs—always dominated by the contentious clerical question—had to offer. The religious problem was traditionally virulent in Mexico. Although the clergy had given Hidalgo[1] and Morelos,[2] the two most vigorous fighters to the struggle for independence, they were now, by a curious contrast, the yeast of all civil discord in the Republic. Juárez had, at length, subdued the priests by the Reform Laws; Lerdo had incorporated these in the Constitution, and

[1] Miguel Hidalgo (1753-1811): the Mexican priest who started the movement for independence from Spain. He rose against the colonial government the night of the 15th of September, 1810, with the cry of "Long Live the Virgin of Guadalupe, and death to the *gachupines*" (i.e. the Spaniards). This has ever since been called, in Mexican history "the Cry of Dolores" from the small town in which it was uttered. After leading an intense guerrilla war against the loyalists, Hidalgo was taken prisoner and shot, together with twenty-seven companions.

[2] José María Morelos (1780-1815): the other famous priest who, like Father Hidalgo, was one of the founders of the Mexican Republic. At the death of Hidalgo, he led the fight for independence, which he proclaimed in 1813, after the victory of Palmar. But he, too, was defeated and shot by the Spaniards.

had enlivened his anti-clerical program with a sensational expulsion of monks and Jesuits.

These measures inflamed public opinion even more. Traditional religious zeal defended itself against the unceasing attacks of liberal writers, for whom positivism was a weapon against romantic blandness. President Lerdo had quite recently blessed the new Vera Cruz-Mexico railroad, and Gabino Barreda, the taste for Comte's philosophy.

Positivism and secularism went hand in hand in the new climate of materialism. But since romanticism was not entirely overthrown, the negation of spiritual values met resistance even in the liberal movement itself, where religious feeling, divorced from the Church, chose to avail itself of the hospitable gospels of Allan Kardek.[1]

This doctrine had raised such a stir that the extremely cautious Liceo Hidalgo had ventured, not without scandal, to propose as a topic for one of its public forums: "The influence of spiritism on the study of the sciences in general." Martí, who had been admitted as a member of the Liceo a month before, spoke during the first session, achieving in his first appearance before a Mexican audience what the *Revista* called "an enviable triumph."

At the second forum session the discussion was to come to a climax. Expectation ran high. The small Conservatory Theatre was not large enough and the tournament had to be concluded in a larger arena. Gustavo Baz, who had taken the offensive against spiritualism, displayed the tactics of logic. His opponent was strong in sentimental values.

Martí had listened to the godless voices and examined his own conscience. As always, when he looked deeply within

[1] Allan Kardek: One of the earliest exponents, and certainly the most popular, of so-called "spiritism" in the 19th Century. In 1861, his works had made such inroads in Spain that they were publicly burned; notwithstanding this, they continued to be translated and published in Spain during the '60's and '70's, reaching Spanish America, where you will still find the constant new editions in every bookshop.

himself, he saw two very different men: One, an idealist for whom life held no meaning except as an adventure of the spirit; and the rationalist that wide reading and the temper of the times were painting in over the earlier portrait. The years in Spain had impressed him, too, with the philosophy of Krause and vague Oriental mysticism, which had stored up in him convictions on universal harmony, immortality of the soul and its progressive purification through "forelives and afterlives." Allied to the romantic impulse, these ideas rebelled against negation of the spiritual, but without anchoring him too closely.

> "I come to this discussion in the spirit of conciliation which regulates all the acts of my life. I stand between materialism, which is the exaggeration of matter, and spiritualism, which is the exaggeration of the spiritual."

This simple, half-way position proved to be sensational. But Martí's innermost experience actually inclined him more to the spiritual. Gustavo Baz was witty and ironic. The public, however, which wore its heart on its sleeve and knew nothing of dialectics, was conquered by the eager affirmations of the young Cuban, even though the general staff of materialism found Martí's statements incurably lyrical.

In commenting on the forum discussion, the newspapers larded their praise of Martí with reservations. "Whatever we might say about his speech," wrote *El Federalista*, "would be pallid. It was a cascade, a torrent, of ideas bubbling with brilliance and colors." . . . In the *Eco de Ambos Mundos*, "a person who would judge impartially the dramatic incidents of the debate" wrote:

> "This young man would be formidable in public gatherings in a time of popular unrest; he can wring tears from a corpse; he will be the favorite orator of women,

children and the non-critical; but he will never—and this is due to his nervous intensity, his lively and impetuous imagination—never will he be convincing in a parliament, nor will he be at advantage in the cool and serene discussions of science."

There was considerable justice in this analysis. But the critic forgot that Señor Martí was only twenty-two.

Rosario cherished him all the more for those fiery demonstrations. His friendship with the Muse became much more intimate, but he was still kept at arm's length—much to his regret, for he was impetuously eager. From his reporter's desk in the Congress, when he should have been keeping notes on the session, he would send Rosario nostalgic messages in which he fondly recalled

> ". . . the unforgettable gratitude that my lips would like to press into your hands. But Ramírez plagues me too much today . . ."

"The Magician," even though checked by awareness of his own old age—"A cypress growing in a tomb"—was still pursuing Rosario like a love-sick swain and was as persistent in being ironic about Martí's love as that young man was in convincing himself of the authenticity of his emotion.

Pepe's protestations, which reflected doubt and vehemence at the same time, did not really convince Rosario. Yet, what a complex sincerity, deeper no doubt than any personal attachment, was in that idealized emotional outpouring! From what heights did the youth gaze when he wrote to her: "Rosario mine. My woman is more than an ordinary woman"? And how was that incredible naïveté to be explained—"so in love with light that it was necessary for him to see his love without cloud and without shadow"?

Rosario was disconcerted. She had begun by taking Pepe

Martí for a polished courtier and had amused herself with him. But he had been converted into an almost mystically passionate admirer, with the accents and attitudes of extravagant worship. From joviality he would abruptly change to melancholy and his talk would become like a well of ancient sorrows.

One evening Rosario attempted to explore that disturbed soul. The letter she received the following day answering her "shy or calculatingly cold" note was a complete confession.

> "Love in me—and I express in these words all the belief in my soul—is so strong . . . that no matter where I go on this narrow earth, it has not yet found a perfect resting place. . . . To feel intensely alive and full of tenderness is anguish . . . anguish to be in this tepid atmosphere, in this insupportable littleness, this monotonous sameness, this measured life, in this emptiness of love weighing upon my flesh. The sickness of life: Acuña died of this sickness."

The rest of the letter was a desperate supplication of the Muse:

> "Rosario, awaken me. Since to live is a burden, for that I live; because to live is suffering, I live; I live because I must be stronger than every obstacle and every valour. Force yourself, conquer me. I must find in my soul an explanation, a desire, a just motive, a noble cause for my existence. Of all I have seen, no one but you could do. And for the last four or six days I have been cold."

After reading and re-reading the letter, Rosario believed she finally understood. Now she could see why he had signed this letter, like all the others, with his given name and surname: José Martí. She had thought before it was a display of timidness, even vanity, perhaps. As if by magic the letters now grew before her eyes. The full name took on an inscription-like austerity. In the light of those ardent paragraphs Martí revealed and lost himself simultaneously as if he were an image projected upon a gigantic, unknown destiny. No: he was nothing like Acuña; his despair was not a simple romantic fatigue, nor a frustrated desire for a woman. Pepe Martí evidently harbored a greater rebellion and a greater ambition. His love was merely a burning desire for action obliged to sublimate itself into passion.

Frightened, Rosario felt unequal to the task of inspiration which that young crusader for heroism asked of her. On the 17th of April, Martí wrote a beautiful poem entitled "Without Love," an elegy to his own sentimental fiction.

O my soul, poor and dun,
Seared by the fire of its own sun.[1]

[1] ¡Oh, pobre ánima mía,
quemada al fuego de su propio día!

Chapter Ten

"ORESTES" AND THE FURIES

He loved purely, which is to redeem oneself from horrible dreams. And, laden with duty, he loved life."
Martí: Eulogy of Torroella

On the fifth of May, a patriotic anniversary, beginning early in the morning the joyful reports of exploding fire-crackers punctuated the music of brass bands and ballad-singing guitarists. Gaudily dressed women made flowery every street, and the plaza was filled with Sunday finery, rich shawls, many-colored *serapes*, elegantly trimmed hats and jackets. Occasionally the glitter of a knife-blade interrupted the festivities in the taverns, but quarrels soon gave way to patriotic vows.

Martí wanted to take the pulse of this fever of patriotism which his own land—alas!—did not yet know. Snatches of conversation overheard in passing were dramatic and bawdily pungent. When *pulque* loosened tongues, allusions to political figures were apt to take on a vindictive tone. It seemed that in celebrating the multitude felt liberated from some customary repression.

On the following day Martí, whose literary stature had grown considerably since his speech at the Liceo Hidalgo, began to function as one of the group of editors of *La Revista.* He made his début with a meditative essay on the patriotic holiday, striving to show that, in the new age of reason, the cult of saints had been replaced by the cult of heroes. But as it chanced he was only rationalizing his own feeling. The merrymaking and holiday spirit, marking the eve of the anniversary, was purely *mestizo* in character. The *pelaos*, of pure Indian stock, kept well outside the bounds of popular rejoicing, their minds indelibly stamped with the apathy of centuries. They wore no fiesta clothing. And when intellectuals delivered their ringing orations on Liberty and Progress, they seemed not to understand what it was all about.

Martí began to perceive the vast incoherence of America. He saw the isolation and rancorous silence of the Indian, most American of them all; the irresponsibility and blindness of the others, the fairer-skinned men of sword or pen who had not, even yet, felt the innermost stirrings of the new world. Was not here the great duty of the new Americans?

For the first time the idea of a higher, continental responsibility invaded his spirit, which was longing for love and duty. He surrendered himself to it. Entrusted by the *Revista* with one of its more delicate tasks as a commentator, Martí found it wise to sign his editorial opinions with a pseudonym, "Orestes," which would allow him to comment freely on Mexico's part in the formation of a new America. From the beginning, the articles were devoted to large issues, and discussed principles, a rather surprising thing in the petty and partisan press which prevailed in Mexico at the time, as well as in Cuba. The well-educated found in these articles also a quality of style which was both new and antique—a classical structure with colorful nuances and temperature.

Martí put into his new task an American ardor which consoled him a little for his forced inactivity regarding Cuba. But each fragment of good news about the revolution going on in the Island steeped him in successive moods of joy and melancholy. "I have before me, and all my soul goes out to it, one of the newspapers published in the camp of the revolutionaries in Cuba." He recounted the feats of valor of the earliest insurrectos, already so ancient as to be almost legendary. "Retribution and shame to those of us who do not fight side by side with them!"

And the journalist never lost an opportunity to do whatever he could to further the Cuban cause. So much so, in fact, that the good don Anselmo de la Portilla, publisher of *La Iberia*, considered it in order to write in his paper reprimanding "the estimable writer who persists in taking such pains to make public issue of the Cuban question in *La Revista*." Martí could not forget that don Anselmo had done him "an extremely personal favor" during the trials he suffered the first few months after arriving in Mexico. This knowledge had restrained him from commenting on certain previous unfriendly allusions to the cause of Cuba in *La Iberia*. But now, actually accused of abuse of journalistic hospitality, he found it necessary to protest: No one was more aware than he of the prudent conduct owed to a country "which nevertheless has not wanted to treat him as a stranger." But he could not stand quietly by when he was able to refute erroneous and unjust opinions about the efforts of his countrymen to achieve their liberty. Having affirmed the justice of his actions, he concluded by again thanking publicly Señor de Portilla for the assistance for which he was indebted.

This good taste moved the publisher of *La Iberia*, and the polemical skirmish came to an end with cordial explanations from both sides. The topic of Cuba continued to receive occasional but brief mention in *La Revista*. The subject touched Martí deeply but he stifled his impatience. Only in lively discussions with other Cuban expatriates did he unburden himself; with Antenor Lescano, already somewhat Mexicanized; with the good and austere Nicolás Domínguez Cowan; with Romero Cuyás, and above all with the poet

Alfredo Torroella,[1] an indomitable spirit whose seven years in the Anáhuac had not cooled his burning homesickness for the Island.

A generous and ironic destiny united Martí also in his exile with a Cuban who had always been very close to him and yet very distant: the illustrious Nicolás Azcárate.[2] Martí's reverence for him since childhood was a reflection of Mendive's opinion. Azcárate had been, before the insurrection of '68, a lawyer of note, a patron of literature and one of the "seven sages" of Havana. He had gone with the Commission of Inquiry to Spain, where he had defended his reformist ideals with nobility and eloquence. Pepe Martí had heard a great deal in Madrid about the aristocratic gatherings at Azcárate's house, about his anti-slavery campaigns in the newspaper which ate up his fortune but not his hope in Spanish justice. A few months after returning to Cuba, ruined and disillusioned, Valmaseda[3] rewarded his loyalty

[1] Alfredo Torroella (1845-1879): A Cuban poet and playwright of the romantic generation. In 1868, undoubtedly because of his revolutionary ideas, he emigrated to Mexico, where he continued his literary and journalistic activity, contributing, like Martí, to *El Federalista*. In the late seventies he returned to Cuba because of his severe illness, and died in 1879.

[2] Nicolás Azcárate (1828-1894): A Cuban lawyer. Before 1875 he had been active in the Reform movement in the Island. Because of his liberal attitude he had to seek refuge in Mexico. He returned to Cuba in 1878 and resumed his literary activity, not as a writer but as the host for certain famed *tertulias* or gatherings of men of letters in his home. These *noches literarias* had quite an influence on Cuban letters. He was the first president of the also famous Liceo de Guanabacoa.

[3] Valmaseda: Blas Villate y de la Hera, Count of Valmaseda (1824-1882), one of the "strong" military chiefs to whom Spain resorted when things went wrong in Cuba. Perhaps he was the most ferocious and also the ablest of them all. He was sent to Cuba for the first time in 1844, again in 1860 and in 1867, when Lersundi proved too weak for the taste of the Spanish "volunteers." During the first years of the Revolution of 1868 he led a savage war to the death against the Cuban insurrectos which did much to check the movement but also much to deepen Cuban rancor. He was finally replaced by Jovellar in 1875.

to Spain by ordering Azcárate to leave for other parts, bag and baggage. And now here he was in Mexico with nothing more than his literary taste and his aristocratic Basque bearing, earning a living as a clerk in a law office and as re-write man for *El Eco de Ambos Mundos.*

Their common love of Cuba and literature united the two Cubans, so long in meeting each other. Martí often went to the Hotel Iturbide to visit Azcárate and together they went walking, wrangling in tremendous discussions on literature and politics. They never agreed. They were apt to part in a disgruntled mood but the next day they could again be seen gesticulating along the Alameda or seated together in the orchestra of the Teatro Principal.

Mexico became, for the young Cuban journalist, more and more an absorbing preoccupation. His serious frame of mind, by nature attracted to "the absolute and the abstract," found unsuspected depths in the most casual subjects, and he set himself to try to deduce the future from the chronic problems of the country: the social parasitism of the Hispanic Mexicans, who used their intelligence solely for personal gain or snobbish ornament; the unstable economy; the need for compulsory and secular education; and, above all, the exploitation of agricultural labor and the fate of the native Indian race. At a time when no one was thinking about this semi-slavery except in a vague, philanthropic way, Martí began to advocate a long-range policy aimed at redeeming the Indian through "contact, personal attention, and remunerative employment."

Since *La Revista* was widely read, even in distant Mexican states, the identity of the writer who showed such a bold outlook for the future and such a lively concern for the submerged, but who hid behind the pen name Orestes, soon became known. Martí's name was mentioned among the workers of Chihuahua to represent them in a workers' congress. In intellectual circles where every comment in *La Revista* was a topic for discussion, the generous talents of Peón y Contreras or of Justo Serra went to the defense of Pepe Martí when he was accused of being a false prophet or of writing in an inflated style. Martí himself tried to disarm petty jealousies with a smile. He even won over to his extreme unorthodoxy the parochial minds enthusiastic about the "glorious heights" to which Mexican literature was rising. There was much too much aping and imitating; he wanted to hurl down upon the country Victor Hugo's "masses of light," but to keep Mexico true to itself, true to its American destiny or vocation.

When the actor Enrique Guasp de Peris obtained President Lerdo's sponsorship of a project for the revival of literary and dramatic art in Mexico, Martí applauded the official approval and meditated with the emotion of an as yet untried author on the cultural effectiveness of the theatre "by means of which one spirit can influence other distant ones."

Established dramatic poets were already sharpening their pens and their creative abilities for the opening, which Guasp promised would be held at the Teatro Principal, subsidized by the government. And Guasp insisted that Martí should write something for it. A close friendship united them through Azcárate, who had known the actor ever since the time, years ago, when, while adjutant to Lersundi in Havana, Guasp had been the "romantic juvenile" of the amateur theatrical productions of the Liceo de Guanabacoa and had, on the fall of Isabel II, gone on the professional stage to realize the dream of his life. Now he was the theatrical idol of a bored and sentimental Mexico.

Guasp's insistence finally persuaded Martí to write a short

theatrical sketch, a proverb in verse, entitled *Amor, con amor se paga* [Love for Love]:

> *Whimsical diversion*
> *Of an unhappy heart*
> *Sighing to find itself.*[1]

The heart he found, however, was that of Concha Padilla, the pretty Mexican actress who played opposite Guasp in a dialogue of flirtatious courtship. In the course of directing her during rehearsals as to the manner in which she was to allow the *Julian* of the sketch to make love to her, the young playwright fell in love with Concha, and she with him.

This affair was a new storm of love, but this time without overtones of literature and introspective suffering. The stage had not yet taken from Concha her middle-class respectability, but it had certainly infected her with an aptitude for sudden dramatics. And since Concha was of a jealous disposition and Pepe not at all repulsive to women, this idyll from its very start veered from calm to tempest.

On the night of the opening of *Amor, con amor se paga*, all of literary Mexico, and no meagre representation from society, filled the Teatro Principal. In the wings, hanging on his beloved's every word, Martí went through all the opening night anguish. When Concha finished speaking the final lines:

> "*A man with no homeland to live in*
> *Nor a woman for whom to die*
> *Nor proud ambition to satisfy*

[1] caprichosa distracción
de un mísero corazón
que por hallarse suspira.

Has naught better which can be given
Than this flattering thought above
All else, as he suffers, confused:
At least good audiences are used
To giving love for love"[1]

the good public paid with great applause. But Martí, before the footlights, refused to let Guasp and his friends actually place on his head the laurel crown which they presented him in reward for his efforts.

In a box adjoining the one occupied by the daughters of the great Juárez and the Cuban poet Pedro Santacilia, husband of one of them, sat doña Leonor, don Mariano and the girls, wiping tears from their eyes. In another box occupied by Cubans, on the opposite side of the horseshoe, a Cuban girl attracted everyone's attention by her beauty and distinction. It was rumored that she had recently come to Mexico with her father. Martí asked who she was: She was the Señorita Carmen Zayas Bazán.

The clatter of applause was rewarding to one who felt called to a social vocation. Martí now felt he possessed enough authority to encourage through *La Revista* the formation of a new Mexican theatre with a democratic inspiration—and he discovered that he was not preaching to the deaf. A group called the Alarcón Society was formed, its object being to provide an extensive repertory for Enrique Guasp. The already established Gorostiza Society resented

[1] Nada mejor puede dar
quien, sin patria en que vivir,
ni mujer por quien morir,
ni soberbia que tentar,
sufre y vacila, y se halaga
imaginando que, al menos
entre los públicos buenos,
amor con amor se paga.

the threat of competition, and jealousy spread dissension among the Mexican drama lovers.

But, as it happened, other and more serious circumstances prevented the rebirth of the theatre. Politics took on a grimmer aspect and President Lerdo was getting to seem more like a protégé than a patron. His opponents accused him of favoritism and administrative irregularities. Followers of Porfirio Díaz were again openly revealing their ambitions. *El Siglo*, *El Monitor*, *El Pájaro Verde*, never tired of calling tyrant the very man who allowed them the liberty of hurling these and other insults at him. A liberal with solid Juárez background, a man of great ability and a sense of humor, don Sebastian paid little attention to these attacks. *El Eco de Ambos Mundos* and *La Revista,* however, were not slow in his defense.

Martí's status as foreigner braked to a degree his expression of opinion on partisan politics. Forgetting this had already cost Azcárate a lively controversy. But "Orestes" owed certain duties to *La Revista,* and when General Riva Palacio opened a violent campaign against President Lerdo on the pretext of vague administrative reforms, the Cuban commentator judged the time ripe to pour the oil of good sense on troubled waters. He also took part in the rebuke his paper addressed to Porfirio Díaz on the occasion of certain ominous requests made by the high clergy. Finally, he participated in banquets in honor of the President and even helped in the propaganda urging him to run again. Partisans of Porfirio Díaz kept a careful memory of these activities but chose to forget that the Cuban had declined an offer to make him Secretary of the state of Puebla.

At the beginning of 1876, *La Revista Universal* formally launched Lerdo's candidacy for re-election. The anti-Lerdo forces, which up to this point had been held in some restraint by the hope of a complete political renovation, came out into the open. In early February there were excited rumors of the revolutionary plans agreed upon by Generals Díaz and Donato Guerra, whose program was boldly published in the opposition papers "in view of the fact that the Mexican Republic is run by a government that has erected corruption into a political system."

Martí viewed events with a mixture of impatience and a calm sense of history. The repressed man of action in him would have liked now and then to leap over the barriers of discretion and get into the thick of the fight. On the other hand, the whole thing seemed to him to be an organic convulsion—freedom was not achieved in a day; it was a process:

> "The formation of a people is begun by war, continued through tyranny, renewed by revolution and is secured by peace. Peace is never perfect, but is constantly perfecting itself."

The journalist did not attempt to define in which stage Mexico was, nor whether the revolution spreading rapidly in Oaxaca and other states represented a renewal, a seeding-time of the people. But the article expressing his views was reprinted in the *Eco* as "timely in the present state of the Republic." Followers of Díaz made careful note of all this, too.

Neither the *Eco* nor the *Porfiristas* took heed of one of Martí's other paragraphs which was probably meant as a profound judgment of the President.

> "By being men we draw from life itself the principle of liberty; and as intelligent men, we have the duty of achieving liberty. One is liberal by being a man. But one must study, guess, foresee and create much in the applied art of being an American liberal."

Perhaps Lerdo had not known fully how to be one. That

Es ahora un hombre de treinta y cinco años. El pelo fino se le ha ido retirando hasta formar, en torno a la frente acupulada, una leve ola oscura. El bigote y la mosca negrísimos le encierran la sonrisa. Los ojos almendrados parecen más distantes entre sí y más melancólicos..

J. M.

MARTÍ AT TWENTY-FIVE

A drawing by Jorge Mañach as a frontispiece for Emeterio S. Santovenia's *Bolívar y Martí*, Havana, 1934. The legend paraphrases the description of Martí on pp. 115-116 "simple and modest" man to whom Martí listened with pleasure when he spoke "of all the noble principles and sound ideas that warm a superior democratic intelligence"; that ingenious and worldly gentleman who governed somewhat frivolously, was perhaps too self-confident, had too much of the academic in him, and lacked a feeling for the dramatic reality with which he had to contend. Yet infinitely more deserving of blame than Lerdo's liberalism-without-tact was the ambitious militarism which would again submerge Mexico in a civil war.

By March the revolution had spread to the state of Puebla. The government press did not conceal its alarm. Conscription and war-time taxes had made silent sympathizers for the Porfiristas. Men were beginning to desert the floundering government. One manifesto followed another. Mexico was in a convulsion.

Chapter Eleven

CRISIS

MARTÍ, MEANWHILE, was battling with love within himself. His romance with the Padilla girl was beset by a conspiracy of forces. Doña Leonor did not look kindly on the affair. The girl might be as decent and respectable as one could ask; nevertheless, she was on the stage: Martí's sisters were strictly forbidden to call on her. A theatrical gossip called "Cross-eyed Juvenal" because his gaze was as uncertain as his motives, had written a cheap crack about Martí's ovation, and now his insinuations about the love affair of the Cuban and the actress had infuriated doña Leonor.

On her part, Concha demanded more and more attention from her swain who, to tell the truth, was lavish in his courtesies to too many women. But what could be done about it? A certain General's daughter was notoriously taken with him, and Edelmira Borrell, the clothing contractor's daughter, was in and out of the Martí home frequently on pretended errands for her father but in reality attracted by Pepe's troubadour gesture of kissing her hand whenever she came. Nicolás Azcárate affectionately nicknamed him "Cavalier" and Martí actually confessed to his mother, who was secretly rather proud of his popularity, that he "should like to divide himself into little pieces."

The young Cuban was not at all unattractive. At twenty-three, although slender, and not taller than average, he had filled out a little; his dark eyes slanted slightly upward at the temples like his mother's, and during moments of silence they had a far-away and dreamy expression which lighted up brilliantly in conversation. A small mustache accented his easy smile. His naturally curly hair—doña Leonor called it "choppy"—was already beginning to recede from the very pale forehead. But what women liked most about him was his command of language, rich in every shade of meaning; his extreme courtliness; his clear, musical laughter; the romantic halo of the exile and literary fame.

> "Has it ever occurred to you when talking with M——," a lady asked Nicolás Azcárate in an anonymous letter which the *Eco* published, "that his head cannot contain his genius, and that between noble aspirations and gigantic fantasies, his brain works with the expansive force of steam? And this, no doubt gives M—— that peculiar restless intensity which characterises him."

Since he was the object of so much admiration, it was not strange that when he became ill, perfumed notes and gifts of sweets reached his bedside. Concha Padilla's "little piece" of him was noticeably growing smaller. And to doña Leonor's amen, Manuel Mercado was doing his best to break up his friend's stage romance by "parading before him"—according to the girls—the lovely Cuban, Carmen Zayas Bazán, so delicate and fashionable.

Martí, on meeting her at a dance, days after the opening of *Amor con amor se paga*, had found in her the traditional charm and aristocratic bearing of the women of Camagüey. He had soon begun to escort her on Sunday afternoons on walks along the Alameda, where the Cuban girl attracted everyone's admiring glances for "her coiffure and the long train of her gown, in the style of Mamá Carlota." [1] Pepe called at her home every night before going to the theatre. He argued with his sister that a turned-up nose—in Carmen—was a sign of aristocratic lineage. And when Car-

[1] Empress Carlota, Maximilian's wife.

men objected to Pepe's presence on the stage to take curtain calls hand in hand with Concha at the end of his play, the public had to locate him in one of the orchestra seats to single him out for applause.

In the Spring, Martí again fell ill from his old malady, which from time to time prodded his flesh with memories of the Presidio. One day during his convalescence he was unable to find under the bed the small satchel in which he kept all his love letters. Suspecting Carmen, who had been there to visit him while he slept, he wanted to go retrieve the compromising documents. Doña Leonor objected: He was still altogether too feeble. She turned the key in the lock—but Pepe escaped through the transom.

The incident had as a natural consequence the absolute forgiveness of the past in exchange for a single, solemn pledge for the future: Carmen.

His physical suffering, nightmare memories of court-room and prison days, while he lay on his sickbed, and now the latest news from Cuba, all revived ancient longings which confronted the solemn pledge of the two young lovers. All through these months in which he had wished "to live in peace with the kind of life he disliked," the unfulfilled duty he owed to Cuba worked silently and tirelessly within him. More than once his poetry expressed the necessity to apologize for his inaction.

If more as martyr than as coward
I loose bitter words about that distant land—
Martyr more than coward do I love her:
Bondage, not caution, ties my hand.[1]

[1] Y si, más mártir que cobarde, libro
tanta amargura de aquel sol lejano,
mártir, mas que cobarde, aquí lo adoro.
Atada está, no tímida, mi mano.

After his illness the "sleeping birds" awakened anxious for flight. But it was already too late; now his impulses were tethered by the pleasant reins of a newfound love.

The voice of the woman I love
Spoke of love in her accents soft
And, in a flock, the rebel birds
A-tremble, wheeling aloft,
Found rest within my mind and in my breast,
Their wings by prison bars confined and vexed.[1]

Ashamed of this admission, he began to doubt himself. When in a ringing letter in verse he reproached the Cuban poetess, Rosario Acuña, for "cutting laurels" in Spain, he could not forget his own desertion and described himself as "wretched, with the soul of a woman and the shell of a man." But the following verses vindicated his manhood and suggested the real source of his inhibition:

Forgive me, God! If valor's bud
Because of destitution stark is plucked
By old and young who are my flesh and blood.[2]

No, he could not have gone to Cuba, leaving his home, which bravely struggled against poverty, without his necessary assistance. He would have to resign himself as yet, until

[1] La voz de la mujer amada
habló de amor con sus accentos suaves,
y las rebeldes aves,
en trémula bandada,
las alas que su cárcel fatigaron
en mi cráneo y mi pecho reposaron.

[2] ¡Perdónemelo Dios!, porque mis bríos
con su miseria el hálito han cortado
viejos y niños, carne y huesos míos.

the arrival of "adventurous days of cloudless space and unlimited flight."

Another newspaper man, less discreet and courteous than don Anselmo of *La Iberia*, found proof that Martí's pen was always ready for every necessary defense of Cuba. Adolfo Llanos edited the newspaper *La Colonia Española* with a pro-Spanish attitude towards colonial history. He had published a book entitled *Don't Come to America* and in his newspaper had exaggerated unpleasantness so outrageously that Mexican newspaper men collected a fund of $700 so that he could go back to Spain. But he had stayed on in Mexico. He had recently visited the United States, which was celebrating the 100th anniversary of its independence with the Centennial Exposition at Philadelphia. And now Llanos reported in his paper that very scant attention was being given up there to the Cuban revolution, and that the United States was not at all inclined to grant belligerency status to the insurgents.

As soon as Martí could find space in *La Revista*, which was crowded with articles and commentaries on the Porfirista rebellion, he answered Llanos. He overwhelmed *La Colonia* with proofs of United States' interest in Cuban affairs and when Llanos answered saying that Martí was living on illusions, Martí replied:

> "Those who live on illusions are those who deny to men the beautiful rights of compassion and admiration. I do not deduce the recognition of Cuban rights by the United States from mere eulogies: I have faith in the recognition of martyrdom and respect for heroism. We are not waiting for recognition, nor do we need it to triumph."

His optimism was to deceive him; but one month later *La Revista* reprinted an article from New York which supported Martí's position in regard to North American interest in the Cuban revolution.

The last months of 1876 were at hand. The political situation in Mexico was becoming more precarious each succeeding day. As if the persistent military advances were not enough, the men of force were now joined by men of law. Foreseeing that a reëlection of Lerdo—even if possible in such troubled times—would do nothing to bring order out of chaos, the President of the Supreme Court, Iglesias, went over to the side of Díaz. That "hero of Puebla" was now at the gates of the capital. Lerdo, heir of Juárez, hated by the clergy, never popular with fickle crowds fascinated by the glitter of weapons and military uniforms, now deserted by his own followers, could feel judgment day closing in upon him.

The opposition press, already certain of its triumph, and the opportunist press, which took its stand when it could see the political harvest coming, began to denounce the supporters of the tottering Lerdo régime and suggested a St. Bartholomew's Day for the President's followers. The antipathy which *La Revista* had earned by launching the campaign for Lerdo's reëlection was reflected on the best-known members of its editorial staff and especially on those who had advocated respect for the Government. Veiled threats were made. Friends of Martí urged him, in any case, to seek safety.

To reassure his friends, Martí hid in Domínguez Cowan's house on the day—November 24, 1876—when Porfirio Díaz entered the capital, from which Lerdo had secretly fled the night before. The "hero of Puebla" marched in, leading his ragged troops amid banners and the ringing of bells.

Reprisals did not reach the feared excesses. Martí was very well protected by the esteem and affection of those intellectual circles on whom Díaz, the budding Caesar, was going to rely for an era of intelligent despotism. With its very first measures, the new government began a policy of active conciliation.

But it was no longer the sort of spontaneous hospitality which an exile like Martí could find congenial. And besides, a more profound unrest made him anxious to find other roads. He had been in Mexico for two years without being able to make a better than moderate living. His family still had a hard time of it and he had undertaken a new obligation: He was engaged to a woman of a wealthy family, impatient to marry. What was he to do?

He went through a time of painful indecision. His heart on one side, his mind on the other. In Mexico he had heard much about neighboring Guatemala, a new land seeking new blood. In addition to the hope of being able to establish a home there in sound security, a burning curiosity about America attracted him. Cuba also called him, and a greater duty, a duty without pleasure. He felt within himself the maturing of a conflict until now retarded by youthful confusion—between his private interest and public vocation.

At the starting point of these two divergent roads he decided—but still tentatively—to follow the road of public duty. He would tell his parents, his fiancée, that he was going to Cuba to procure from Fermín's father letters of introduction to use in his Guatemala venture. But the excuse was obviously weak: An exile does not return to his forbidden country under an assumed name for such a frivolous reason. Actually, he himself did not know why he was going. He went, drawn by homesickness, illusion and a sense of duty. He made sensible promises to his family: No, he would not yield to patriotic rapture and become part of a lost cause.

But was the cause a lost one?

When at dawn on the 5th of January he sighted from the deck of the *S.S. Ebro,* which had brought him from Vera

Cruz, the flickering little lights of sleeping Havana, he was shaken with emotion. There, far away behind the forbidding mass of the Santa Clara Battery looming above the slate-smooth sea, lay the quarries. With that bitter recollection was mingled the joy of perceiving again the fragrance of his Island—and his melancholy at arriving secretly after six years' absence, and, pervading all his memories, the evocation of a moonlit night in the country, startled by the occasional sibilant noises of insects stirring in the grass. . . .

In the morning he could not suppress a certain anxiety upon seeing Spanish uniforms . . . the walls. . . . It was not fear of danger itself, but the possibility of a careless, meaningless slip. The sergeant of carabineers looked carefully at the blushing face and the Mexican passport which Martí had taken out under his middle name and his mother's maiden name; since he did not want to be . . . "more hypocritical than necessary."

Vigilant authority never found out that the "J. Pérez" whose name was listed among "Passengers Arrived" in the *Diario de la Marina*, "official publication of the naval station," on the 7th was a troublesome exile. There were other things in the papers of greater importance to the authorities, as well as to Martí himself, principally the "march of progress" of the most excellent Captain-General Martínez Campos who, after restoring the Bourbons in Spain, had arrived, determined to pacify Cuba.

Official bulletins invariably gave an account favorable to the cause of "order and integrity." While the Captain-General completed his preparations to "free the towns from the scourge of war" his flying columns struck with "unfailing heroism" against the "paltry gangs of bandits" encountered in the sugar-growing regions.

It was obvious that one could not put much faith in those official releases. But trustworthy sources of information which Martí sought out immediately did not reveal much activity on the part of the Insurgents. The Cuban press, Cuban gatherings, homes which had sons dedicated to the Cuban cause, and groups of youthful gossipers on the Acera del Louvre, overflowed with tid-bits of rumor. Some die-hard optimists claimed that Máximo Gómez was already in the province of Havana and that the extreme east portion of the Island was all but controlled by the Republic-in-arms. More credible informants, however, drew a very different picture. Serious dissensions were known to exist among the Insurgents. Cubans in New York were also divided among themselves and, almost disbanded, were not sending military supplies to further the revolution. The Insurgent army had no other weapons than those they could snatch from the enemy, no food other than roots and palm seeds taken in the field. The Republic-in-arms lived a nomadic and precarious existence, weakened by the struggle between its civil and military factions. . . . All these factors, plus the arrival of Martínez Campos in October with large reënforcements, and the conciliatory attitude which the new Captain-General immediately showed, had virtually brought the revolution to an end.

In Havana itself, Martí found an atmosphere of profound weariness. Weak, battered, consumed with fever, the Spanish soldiers on furlough or about to be returned to Spain could be seen sitting in despondent rows along the curbs of the sidewalks; it was easy to imagine how much greater was the suffering and despair of the besieged men in the field—with so much less medical attention. The desire for an immediate end of the struggle was no longer even disguised. The war had already taken a great toll in taxes and "fires" in sugar-mills and plantations. The romantic spirit which had enlisted the men of letters in support of the war had given way to a cold, analytical mood. The *Revista de Cuba* had just been started, and with it, positivism.

Having taken the pulse of failure on every side, Martí was haunted by an heroic temptation: If the cause were on the point of being lost, then, more than ever, it needed fresh enthusiasms. But—was not the revolution completely frustrated because of its incoherence, its lack of unity? Without favorable support in the cities, without aid from the outside, on what material sources or moral forces could it sustain itself? And what authority or power did he himself have with which to improvise new strength?

Romantic patriotism is not prone to reason; but Martí's political sense had thrown off much of its load of romanticism. And besides, at twenty-four, only his capacity for personal love had matured. His romantic adolescence was over; other sentimental interests had entered his life. So his duties still loomed up before him in the pattern woven of family ties, of the obligations of private life. He did not feel that he had a right to sacrifice his immediate duties to a desire, certainly vain as yet, for patriotic service. His time would come.

But this intense struggle between two urges lacerated his mind. When, a month later, he decided to go to Guatemala, he felt as if he were tearing his heart out of his body. Egoism and realistic estimate had triumphed, leaving open an internal wound to bleed within him.

Chapter Twelve

"DR TORRENT"

He arrived in Guatemala "poor, unknown, proud and sad." Fermín's father and Antonio Carrillo—an old comrade in Seville—had furnished him with letters of recommendation to prominent people in that Republic, including the President, don Justo Rufino Barrios, who had been a pupil of Fermín's father. Valdés Domínguez had rounded out his kindness by giving Martí a thousand pesos.

Even without such help it would not have been difficult to make himself quickly and favorably known: Guatemala was a Central American republic in the process of formation, and as in all frontier civilizations, people lived there in a kind of national intimacy. During his brisk morning and afternoon walks, President Barrios, in wide-brimmed hat, leggings and riding-crop, was greeted by everyone in a manner something between familiarity and reverence.

He was then just beginning his fifth year in office and was handling his whip with singular efficacy. After suppressing the clerical reaction against his government with a heavy hand, he had begun a general renovation of public institutions and even of customs. He had decided to "modernize" the country, develop its riches, and above all, to educate it—by force if necessary. He had multiplied the number of schools, kept the University open to all talented applicants, and founded the Normal School. For its Director he had brought from New York José María Izaguirre, a former teacher in Bayamo, Cuba, exiled after a short time with the insurgents of 1868.

Martí had heard vague reports in Mexico about the success achieved in the neighboring republic by his compatriot, and upon arriving in Guatemala he had hardly shaken off the dust of the road before he sought out Izaguirre and asked him for a teaching position. The Cuban from Bayamo liked Martí's "pleasing and respectable" appearance, his "easy and charming manner of speaking" and remembered in a hazy sort of way having read Martí's pamphlet on his prison experiences. These were recommendations enough. Martí was appointed a member of the Normal School faculty, to give courses in history and literature.

At the end of his first day in the classroom, the pupils—young women as well as youths—left the campus praising the new professor, talking of his charm and eloquence. Particularly lavish in her praise was one of the older girls, María García Granados, daughter of President Barrios' liberal predecessor. Through her "the best people" of Guatemala learned that night that an important new Cuban had arrived. Martí could notice how the venetian blinds quivered as he walked along the streets.

On his way toward Guatemala City, "his mind warm with dreams and his heart chilled by exile," as he walked along the "proud coast of the Atlantic" the friendliness and informality of the new country announced itself in primitive and symbolic form: that of a splendid Indian Venus who was bathing in a brook—a vision altogether appropriate for a fleeting forest idyll. And the genuine hospitality of the city proved to be no less generous. He soon found himself in the company of the leading figures of liberal politics. The President himself received Martí in audience, introduced by Izaguirre.

Barrios was a stocky, robust man with short-cropped hair and Indian features. He put his curiously small and well-cared-for hand, whip and all, on Martí's shoulder. "Well, well, a Cuban, eh? We like Cubans here, don't we, Izaguirre?"

The Cuban from Bayamo agreed while Martí pondered the homespun language and familiar gesture. He had admired Barrios for two years, ever since he had dared to decree official recognition of Cuban independence, thereby precipitating a full-fledged diplomatic crisis. Izaguirre, however, had warned him about the temper of that strong man who was literally kicking and shoving his country ahead.

Such tactics did not please Martí. Gentle strength also worked wonders without infringing on human dignity. But perhaps America still needed in some measure these great, vital men of the people to tame her impulses and "open new roads" quickly. In any event, he would observe, study and, tutored by his Mexican experience, hold his tongue on matters not deserving legitimate praise.

Thus he wrote to Señor Macal, Minister of the Interior, who had invited him to write something about the new Guatemalan civil code.

> "Never will I disturb, by speech, deeds or writing, the peace of a people who receive me. I come to communicate the little that I know and to learn much that I do not yet know. I come to drown my grief at not being able to fight on my country's battlefields, to lose myself in the consolations of honorable work and in preparing myself for active combat. There is a great universal politics, and that is the one I follow: the politics of new doctrines."

His eulogy on the civil code gave him a chance to state and evaluate this great politics. Although he discreetly claimed for it universality, he was thinking especially of America. He had already seen enough of its Hispanic areas to explain the essence of America. At first he had been baffled and harassed by the general primitiveness of these new peoples oscillating between anarchy and despotism; but slowly an interpretation of the dramatic problem of

America had taken shape in his mind. The Spanish Conquest had interrupted and frustrated the march of the great native cultures, superimposing on them forms alien to their nature. America needed to resume its own shape, under the new era's spirit of investigation and analysis. This correlation with actual environment gave its value to the new piece of Guatemalan legislation, for example.

Among Barrios' jurists this opinion was received with much satisfaction and admiration. The realistic liberalism of Martí impressed them. Never had the philosophy governing their legal heresies been explained so brilliantly. Nor had they read a style so vivid and vigorous.

Naturally, Guatemala could not allow that pen to remain idle; he was invited to help edit the *Revista de La Universidad*. From this point, admission as a member of the University faculty was but a step and, as Barrios was all-powerful and his determination to procure shining lights for his country was not to be stopped by any mere consideration that the University was already providing a generously rich program, Martí was named Professor of practically everything human and divine: history, philosophy, first principles, and literatures.

What did it matter if he was not equally competent in so many varied subjects? The question was one of imparting ideas, and the young Cuban had, in addition to the extensive culture acquired from books and academic training, an asset which those rhetorical universities liked most—the gift of rhapsodic speech. Plato, Schelling, and metaphysical argument lent themselves equally well to brilliant improvisations, argosies filled with liberalism and references to "universal harmony."

The resultant heterodoxy did not at all please the clericals, who, reduced to silent conspiracy against Barrios and all his works, took revenge on the oratorical exuberance of the Cuban. The nickname "Doctor Torrent" was given him in such circles of wounded conservatism. But in the University as well as in the Normal School, that torrent's waters were intoxicating young minds with an almost mystic sense of the great human task, and with a passion for Duty, Beauty and America.

When he spoke on oratory at one of the evening Literary and Art functions of the Normal School, even Izaguirre himself was struck with wonder. Martí's voice, at once delicate and strong, his intensity of gesture, magnificent imagery which could aptly associate a forget-me-not and a flash of lightning, astonished the learned and made women shiver with excitement. María García Granados listened in rapture. All the recruits of the "Central American Poetic Gallery" enthusiastically applauded the golden-tongued Cuban, and after the speech pressed about him to ask for information about Victor Hugo.

On the following day, *El Progreso* praised Martí's speech at great length, and the group of young people voted to make him vice-president of a brand new literary society, "El Porvenir" [The Future].

The exile already felt roots taking hold in that "hospitable, wealthy and open-hearted country."

From Mexico, doña Leonor wrote him that the family was returning to Cuba. Antoñica's heart had also been affected by the rarified air of the plateau, and the memory of poor Ana's fate was decisive. Besides, don Mariano "would fare better" on the Island.

His mind at rest in this hope, Martí could now allow his longing for a home of his own to possess him. He needed an affectionate environment to assuage the muted unrest which was always with him. He wrote now to Carmen Zayas, who was waiting for him in Mexico, telling her about the cordial reception he had received in Guatemala. He believed he could establish his home there. As soon as it was possible without violating his duties he would come to marry her and take her back with him. He had already hinted this to Izaguirre.

His new duties and plans did not, however, succeed in quieting the demands of a less precise but much graver responsibility. The sadness of exile was the central core of his life and, embedded in it, awareness of the vow he had made in Madrid, an obligation for life. At times, when talking with Izaguirre or the poet José Joaquín Palma, who had been Céspedes' adjutant in the war, Martí suddenly fell into abrupt and troubled silences, as if a temptation or a rebuke greater than words had suddenly subdued him. He would come out of these trances with a short sigh and a sad gesture of humility.

To escape from himself a little he visited in the friendly homes of liberals where he found the "seductive face of Guatemalan life. Uncorrupted love, genial hospitality, storied trustfulness, family life at its best." All this was to him a "great salvation."

The home he most frequently visited was that of General García Granados.

After Martí's arrival, theatrical productions at the Normal School were more brilliant in performance than ever before. María García Granados invariably took part in them. She was twenty years old, had a beautiful voice and pale, fine features. Martí had quickly perceived a "dormant love in her brilliant and gentle glances." The verses he had written in her album said other courtly things. When María, at the piano, played Catulle Mendès' "Pensamento" or one of Arditi's waltzes, Martí could not help feeling an overflowing tenderness welling within him. At times, if the General were engrossed in his chess game and the ladies were chatting in the drawing-room, the visitor could sigh with happiness and lean relaxed over the piano.

"With fraternal love alone the exile speaks," one of the

verses in the album had stated baldly. Why then, had he never mentioned Carmen at the General's house, or his engagement? What shyness born of insecure feeling, or of one too overwhelming and profound, made him conceal his engagement from everyone except Palma and Izaguirre? He did not ask himself this question, perhaps unconsciously to avoid baring his own innate reserve, or perhaps in fear of the ambiguity of his feeling for his fiancée, which, nourished on everyone's advice and dreamy Cuban memories, had come at a time to heal a more turbulent emotion. . . .

He did not notice that in the shadow of his silence another illusion had been taking root. Whenever he came to call on her, María would suddenly grow pale and then blush. If he immediately asked her to sing, as he usually did, she would prefer to wait until her sisters withdrew and the excitement yielded to a pleasant dialogue. All he realized at the beginning was that he was happy in the General's house with its wealth of kindness. And he needed so much to warm himself in the sunlight of other people's happiness. But one day a suspicion of the truth crossed his mind: María asked him for a new poem, not to be written in the album for all to see, but for her alone. . . . There was in her voice an unusually caressing quality, and her eyes betrayed her. In the long poem which he wrote for her that evening, classical thought went hand in hand with brotherly reserve. "You ask of me verses to friendship

> *And to you goes out in joy my song as brother.*
> *What another song it would be*
> *If on the strands of your tresses it could play!*"[1]

In this struggle of fine scruple against burning temptation, memories came to his aid—"memory is the nobility of man."

[1] "y a ti va alegre mi canción de hermano.
¡Cuán otro el canto fuera
si en hebras de tu trenza se tañera!"

The poem recalled other episodes of friendship in his life, and it warned him not to barter those genuine realities of affection for other feelings more ephemeral, and asked María to wear the "flower of friendship" in her hair. But there was also in the poem an illusion to a certain critical situation in Mexico and to "his wife, kneeling . . ."

His wife . . . But Martí had not yet married Carmen. What hidden meaning and secret exactitude were held in this inaccuracy? María read the poem sorrowfully. The lie which was intended to be merciful was a cruel revelation. When he tried to take her hand in his as a pledge of friendship she suddenly put her handkerchief to her eyes and fled from the balcony into the depths of the house.

He did not call again nor did he see María until weeks later at the Jocotenango Fair, a traditional occasion for merry-making. Excited about everything of American folk nature, Martí went to this typical festival where high and low met on common ground and even the redoubtable President himself was lost in the crowd, pushed around and forced to move with its currents. Under the bright August sun the spectacle was strikingly lively and colorful. Martí saw the aged García Granados, every inch a soldier, pass by in his carriage with his wife and family. Shortly after noon he received from Granados an invitation to join them in the classic *merienda*—a picnic banquet of Indian fricassee and a variety of sugar delicacies served on palm-leaf mats. María was paler than ever. Dressed in filmy folds of muslin, and abstracted, detached in manner, she seemed infinitely ethereal. He was able only to exchange a few difficult and careful phrases with her. When the festivities came to an end Pepe asked to be excused from returning with the General and his party. The day had melted into a blood-red sunset and the young poet was frightened by the prospect of a summer night filled with emotional strain, heady fragrances and the stars.

On the 15th of September, at one of the public ceremonies commemorating the patriotic anniversary, the General showered him with affectionate reproaches for not having been to visit them. Martí apologized—his teaching duties, the editorial sessions at "El Porvenir," and a book he was writing on Guatemala to make that country better known in Mexico, now that—he thought of María and ended with a certain defensiveness—now that he was going there soon to get married. The General chided him paternally: Weren't there any girls pretty enough for him in Guatemala?

A month later the city was in an uproar. Something serious had happened: The conspiracy of the clericals, which had been a topic for rumor and old wives' tales, had turned out to have something to it. An old woman for whom the President had done a favor the year before had gone to him and assured him that the "serviles" had formed a plot to assassinate him. She revealed the meeting place of the conspirators. That same night, whip in hand, Barrios went alone to their hideout, kicked open the door and flogged the astonished plotters out into the open, where they were later caught.

Among them were persons of some standing, restless youths and former convicts. All Guatemala wondered what the "terrible backwoodsman" would do with his captives. Weeks later he had them shot in the very Plaza de Armas where they were captured.

Disturbed by that typically American incident, Martí went to drown his civic sorrow in private emotion. He went to visit the García Granados family. The General tried to get him to listen to his diatribe against local reactionaries, but Martí preferred to be drawn by María's aloof sadness. As usual, the girls became bored with the conversation and left the couple alone. Their talk became dangerously intimate. María, who had learned from her father about Martí's approaching trip and its purpose, referred to this in a way that reproached him for the lie in the poem. He tried to justify the misrepresentation as poetic license, but never had he felt so keenly the helpless futility of every single word.

Just as his holiday for the trip to Mexico was at hand, Izaguirre spoke to him about María's state: How could Pepe imagine that no one had noticed? The girls themselves had made jokes at María's expense until one day she began to cry. Now they were saying that their sister was heartbroken.

Martí was overwhelmed by an acute, compassionate sense of responsibility. Many times—as the very poem in her album expressed it—he would have liked to "hang about her neck the chain of his love," but in truth he had never spoken to her except "with brotherly love." He reproached himself only for his blindness, the injury he had not known how to prevent. What strange mixture of love and self-pity did his repentance hold? He would have liked, at that moment, to annul all his promises.

But duty won out. When he went to take leave of the General and his family, the night before he was to go away, his speech and bearing were more confused than ever before in his life. María desperately controlled her anguish. In a fleeting moment aside she gave him a small, pillow-shaped *sachet*, beautifully embroidered. She was scarcely able to murmur in a hushed voice: "Keep it, Pepe. . . . For good luck." The only answer he could make was to kiss her impulsively on the forehead. And that quick caress told him that she was hot with fever.

Eager to make his trip useful in rounding out his knowledge of the country, he returned to Mexico overland, crossing the Río Grande and over the Sierra de las Minas on horseback to Cobán, from which point he could reach the border. It was a country of forests and volcanoes where, at intervals, coffee plantations broke the rugged landscape and where the *quetzal*,[1] symbol of an untamed America, hid the useless luxury of its plumage from the curious gaze of the wayfarer.

This strenuous immersion in vast, primeval Nature enriched his sense of America: That trip was a definite documentation. He arrived in Mexico intoxicated with the magnificent panoramas and a vast hope. Guillermo Prieto, Justo Sierra, Peza, Mercado, all his friends, listened to him speak of America and the Indian in phrases which seemed to draw their wealth from the very Nature they were describing: "America is destined to give warmth and animation to everything!"

During the trip he had completed his eulogy of Guatemala, a fistful of rapturous pages. When the Guatemalan Uriarte was given the essay to take to the printer, he read it with such excitement that he took it upon himself to write a foreword.

Martí's stay in Mexico was brief. His month's leave of absence coincided with the Christmas vacation and he had to be back when classes began again, right after the New Year. The wedding had a happy setting as a climax of Christmas merry-making, and in Mercado's house, where the ceremony was performed, the flower of Mexican literary life were gathered together. A splendid album was presented to Carmen, filled with the compliments and poetic good wishes of all, beginning with don Justo Sierra and ending with don Anselmo de la Portilla himself, Pepe's old-time adversary of *La Iberia*. Nicolás Azcárate wished for "the brilliant couple of which our Cuba is proud" that they might never reach the stage of "bitter tears contemplating the crumbled altars of their temple."

[1] The *quetzal* is a bird which is said always to die when reduced to captivity. It is used as a motif in the coat of arms of Guatemala.

On the very day that Martí's leave expired—one of the first days of the new year of 1878—the newlyweds arrived in Guatemala. That afternoon when Martí, with Carmen on his arm, strolled past the Granados home, he thought he saw a silhouette clearly move in the depths of the balcony and for a fugitive moment he felt the subtle, oppressive presence of tragic finality.

The General was not long in paying them a visit of welcome. With the candor that comes from too much experience, he regretted that María was not well enough to visit them. One afternoon, late, she had gone bathing in the river, just as the sun had nearly set, and ever since that time she had been suffering from attacks of fever. . . . "The madness of young people" was the old veteran's comment. They must come to the house so the girls could meet the attractive Cuban bride.

A few days later, Izaguirre brought the news that María's condition was extremely grave. Martí, greatly distressed, wondered if he should visit her. The very next morning the bells of the Church of la Recolección were tolling her death. He saw her then in the large "cold vault." Under the gaze of hundreds of weeping mourners, he approached the white silk-upholstered coffin and kissed the dead girl's thin hand.

All Guatemala gathered in the streets to watch the funeral procession of "The General's Daughter" with its wealth of floral tributes and the neat white casket borne on the shoulders of her friends. When the burial was over, Martí, Izaguirre and Palma remained standing where they were. They stared at each other and finally left the cemetery without speaking. Carmen never understood why her husband returned so shaken by a stranger's funeral. He already carried within him the poignant remorse that would find expression in a future poem:

Of a chill they say she died:
I know that she died of love. . . .[1]

Arrival of Martí's booklet praising the country was a great event. Never had the little country been so generously appreciated. There was no aspect of either landscape or Guatamalan life which did not receive its full due. The little book was almost too generous, for Martí had written it as an obligation of gratitude and a tribute to America. Guatamala had given him a home; it had made him a teacher, thereby "making him a creator." He had there found scope for his "unbounded American restlessness."

But there was another, a more urgent, reason for its praise: America was divided and it was essential to unite her through knowledge of herself. "Since disunity was our death, what little mind or mean heart needs to be told that our life depends on unity?" Everyone should do his part; he would not shun his. "I live to unite what ill fortune has separated."

No language could be more pleasing to those federalist liberals whose only god was Bolívar. For many weeks Guatemalan literary circles talked of nothing else but this magnificent evaluation of their country. Some young poets were irritated by the fact that they had not been singled out for mention, but all agreed that never had they noted adjectives so exact or descriptions so vivid and beautiful.

As married life had increased his economic responsibilities and, aside from that, his classes were only a limited forum, Martí took advantage of his success to start a project for a Guatemalan *Review*. A carefully thought out and persuasive announcement went to press announcing the coming publication.

[1] . . . dicen que murió de frío:
yo sé que murió de amor.

Then something happened as serious as it was unforeseen. On Izaguirre's name day a party was given in his honor in the Normal School auditorium. Teachers from other subordinate institutions, who for some time had been waging a silent war against Izaguirre because they had been obscured in the shadow of his success, took advantage of this opportunity to accuse him of self-admiration and dereliction of duty. This accusation was relayed to the President himself. It reached don Rufino on one of the days when he was easily provoked and Izaguirre was summoned before the august presence. Barrios was not a man to listen to excuses nor was Izaguirre a man to make them. Izaguirre limited himself to the statement that he had always fulfilled his duties and handed in his resignation.

No sooner had Martí found out what had happened, when he hastened to Izaguirre's side and announced that he, too, would resign immediately. The older Cuban tried to dissuade him. Martí insisted on the decision he had made.

"What they have done to you is contemptible. I shall resign."

"But Martí! Your salary as professor is your only income; how are you going to support your wife?"

"I shall resign even though my wife and I were to starve."

What mysterious fate joined, once again, the vicissitudes of his life to those of his beloved native Island?

While Martí, longing for Cuba, was finding consolation in his passion for all things American and in "preparation for a vigorous fight," in the Island itself the Revolution had almost completely petered out. Only vague and fragmentary bits of news reached Guatemala. The Mexican papers scarcely mentioned the Cuban cause, and letters from his family and friends contained only allusions indicating discouragement—or satisfaction—over the fact that the whole thing "will soon come to an end."

GENERAL MÁXIMO GÓMEZ

But it was impossible for him to return as yet. And now, suddenly cast adrift in Guatemala when he had begun to feel his love and respect taking root there, what was there for him to do but go to another American country, to Venezuela, perhaps, mother of them all?

While he was trying to come to a decision, newspapers from abroad arrived with the sorrowful, or happy, news: The war in Cuba was over. Spaniards and Insurgents had come to terms on a basis other than independence. To all appearances there were still some doubts and dissensions. General Maceo was as untamed as ever. . . . Martí waited. By summer, letters from Cuba assured him that it was all over, but he felt even then the inevitability of "future new struggles for the Motherland" and embarked with his wife for Havana.

He borrowed, to read en route, a copy of Pozos Dulces' *Collection of Studies on Agriculture*, in which he would find many things he had been thinking "and others he never would have been capable of thinking." In Carmen's album General García Granados wrote a few faithful lines of farewell on July 26, 1878.

Chapter Thirteen

"FORGETTING THE PAST"

"He belonged to the select race of those who do not work for success but against it."

Martí: Amistad funesta

THE ZANJÓN PACT made it possible for hundreds of Cuban expatriates to return to Cuba from exile, principally from the United States and other American countries. Many had gone into exile at the beginning of the war in '68; after ten years of anxious expectancy and, in not a few cases, of untold hardship and work they were returning, like swallows to their perches after a storm.

The second stipulation in the Pact was phrased ambiguously. General Martínez Campos had proposed "a general pardon." The Insurgents repudiated the implication of guilt and suggested "general amnesty." But this, in turn, had appeared to imply too great a recognition of belligerent rights. The phrase agreed upon as a compromise was "forgetting the past." The ironic doom of the phrase, which covered all attitudes but left all standards undefined, could not yet be perceived in those summer days of 1878 when Martí returned to Cuba with an accent slightly Mexican and noticeably excited by the fact of his wife's pregnancy.

The heavy atmosphere of dog days was still charged with a vague excitement, an enthusiasm somewhat induced by strong doses of "fraternity," "harmony," "race" and similar hopeful watchwords. Spain had won; but the Peninsulars, inspired by the gentlemanly Martínez Campos, concealed their joy at keeping Cuba for Spain, sublimating it into channels of consideration and courtesy. Their uniforms and red and yellow cockades had been discreetly put aside. As for the Insurgents, Maceo, Máximo Gómez and other important leaders had preferred to leave the Island; the majority had returned to their own villages and farms; some could be seen in Havana's Acera del Louvre, where they were stared at in admiration. In the open entrances to certain photographic studios groups of people, arguing or ironically silent, looked at pictures of Insurrecto soldiers, almost all of them taken in pairs with their machetes crossed above their straw sombreros. Near by on large easels were pictures of Generals Jovellar and Martínez Campos, their chests blazing with decorations and medals.

Newspapers were still extracting tid-bits of comment on the speeches delivered at the banquet which peaceable and liberal-minded Cubans had given "The Peacemaker"—Martínez Campos—at the Tacón Theatre a few weeks back. Don Pedro Gonzáles Llorente, the prominent lawyer, had been eloquent in defending, and explicit in explaining, the doctrine which had restored peace: "We want, consistent with our ancient national unity, what we believe to be our rights, but we want to achieve them, enjoy them, and defend them, through legal means." The General had conceded these concepts "as an expression of the country's sentiments" and recalled that the reforms just yielded by Spain to Cuba were only provisional, not prejudicing those rights which the Island might later obtain through its representation in the Cortes "if it nourished greater aspirations."

The reforms, in reality, could not have been more stingy. The Cuban signers of the Pact had asked for a "status" for Cuba equal to that of the provinces in Spain. At Zanjón Martínez Campos did not want to promise anything more than political rights equal to those Puerto Rico had enjoyed since the September Revolution in Spain. When the Cubans asked to have these rights defined—they were spoken of as a panacea—the General found himself in a tight spot and consulted his associate in command by telephone. Jovellar had answered from Havana that he did not know them in detail, but that "it could be said" that the Province of Puerto Rico and the provinces of Spain possessed "substantially the same status." The Insurgents accepted on this basis.

Now, after several months, they learned to their surprise that Puerto Rico was still legally in a state of siege! In 1874 a captain-general had suspended the "glorious concesssions" made by the Spanish September Revolution, and Cuba's West Indian neighbor enjoyed no other political right than representation in the Cortes, which, therefore, turned out to be the only right granted to Cuba for the time being. . . . The Pact was a cruel joke. Cubans who had not sympathized with Maceo now began to understand why he had skeptically refused to come to an understanding with Martínez Campos under the remote mango groves of Baraguá and had pronounced for continued opposition.

But a mood of confidence, none the less, prevailed: The Peacemaker was without any doubt a man of good faith. He himself had advised Cánovas "to entertain frankly the question of liberties." Representative groups on the Island were, for the most part, divided in their attitudes on different matters. In August the Liberals formed a party to advocate "application to the Antilles of all rights granted to all Spaniards in Section I of the Constitution." Days later, the Conservatives, or "unconditional Spaniards," organized themselves under a program calculated in its vagueness: "to reconcile the tradition of an indispensable past with the legitimate exigencies of the present and noble aspirations for the future."

Two months later, in a modest office on San Ignacio Street, two lawyers were heatedly discussing the various new courses of action open to the Island. One of them was don Nicolás Azcárate who, as soon as he heard the news in

Mexico of the Zanjón Pact, had shaken off his rôle of poverty and returned to Cuba. The other lawyer was Martí.

When Martí had returned to Havana, Azcárate had already opened a law office, and when his old friend invited Martí to work with him, he accepted. Since lawsuits were not numerous the eternal dissenters debated with each other over politics every afternoon. Behind the ornately carved table, completely barren of papers, don Nicolás sat erect, barrel chest extended and great leonine head held high.

"But don't you see, Pepe, that. . . ."

Incapable of standing still, Martí walked from one end of the office to the other, his hands in the armholes of his vest, shaking his head negatively: No. The "assimilation" theory of old-time reformism could not convince him. "Assimilation!" The word itself was absurd. How could Cuba, an American land, the cradle of a people who had just gone through a courageous ten-year struggle for independence, resign itself to being merely "assimilated" as a Spanish province? Race, language, tradition, these were all very well, but above all there was the will, already mature, to create a separate entity: the American vocation of Cuba. "Assimilation" as a province of Spain was too niggardly a solution:

"But you will see, Nicolás, that Spain will never want to give us even that."

Azcárate, as intolerant of contrary opinions as he was vehement in defending his own, insisted on his long-standing prejudices. Independence was the Yankee peril, or the Negro peril. There you had Maceo's objection to Zanjón, an objection motivated by racial ambition. . . . Those people wanted liberty only for themselves. . . .

He suddenly stopped. At the door there appeared, as if called up by that very allusion, a young colored man slight of build, very properly dressed in a frock coat and silk hat.

Azcárate introduced him to Martí. "Juan Gualberto Gómez, a friend of mine from Mexico." And smilingly he added, "But he is one of us."

The new arrival did not realize the meaning of the characterization. He looked at don Nicolás with hero-worship in his eyes, eagerly shook hands with Martí, and proceeded to make himself comfortable in an arm chair, taking out a large home-made cigar and twisting the end of it in his thick lips with gusto.

Conversation was threaded in and out with reminiscences of fairly-recent days in Mexico, where the colored youth had met Azcárate. Martí discreetly asked about the visitor's past and he spoke of it without hesitation. When still a boy, he had been sent to France by his parents to learn the only thing colored people could usefully engage in at that time in Cuba—a trade. Only, Juan had taken advantage of his stay in Paris to acquire a French education in addition to learning the technical phases of carriage making. When the old patriot Francisco Vicente Aguilera went there to win over the wealthy Cubans in Paris to the revolution, he found no one more ready or disposed to take charge of his correspondence than the little mulatto. He made Juan Gualberto a politician and a Separatist. Years later, an exile in Mexico, how many times had he discussed independence with Azcárate in the dining-room of the Hotel Iturbide! . . . But what Juan Gualberto always admired about don Nicolás was the tenacity with which he had fought for the redemption of the colored race.

He expressed himself fluently and vivaciously. Every part of him expressed the happy frankness of a child, a refreshing loyalty. Martí listened to him with delight and when he had finished, he gripped his hand in silence and gave Azcárate a look that said: "Don't you see? Don't you see? We are all one!"

From that day on, Juan Gualberto made it his habit to go

to the office every day to talk with the leisurely lawyers. Favorite topics were the past war with its ten years of illusionary struggle, its magnificent feats of heroism and regrettable streaks of meanness, with its Agramontes[1] and its double-dealers . . . the weariness at the end, Maceo's absolute refusal to give up, the nothingness of disillusion, and now, the bad feeling, increasing every day, between the two Cuban groups on the Island. . . . Both groups were campaigning vigorously. The Constitutional Union party wanted nothing more than status quo, frankly confessing that it was against abolition of slavery. And the Liberals were already becoming impatient for the promised reforms and were talking about self-government.

At other times Juan Gualberto would find Martí and Azcárate involved in literary matters. Don Nicolás had resumed his old hobby of being a patron of belles lettres. The Guanabacoa Liceo, which he had assisted in founding prior to the rising of '61, and which had suspended its activities during the long war, now reopened its doors. In the quaint old "town of hills" near the city, where numerous prominent people of Havana lived, this occasioned a great deal of enthusiasm: The Liceo was a local pride reborn.

Azcárate immediately enlisted Martí's help, and had him named a member of the literary committee. Martí was not long in proving his competency. Literary men of Guanabacoa praised the eloquence and natural air of authority of the young man nobody knew, who spoke so fluently—although his s's were a little too sibilant—and who modestly inquired after his every suggestion, "No?" One always had to agree with him: The literary programs he planned were perfect.

A private event obliged Martí to make plans more serious and intimate, however, than these. On November 12 his first

[1] Ignacio Agramonte y Loynaz (1841-1873): Major General and one of the great heroes of the Ten Years War. He was a member of the first Constituent Assembly at Guáimaro, 1869. Was killed in a skirmish at Jimaguayó.

child, a son, was born. Life suddenly became filled with responsibility. He could no longer continue to live with Fermín Valdés Domínguez who, although he was married, had taken Martí to share his house the first few months after his return to Cuba. Nor would the small amount of money he was earning in Azcárate's office be sufficient. Luckily, the attorney Miguel Viondi, one of the leading men of Guanabacoa, needed someone to help him with his large clientèle. Martí entered his office as assistant.

Juan Gualberto continued to visit him frequently at his new office; a brotherly friendship had grown up between the two young men. Martí came to appreciate more every day the intelligence and likeable traits of his colored friend, who was then writing courageous political articles for *La Libertad*, a daily paper owned by Márquez Sterling. Contact with the newspaper world through Juan Gualberto excited Martí's natural inclinations greatly, but he held himself in check.

Marriage and fatherhood were "weights on his wings" but were a great consolation after a long day's work at the law office, after "court clashes which at times caused him anxiety and disgust"—as he was to write in the future, recording his own image in the leading character of one of his novels—and they were a relief from the drabness and timidity of a provincial life, goaded on by material necessity. As in Mexico and in Guatemala, so he now felt in Cuba the tragedy of the intellectuals, one common to the undeveloped countries of America, where education—far too literary and scholastic—was divorced from real needs and possibilities. What else could be expected but greedy political shuffling, vain discord and tolerance of corruption? Reduced by present necessities and duty to practice his "deceitful profession" as a lawyer, he was trying to practice it at least without sacrificing his independence and his integrity.

Month after month passed by and the promises made at

Zanjón were not being carried out beyond meager representation in the Cortes, where the Cubans already had had to listen to a spate of contempt from General Salamanca, bitter enemy of Martínez Campos and all his works. The Peacemaker had written his Government a hundred times asking for betterment of conditions on the Island:

"It must be emphasized: The inhabitants of this *province* wish to be a province and I am not here recording their complaints—which today they present in a calm voice and which tomorrow they may demand too loudly and violently—because it is not my task to echo them, and above all because they cannot fail to have reached the high discernment of Your Majesty and of the Government."

Martínez Campos was not writing about bonfires. Although he was flattered upon hearing himself called the Peacemaker he knew that peace was still a very tender sprout. If his political astuteness had not become aware that for the Cuban patriots Zanjón was only a truce, not a surrender, at least his military shrewdness made him realize that the fires of insurrection were banked but not extinct. There were still independent bands of men causing trouble in the jungle; a fresh spark of anger over defrauded hopes could set the fires of war ablaze again.

Nor was the General overlooking the fact that the emigrés in New York who favored independence were far from being idle. The Revolutionary Committee which had been established there within three months after the Zanjón Pact was now intensifying its activities under the direction of one of the few leaders of the revolution who had not signed the Pact and maintained his prestige unscathed: General Calixto García. Spain's representative in Washington assured him that funds from Havana were reaching the Committee

GENERAL ANTONIO MACEO

and that something serious was again being hatched on the Island. Could not the Government of Spain see that it was flagrant folly to delay the too-often promised reforms any longer?

The General's insistence began to annoy the leaders of the clique in Madrid. Martínez Campos had certainly become "more Catholic than the Pope." His presence in Cuba was becoming a nuisance, and Cánovas finally decided to recall him and make him a cabinet minister for a time in order to silence his presumption. The Peacemaker announced his return to the Peninsula at the beginning of January.

With Spain's slowness of action, Martí saw distrust and suspicion growing, stimulated by the bad economic situation. He came across a copy of a manifesto published in August by the New York committee, urging Separatists on the Island to organize in secret groups "to work by all means conducive to the achievement of independence, contriving and collecting financial resources and material for war."

He had just recently arrived in Cuba after eight difficult years of absence. He had a wife and child. And his country was now calling him again. On which side lay the higher duty? That afternoon, as on every afternoon, news hawkers of Márquez Sterling's paper—first to hit the streets in Cuba—went by, filling the afternoon air with the shout: "*La Libertad! La Libertad!*" Liberty! Martí trembled.

The following day his conversation with Juan Gualberto was longer and more intimate than ever.

Chapter Fourteen

CONSPIRATOR

VERY SOON there was opportunity for Martí to reveal his own convictions.

Alfredo Torroella died. He had come from Mexico, a swan song on his lips, to rest at last in the land he loved. The Liceo, in whose literary section he had been prominent, gave the public a chance to see the poet lying in state in its auditorium. On that sad occasion a group of friends were reunited. Azcárate spoke a few trembling words standing at the coffin. Luis Victoriano Betancourt, a writer of light verse, read some melancholy *quintillas.* Then Martí spoke. He spoke quietly, in an almost confidential voice, of the time of their common exile, shared under the star-lit nights on Mexico's high plateau, the agonies of romantic youth, camaraderie in friendship and in love affairs. In the silent hall, the evocation of the past, so pregnant with sadness, stirred everyone with its prose strophes of lacerating beauty. The light of the flickering altar candles was reflected, sparkling, in the eyes of all, eyes wet with tears.

In another instant these eyes were staring at each other in alarm. Martí had lost his bearings a little, had raised his voice, and in referring to exile was saying very harsh things of Spain. He stopped speaking in an atmosphere charged with fear. Azcárate shook his huge head in disapproval.

However, this did not prevent him, a few days later, from entrusting to Martí the eulogy to be given at the formal convocation the Liceo appointed to honor Torroella's memory. "Don't be reckless, Pepe . . ." was Azcárate's only advice.

It was Martí's debut in Cuba before a large audience. Azcárate introduced him with generous commendation. Very pale, but "blushing at each glance like a school girl," the new orator entered the famous pulpit.

> "Today we do not need the fiery word in flowers of sorrow which the wind snatches away, to pay fleeting tribute to the dead, so well loved by his Country. Although, if his Nation loves him, he is not dead. . . . His good friends wish my trembling hand, still warm with the fire that in life consumed his own generous hand, to be one to portray the sincere and original spirit with which he placed many laurels on the gloomy brow of our Nation, now laden with wreaths of mourning . . ."

These references to "Our Nation" at a time when it was customary to say "The Island" or "the Country," and those to "gloomy brow" and "laden with wreaths of mourning" disturbed Azcárate, making him move uneasily in the presiding officer's chair. The audience, however, was spellbound by that melodious voice vibrant with power at one moment and in the next breath quietly hushed in tones of mourning. Martí did nothing more than tell of the poet's life, but his way of telling it was full of reticences and implications so Cuban that the expression on the face of don Nicolás went from astonishment to alarm. When at last Martí concluded with a magnificent invocation to death, the audience was electrified. The mournful silence was broken by a wild ovation and Martí was carried away from the rostrum amid embraces.

He had dedicated himself. Next day the newspapers saluted enthusiastically the "fledgling eagle of our rostrum." When, a week later, it became known that he would take part in a debate the Liceo was sponsoring on "Idealism and

Realism in Art," people packed the hall, the balcony—and even the adjoining courtyard.

> "Irreplaceable losses, grieving voices, majestic spirits, haunt my soul; poor ghosts who do not know what to say, or cannot say what they would . . ."

And since they could not say what they would, they confined themselves to praising, in his hymn to the Liceo and to Guanabacoa, all "these towns, beloved children of the Country, who keep pure and unstained all the glories of the past. . . ."

La Patria, in its news story, lavished praise on the "young and already celebrated orator, Señor Martí": He had introduced to Cuba a style of oratory quite out of the common—eloquence of vigor and brilliance, subtle and intoxicating.

"You are the only ones now conspiring in Cuba," Attorney Viondi used to say, on noticing in the office the frequent and secluded sessions between Juan Gualberto and Martí.

But the lawyer was mistaken. The underground organization recommended by the New York Committee was spreading like a grass fire. General Blanco, who had succeded Martínez Campos as governor was aware of what was going on. According to Polavieja, his officer in command, there was already a movement in Oriente directed by Calixto García from New York and Antonio Maceo from Jamaica. What the Captain-General did not, perhaps, suspect was the extent of the conspiracy in other places on the Island, and in Havana particularly.

Havana did not want to lag behind, this time. Over and above local pride, there were certain lessons learned from the past war, principally the lesson that a merely regional movement was too vulnerable. The effectiveness of a future war would depend upon its being a simultaneous rebellion throughout the whole Island. Calixto García continued to stir up the western portion of the Island and although Oriente, proud of its past deeds, still seemed inclined to act for itself, Colonel Pedro Martínez Freyre took care to maintain liaison from one end of the Island to the other. On his orders José Antonio Aguilera secretly came and went from "Cuba"—as Santiago was often called—to Havana, carrying the personal instructions of Martínez Freyre himself, Flor Crombet and Mayía Rodriguez; stopping in the central Villas to discuss plans with Francisco Carrillo and Serafín Sánchez; and tying them all in, finally, with the commitments in Havana of persons newer to the Cause, such as Martí, Juan Gualberto, Cirilo Pouble.

Martí had now overcome the last resistance counselled by his private interests and a certain temptation to political modesty. When Urbano Sánchez Echevarría, a lawyer from Oriente, at the urging of several liberals of that region, broached to Martí the idea of making him candidate for the Spanish Cortes from that district, Martí answered that should he be elected, he wanted it clearly understood that he would accept the post to defend in the Spanish parliament the only wise course which in his judgment a Cuban could defend: Independence. The bearer and the message fell into the hands of the police. He was, however, put forth as a candidate at the last minute, polling about a hundred votes, and this political inconsistency engraved itself on some invidious memories.

He was not long in indicating his stand publicly. On the 26th of April the Liberal Party held a banquet in honor of Adolfo Márquez Sterling, in return for one previously given by him, with the object of a possible understanding between Liberals and the Republican Party, which Márquez Sterling headed. He entrusted the delivery of the address of thanks to Martí. The function took place in the historic "galleries" of the Louvre. The attorney Gálvez opened the banquet with a circumspect, optimistic speech filled with liberal moderation: a summary of the Liberal Party program. Then, rather unexpectedly to the organizers of the banquet, the floor was turned over to the "Mocking-bird of the Liceo."

Martí's opening phrases revealed how aware he was of his precarious position. He spoke as a "bystander," as a "fiery particle," a flame that would never be extinguished except by "a raging torrent of liberties."

The tone and aspiration of his words surprised the gentlemen at the speakers' table. Especially when Martí, praising the public honesty of the journalist in whose honor the banquet was given, declared forthrightly that "The man who demands is worth more than he who begs . . . ; rights are taken, not asked for; they are seized, not wheedled. . . ." The impact was like that of a cannon ball. At some sections of the table one heard: "Good! Very good!" But Lawyer Gálvez frowned, drank some water and exchanged a quick glance of surprise with Govín, Secretary of the Committee, and Rafael Montoro, the young orator of the Liberals. Faces were tense with expectancy. After alluding to the "incomplete liberty achieved by conquest, not by anybody's gift," Martí launched into a crescendo of hypotheses that took the breath of everyone at the table. If liberal Cuban politics were energetically to work for the radical solution of all the Country's problems

> . . . "for loftiness, for dignity, for energy, I drink a toast to Cuban politics. But if, taking a narrow and winding road, we do not act on the problem in all its aspects and fail, therefore, to arrive at immediate, definite, and concrete solutions; if we forget, as lost or destroyed, social elements which are powerful and vital; if we tighten our hearts to prevent surging from them the truth which

escapes from our lips; if instead of being echoes of our Country we act as a masquerade of our true selves—then I shatter my glass; I do not drink a toast to the politics of Cuba!"

Martí, who had lightly lifted his glass, put it down again on the littered table with trembling hand and when it clinked against other crystal in the tense silence, the tinkling was dramatic.

Eloquence momentarily overcame discretion and timidity; but the final applause was an adjustment between courtesy and party discipline. Kindled by the courageous words, José Rafael Izquierdo gave his enthusiastic vote for the policy Martí had just outlined. Gálvez sent a message to Montoro, and the latter rose to answer. He cut a handsome figure, a solid and classical profile, in contrast to the frail, romantic silhouette who had been the center of attention a few moments earlier. In the congested atmosphere Montoro's tranquil and polished phrases were calming. The young orator of the Liberals praised Martí's eloquence and Señor Izquierdo's enthusiasm. He did not intend to discuss their points of view: He wished only to make clear that they did not represent the philosophy of the Liberal Party, whose doctrine was no more and no less than what was contained in its written platform. The Liberals believed that what was not in harmony with their program was reckless extremism. Every hour had its possibilities; politics was the art of adjusting programs to the possible.

The gentlemen at the speakers' table nodded their heads vigorously in agreement, save for Márquez Sterling, who felt himself restrained by the unforeseen, controversial direction this banquet in his honor had taken. Martí listened, his chin sunk in his locked hands. When Montoro finished, the applause had something orderly and methodical about it—like his speech. Señor Saladrigas, and next Señor Gálvez, finished healing the breach in a diplomatic summation. The banqueters left, at length, in an atmosphere of emotional incoherence.

The lines of division had been dramatically drawn.

Within an hour's time General Blanco had been informed about events at the Louvre. "Who is this Martí?" he asked.

The following day he decided to find out for himself. The Liceo of Guanabacoa had set aside an evening to honor the Cuban violinist, Díaz Albertini. Following the conciliatory policy of Martínez Campos, the new Captain-General decided to ingratiate himself with that nest of talkative Creoles. He had also been tipped off that "that Martí" was going to speak, and although Blanco did not attach much importance to the wild new "mocking-bird," he was curious to see its plumage.

Martí was not niggardly in giving him his opportunity. His praise of the Creole violinist carried such meaning in its reticences, was so direct in its references to "Our Nation" and the future of Cuba, that the pompous Captain-General was shocked. On leaving, stiff with dignity and medals, he commented ominously: "I do not wish to remember the things I have heard—such as I never imagined would be said before me, a representative of the Spanish Government. I am coming to think Martí is a madman—and a dangerous madman."

Nor was the General alone in this opinion. Others, closer to Martí, and inclined to be sympathetic, began to believe that there was something of the eccentric, of the unstable, in that youth of glowing speech and nervous movement who even now was talking of another war. . . . The Ten Years War had cost Spain and Cuba 200,000 dead and 700 million pesos. Wasn't that enough? Could Martí not see that what Cuba wanted was peace, peace as a respite from the all too recent despairs, and to heal the ravages of a decade of destruction and war expense?

To people who felt this way it was not difficult to find evidence in other declarations by Martí that he was a visionary. Food for such judgment was supplied by the state of exaltation, of intoxication with the ideal, in which he lived, as if to defend himself the better from the ordinary temptations to moderation. He was so engrossed in his concern for the deeper reality that he lost at times his sense of touch with daily life. One day an employee at the office mentioned that Attorney Cortina was going to make a speech that evening about "an Englishman who says that man is descended from the monkeys." Martí, ordinarily courteous and understanding, flew into a rage.

"That Englishman is Charles Darwin and his brow is like the side of a mountain!"

To the astonishment of everyone who witnessed the scene, he lectured the terrified lawyer on the theory of the origin of species.

Convinced that Juan Gualberto and Martí had something serious up their sleeves, Viondi finally gave them a back room in the office so that they could conspire to their hearts' content. But whenever the discussion was a vital one Martí preferred it to take place in his own home—a modest second-floor apartment on Industria Street.

He was, with Aguilera, one of the leaders of the Havana underground. His declarations at the Liceo, and above all at the widely talked-about banquet for Márquez Sterling, had made him outstanding. At a secret meeting of the Clubs held in the near-by town of Regla, he had been elected president of the Havana Central Committee, composed of delegates from all the revolutionary organizations of the province. And, the New York Committee had independently named

Aguilera and Martí respectively as their delegate and vice-delegate in Havana.

The underground movement made progress, without let-up. Different groups united. Funds were raised and sent to New York for the purchase of arms. Carrillo, Serafín Sánchez and others were secretly mobilizing the central region. In Oriente alone had there been serious difficulties to face. Polavieja, who was in control there, had deported Flor Crombet, Martínez Freyre and a few others as a precautionary measure. But Oriente, led by its capital city Santiago, would respond; it always responded.

The underground in Havana felt official suspicion thickening about them and its members avoided meeting one another. Martí depended upon Juan Gualberto to maintain his contacts. The Negro intellectual saw him daily at the office or at their "little white nook" on Industria Street, where he was accustomed to drop in and share the restaurant meals "La Perla" provided just for Carmen and Pepe but which were "enough for a regiment." One night Martí arrived unexpectedly on an urgent mission at the tiny little home where Juan Gualberto was visiting his fiancée, a dressmaker. He was so courteous in making his excuses, so genuinely considerate, that the entire family took a great liking to him and not even Juan's betrothed resented it when he took her Juan away with him.

The free Negroes were still treated by the white Creoles of the Island in a manner too reminiscent of the slave-owner. Martí's bearing was sincerely egalitarian, without any trace of condescension. On a day when the Liceo was to hear the violinist, Palmero—introduced by Juan Gualberto, who was sponsoring him—Martí regretted that his many tasks deprived him of the "pleasure of seeing white hands applaud a colored artist."

He was, indeed, far too busy. Classes at the Colegio Plasencia, where he was teaching in order to help earn a living, took up a great deal of time. And every spare moment he used effectively to help Azcárate with his work at the Liceo; he lectured there again on Echegaray's theatre, and once in a while he found time in the evening to visit the Valdés Domínguez home and meet there the aging but always beloved Mendive and other men of learning and letters. On one such occasion he read them a realistic-romantic play he had written: *The Adulteress.*

But all these things were side issues compared with the constant work of the underground. Literary activities were too tinged either with positivist philosophy—and he was an idealist—or with a traditional Spanish classicism of style, and he was so stubbornly American that, half seriously, half in fun, he protested to Viondi about having to write on the kind of paper which was then called "Spanish." He detested every trace of Spanish officiousness. Every afternoon without fail, however, he visited and kissed his Valencian father and his mother, who was born in the Canaries.

Early in August the Liberal Party, feeling the storm coming, decided to deflect its fury by declaring itself—although with considerable timidity—in favor of autonomy. A few days later, Commandante Polavieja advised Blanco that the Separatists were planning a general rising for the end of the month and he proposed to bring it to a head and make it ineffective by seizing the known instigators at once. Blanco, however, still harbored illusions. Govín had assured him that the liberal-autonomist party would stand by him. Polavieja was disgusted with this easy-going attitude.

Events proved Polavieja right. On the 28th of August the Negro leaders José Maceo,[1] Moncada, and Quintín Banderas raised the standard of revolt in Santiago. Other declarations followed in the rest of Oriente and in the central part of the Island. It was known that Calixto García and Antonio Maceo

[1] A brother of Antonio Maceo, then in exile.

were waiting for the right moment to land in Cuba and assume leadership of the movement. Polavieja at last received orders to proceed with a heavy hand and he did so at once and without scruple. Half of Santiago was arrested and thrown into the dungeon of Morro Castle to await the sailing of ships for transportation to the Mahón and Ceuta penitentiaries.

In the house of their co-worker, Anita Pando, Aguilera and Martí received from the hands of Eusebio Hernández a handwritten sheet containing instructions which Antonio Maceo had sent from Jamaica to the Insurrectos of Occidente: Although New York had ordered the rising for the middle of November, it had to be made earlier because of the symptoms Polavieja revealed of jeopardizing the whole movement. There was nothing to do but to go ahead at once. Aguilera, Martí, Hernández, met daily to expedite the shipment of weapons to the interior.

On September 17th, when Juan Gualberto was breakfasting with Martí and Carmen, there was a knock at the street door.

"Pepe, the gentleman who was here to see you before."

Martí went out to the small entrance hall. A moment later he returned, unexcited, and called his wife aside and spoke to her in a low voice. Then he intimated to Juan Gualberto, who was enjoying a leisurely smoke over his coffee, that he had to hurry away on an emergency errand.

As soon as the street door had closed, Carmen gasped in dismay: "They are taking him away, Juan; they've arrested Pepe!"

His friend jumped up and dashed to the street. He could still follow Martí and his captor at a distance. When they took a hack, he followed them in another until they reached police headquarters. Now certain of Martí's fate, he ran to tell Azcárate. That old friend clapped his hands to his head. "It had to be! It had to be!" And, reaching for his silk hat, he went out with Juan Gualberto, without hope, to see what could be done. He was successful in getting permission to talk with Martí. Through his aid, Martí was able to warn Viondi to burn every paper he could find on the conspirators' desk and to deliver to Juan Gualberto, for Aguilera, a small suitcase of the utmost importance.

General Blanco was now amply informed. Searches made in Santiago had brought much to light. Boxes of a shipment sent by Aguilera and Hernández to a town in the interior, had come open accidentally on the station platform, spilling out some of the contents—cartridges. There were other similar "accidents" less easy to account for. The conspirators came to realize—much too late—that they had been spied upon from within their own circle, betrayed. . . .

A few weeks later, Aguilera and Juan Gualberto were prisoners en route to Ceuta; Anita Pando, on the way to Isle of Pines. And while others involved had succeeded in escaping to New York, the movement, frustrated in the Occidente region, spread all through all the eastern portion and hoped for leaders. Bowing to pressure and requests made by friends of Martí, Blanco sent the hint to him that he would not be brought to trial if he declared in the newspapers his adherence to Spain.

"Tell the General that Martí is not the kind of man that can be bought."

On September 25th, he sailed for Spain, on the *Alfonso XII*, under "surveillance."

Chapter Fifteen

RUBICON

AGAIN THE SEA, the sea, great counsellor, silent initiator of self-examination. And again the same gloomy prospect of Spain, the road of nine years ago.

The adolescent of that first taste of exile was now a man, enriched by tenderness, sorrow and thought. He had learned that injustice is not always a design, but an error, of men. Cuba, which then was nothing more than a wound in the soul and in the body of a youth—a mere experience—was now, above all, an idea seeking its destiny.

Was it seeking destiny, or was it awaiting it? What was history, after all—man's work, or his patience? There on the Island in untamed Oriente a few hundred Cubans were again dedicated to the realization of a desire which already seemed doomed by its own impetuous beginning. They represented non-conformity. Their impatience would bring new sorrow and hunger to Cuba. In the Capital, other sincere Cubans preferred to go on winning battles against time. Which attitude would prove to be the right one?

In the blackness of the dark night, Pepe heard footsteps come to a halt beside him and felt a hand rest on his arm. It was a shipboard companion, the Cuban Colonel Ramón Roa, one of the signers of the Zanjón Pact. He was on his way to Spain, so he said, to urge Martínez Campos to fulfill the "secret clauses" of the Treaty. . . . He could not sleep and had come on deck for some fresh air.

Naturally, they spoke of politics.

Martí had proved himself to be an incorrigible dreamer,

hadn't he, by taking part in this new uprising? It surprised him that a man of Martí's talent could have been so deceived. . . . Cuba was not mature enough for independence; he Roa, was saying so, and he had fought in the jungle to the end. There were Cubans who criticized the Pact. To criticize was easy! But it had been inevitable and Cuba now had no alternative but an intelligent peace: to attain the best possible terms from the Pact.

Martí allowed him to go on at length. He could see how the man's thoughts would make sleep impossible for him. One cannot live a great illusion in vain. Nor abandon it with impunity. But that man, who had been a hero in the war, was being lost to Cuba and must be saved. In his own inward self Martí felt some pangs of doubt; but he did not allow the doubt to overcome him, to take shape in a petty opportunism. Cuba was mature enough for independence because it was impossible for her to live soundly without it. Of what importance was it that political oppression had loosened sufficiently to grant make-believe "liberties" when a more subtle and more deeply rooted oppression existed: One which made the Cuban live as a tenant on his own land; which compelled a vegetative and mediocre existence; which limited with the hedges of tradition and old ideas the free expansion of the American spirit, eager for something new. And how could Spain give Cuba something which, through age-long habit, was alien to herself? Separation had become an urgent historical necessity. Even if Cubans were not all of them willing to achieve liberty, duty consisted in working to convince them to take that road, not to betray them with vain hopes.

Appealing to the pride of the former Insurrecto, Martí evoked such precise pictures of the war gone by as to astonish Roa that one who had not fought in it could paint such vivid pictures of it. Martí's argument was a miracle of persuasiveness and faith—a faith defending itself. But Roa kept shaking his head in denial and the passionate speech was carried away by the mighty Atlantic.

On two other occasions during unavoidable encounters of life aboard ship the man who had surrendered insisted on challenging the accusing faith of that "useless Christ," as he ironically called him. Martí met Roa on the ground on which he preferred to argue—political realism. Spain would not give one inch more than she had already conceded. More liberty for the Island would mean—and this Roa would clearly see in Madrid—breaking the ties that still held her; in so far as liberties were granted to Cuba, entrenched material interests in Spain itself would suffer. Cuba had to look to herself.

But the Colonel kept seizing upon unimportant literal phrases, on dotting the i's of certain alleged stipulations implied in the Zanjón Pact. Martí decided to avoid Roa. He preferred to spend the evenings chatting with the ship's purser who, from the first day of the voyage and through a mutual friend in Havana, had courteously offered his services to the exile.

The purser, Señor Viniegra, was a youthful Spaniard, effusive, sentimental, and with a vague leaning toward things intellectual. Unschooled in everything pertaining to politics, he approached the subject with a sort of timid admiration as if it involved some sort of dangerous magic. The mere fact that Martí was a political exile made him seem heroic to Viniegra from the first instant, even though Martí was an advocate of *independence*. As for Martí, a born conversationalist, he needed someone to talk to. Viniegra listened in rapture to the long speculations invited by the inactivity of an uneventful voyage. One night, regretting that such talent was lost to Spain, the purser ventured at last to suggest the political theme: Did not Martí think that the Cubans, in attempting to break away from Spain, were renouncing a glorious nation?

Martí asked him to explain his idea of "nation," and, upon hearing it, judged it to be "charming." Such was the nation Cubans wanted; but it was not the kind Spain had been to them. The dialogue touched lightly on the chain he had worn in prison. "That chain did not mean an injury for me alone; it injured all of America."

The purser gave up, rather sadly; and then they talked of other things. He also had his troubles and, like all sea-faring men, was gnawed by loneliness and eager for companionship. Martí listened to his confidences. When the crew began to swab decks, with the first streaks of dawn breaking over the water, he was still offering the troubled Viniegra the comforts of his own stoicism.

The purser of the *Alfonso XII* could not recall another passenger who had ever impressed him so profoundly. When the ship arrived at Santander the least Viniegra felt he could do was to express his gratitude to Martí in writing.

The modest purser momentarily embodied for the exile that other Spain, noble, generous, also unschooled in politics, which he now could see anew with the same emotion of his youthful memories. More than ever he found her now at odds with her political figures:

> ". . . weary of her servitude to an all-absorbing caste of brilliant and audacious men who forget in the interests of their personal glory the vital and urgent interests of the nation they represent. . . ."

Madrid—always fickle—was preparing to celebrate on a magnificent scale the wedding of young Alfonso XII with the Austrian Princess, María Cristina. Martí visited the Prado, the shrine of the pearly-toned Goyas, the study of the aged painter Madrazo. He spent long hours in the library of the Ateneo, alternating his reading between the classics of political thought—Montesquieu, Rousseau—and classics of Spanish realism and criticism—Quevedo, Saavedra Fajardo, Gracián, Jovellanos. . . .

In the lobby of the Ateneo he often encountered the journalist Julio Burell, who would carry with him a profound impression of that young man "with a Spanish soul" who, without lifting his voice but with his eyes shining had told him, after confessing his love for Spain: ". . . I am a Separatist because Spain is here, but not in Cuba. I, who among you am an equal, would be nothing but a stranger there to you: I would live as a ward, subjected, suspected, all doors closed to my rights if I ask for justice, to my ambition if I legitimately aspire to something. . . ."

And what, if not a lawful ambition, was that impatience for the future which obsessed him, that careful discernment and strict judgment with which he studied the most hidden movements of Spanish politics?

Affairs in Cuba still were causing concern. Cánovas had finally brought matters to a head so that Martínez Campos should come to power and learn that there was a difference between theory and practice. And the poor General, so inured to war, moved timidly between the requests of the deputies for the West Indies—Labra, Bernal, Portuondo—and the passive resistance of his own conservative majority. His rise to power had been interpreted in Cuba as the first step toward the just reforms promised in the Zanjón Pact; but soon it was evident that the Peacemaker, controlled by his own parliamentary majority, was only "holding the fort" for Cánovas against the eagerness of Sagasta's followers to gain control. When the Cortes convened, it was obvious that the Peacemaker was finished.

Martí wrote Viondi his impressions of this political trickery, deaf to the demands of the Island, and added:

> "What am I doing . . . while such a stubborn and useless battle is fought here over my country's affairs? . . . I spend much time in ridding myself of what is worthless and in strengthening my good points. I am studying English with tenacious intensity. And I am collecting all those facts which may be helpful to me in the task which for years I have been planning to do . . ."

He knew that the die was cast, and that the broad Atlantic was again his Rubicon. Although he had few trustworthy reports of the new revolt he had left behind in Cuba, he saw, from a broader perspective, how precarious it was. The Zanjón Pact in its less obvious interpretation had been a truce imposed by the necessity to create a unity of spirit throughout the Island. This requisite, indispensable for a definitive liberation, had not been attained. The new rebellion had been planned while the hopes of many Cubans still rested on reforms. At present, duty urged the support of these Cubans' hopes until their futility was proved; and if they were frustrated, the revolution of the future could only be the result of a long process of maturing and preparation. It was already evident to Martí that this preparation could not be carried out in Cuba. The political base of operations would have to be in the United States, in whose centers of Cuban emigrés the desire for a free homeland was kept alive. Martí, therefore, was studying English with "tenacious intensity."

Certain legal matters that Viondi had entrusted to Martí were to give him an opportunity to meet Cristino Martos, the "able and eloquent coördinator of liberal forces." In the reception room of his house—Martí was to recall, years later—"there were waiting a priest, a journalist whose support could be had for a price, very smooth and urbane; and an unkempt, moody man, his coat-tails falling over the sides of his chair, clenched hands resting on the knob of his walking stick, watch-chain dangling, leather shoes dusty: General Salamanca."[1] Martos, still in bed, received the Cuban lawyer. He was "fat and effeminate, his hair was dishevelled, his eyes outlined by spectacles with black metal rims, and even at that hour his words were meticulously chosen." They discussed a lawsuit contesting the validity of a will in which Martos was lawyer for the plaintiff.

And then they spoke of Cuban politics. Martos wanted to learn from the lips of his guest, so recently arrived from Cuba, the state of affairs on the Island, and Martí made the most of that opportunity. He presented the case of Cuba as he saw it. He outlined the basic and the accidental factors, the natural and the historical, the old and the new: Cubans had grown a distinct personality and their lives, their interests, the rhythm of their development, were contrary to those of Spain. The Zanjón Pact had been a hoax: Cuba was still suffering from oppression and frustration. Revolution was in every heart and, to frustrate it, Spain was not thinking of carrying out reforms but of inciting racial division, making the rebellion appear as a Negro conspiracy. Meanwhile, the prisons of Ceuta, Chafarinas and Mahón were filled with Cuban prisoners, secretly exiled. Even though Spain might want to remedy all this, it would be futile, because Spanish liberalism would always come up against the recalcitrance of the Spaniard in Cuba. Independence was inevitable because it was impossible to reconcile such widely differing sets of interests.

Martos listened religiously, astonished by Martí's fluency and mastery of facts. Finally he exclaimed with a sigh: "Yes, you are right. Nothing can prevent the situation from growing more inflamed every year. It's either you or us."

The following day Martínez Campos proposed that the Cortes adjourn until after the King's marriage. This served

[1] A Spanish general, noted for his political lobbying against political and economic concessions to the colonies.

Martos as a pretext to criticize bitterly the recent attitude of the Government toward Cuba. Martí heard him taunt, from the rostrum, an exasperated House with all the facts he had given him the day before at his bedside. Martos ended by asking "mercy for the unfortunate Island" and as a gesture worthy of the royal wedding, the emancipation of the slaves. Martínez Campos timidly supported the suggestion. Sagasta rose and delivered a speech full of compliments for the Austrian princess. And then the Cortes voted to adjourn.

Days later, Martos wrote to Viondi: "Martí has made such an impression on me that I can tell you he is the most talented man I have ever known."

With the approach of winter, Martí felt more keenly also the chill of absence, nostalgia for the home he had left behind. Still recovering from the first blasts of the mountain cold, he wrote: "It is enough to make one flee from himself, not having a land of one's own to live in, nor one's own child's head to kiss." He was only present in body, an ironic spectator, at the great spectacle of the royal wedding—"a useless, pompous and Byzantine show and, like anything about to perish for lack of real substance, seizing on the shadow for a symbol." The soul of the exile was far away. For he had already made up his mind: As soon as he could get the wherewithal he would go to the United States to spread the idea of a free Cuba. But—always the terrible question—how can the primary duty of a man be sacrificed to this ambition: the duty of a man to his own family?

This conflict between vocation for public duty and his private devotion became more personal and dramatic as it was prodded by events. Engraved on his memory were the words—entreating at first and then more and more reproachful—with which his wife had reacted to his initial activities in the revolutionary underground. Daughter of a well-to-do family, accustomed to a certain idle, provincial snobbery, Carmen's character was by temperament and education diametrically opposed to Martí's. She had dreamed for her husband rank and honors, and if he would but sacrifice his idealism in the same measure that she had yielded to him in her practical tendencies, theirs would be a wonderfully well-balanced union. But Pepe insisted on dreaming. . . . After Zanjón, what illusionary Quixotism could justify his neglect of his profession, in which he could reap so rich a harvest? . . . Her husband placated her with tendernesses; but he could not forget the expression on her face—a mixture of anguish and exasperation—the day they took him prisoner.

Now, with him in exile, their differences were complicated by uncertainties and economic difficulties, which in Carmen's letters were set forth with cold deliberation. Carmen had had to go to Camagüey to live with her father, who had not looked favorably on the marriage. . . . Martí suffered bitterly from this humiliation and he wrote about it to Viondi in a tone of tortured soliloquy. He decided to solve his problem "taking everything into consideration."

> "It would be cowardly to assume a great responsibility and in the moment of trial to cast it on the shoulders of another. And, likewise, it is easy to be successful, if one does not mind being unjust. Let those who are mine come to me. I hold my arms out, open—and they are not slack, or tired."

The opportunity to mock theoretical Spanish vigilance and go to the United States came to him before he thought it would. But first, by a Cabinet crisis at the year's end, he was able to see the bursting of the reformist bubble. Cánovas' ministers in the Martínez Campos cabinet had not been able to agree "either on the twelve-year-old issue of abolition or on the question of coastwise navigation"—even though they were matters of secondary importance. And the weary General turned the Government back to "the Monster." The December crisis frustrated the hopes for reform the crisis in March had raised.

His forecasts on this point confirmed, Martí left for North America by way of France. In Paris, at an entertainment given for the benefit of the victims of the recent flood in Murcia, he met Sarah Bernhardt, dressed as Doña Sol—a Doña Sol "somewhat Asiatic with her eyes at a slant, her slender nose, proud forehead, delicate lips." The visitor recorded in French his impressions of the occasion and of the Jewish actress who was worth "observing as a study of the strength of the human will."

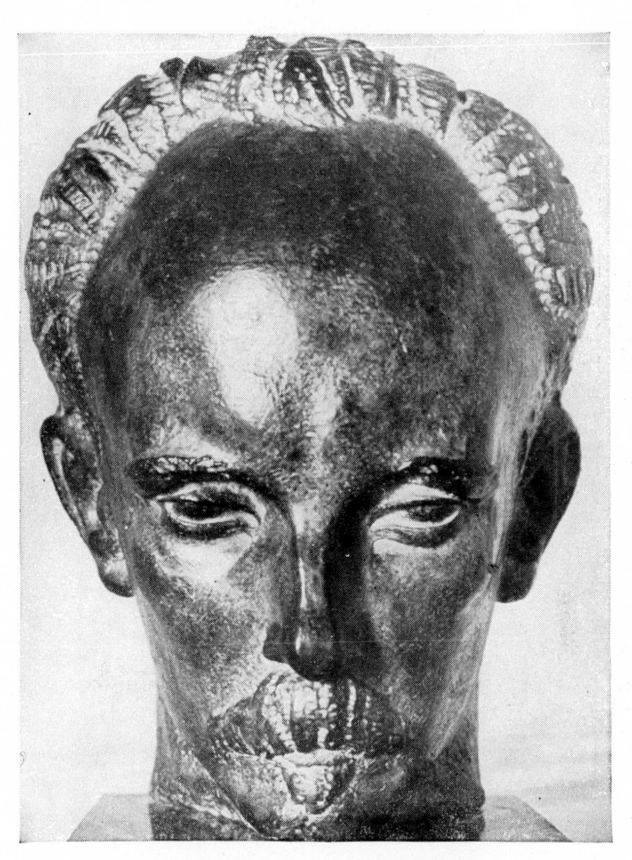

MARTÍ'S PORTRAIT IN BRONZE BY JOSÉ SICRE

—from Márques Sterling:
Martí, Maestro y Apóstol, Havana

DON MARIANO MARTÍ

—from *Papeles de Martí*, Havana

DOÑA LEONOR MARTÍ

—from *Iconografía del Apóstol Martí*, Havana

ONE OF THE EARLIEST PHOTOGRAPHS OF MARTÍ

—from *Iconografía del Apóstol Martí*

MARTÍ IN 1885, FROM A PHOTOGRAPH MADE
BY W. F. BOWERS, BROOKLYN

MARTÍ AND HIS SON, FROM A PHOTOGRAPH
MADE IN NEW YORK ABOUT 1885

—from the archives of Gonzalo de Quesada y Miranda

MARTÍ AND MARÍA MANTILLA, FROM A TINTYPE TAKEN AT BATH BEACH, L. I., IN 1890

—from *Iconografía del Apóstol Martí*

MARTÍ AND FERMÍN VALDÉS DOMÍNGUEZ AT KEY WEST, 1894.
PHOTOGRAPH BY A. J. ESTÉVEZ

Chapter Sixteen

NEW YORK

A NEW YEAR; a new world.

Through the swarming bustle of the down-town section of the city the new-comer walked about, consuming the sights, distances and unexpected misery in his wanderings. He walked miles those first few days, often at random, to escape from himself. He already knew the length and breadth of Manhattan from its most populated area, with its red brick façades, to the semi-rustic region of goats and orchards beyond 59th Street. The brand-new elevated—a dark monster roaring down Ninth Avenue, frightening horses and showering sparks of coal dust—brought him to the financial district where nothing remained that was old except an occasional run-down house reminiscent of Dutch architecture, and those that had seen the Revolution and the early days of the Republic. Everything seemed oppressively concentrated; high, drab gray stone buildings, carriages, horse-cars, mustached men showing off on bicycles, hustling traders, ladies of fashion in bonnet and bustle, tucking up the trains of their gowns in front of every show-window along Ladies' Mile, where the Christmas wreaths were beginning to be dry and brittle.

The winter was mild and cheated the holiday season out of its usual snow. The sky was a yellowish gray, veiling a sun which tried to break through. The immigrant from the tropics walked rapidly, restraining himself from admiration. From his first day in it, this harsh new world, boastful of its youthful energy, depressed him. It forced him to remember with poignant longing the quiet and golden cities that spoke Spanish.

But was it not perhaps because he carried his sorrow within him? He went about "sound of flesh and bone but with my heart greatly—and deeply—wounded by the whitest hand I have ever warmed with mine." One month before, in Camagüey, that hand had written paragraphs which still hurt the traveller's memory.

He felt lost and strange with his misery in this new extrovert world. But when he returned at night to Manuel Mantilla's house, where he had found temporary lodging, he was comforted by the warmth of the pleasant atmosphere and friendly words.

Mantilla was a Cuban. He was married to a Venezuelan, Carmen Miyares, one of whose parents was from Santiago. A girl and a boy made life brighter for the poor parents, who made ends meet by taking in a few Cuban boarders. The father, almost an invalid and often despondent over his health, depended on the physical and spiritual strength of his wife, a robust, talkative woman of captivating charm. Carmita's warm, bright radiance also enlivened the heartsick guest. After a bleak afternoon he could write his friend Viondi: "Perhaps it may be all January clouds that will vanish in February."

Afterwards when he was more acclimated and rested, the stimulus of his new surroundings began to make itself felt. New York had not yet lost its pioneer appearance of rough vigor, confidence in its own strength, accented by the puritanical drive of the North and, above all, by the smug optimism arising from the Union's triumph over the South, the victory of industrial romanticism over the romanticism of a plantation economy based on Negro slavery. The new serfdom to capital was joyfully accepted because everyone believed he could rise to become master. These impressions stirred the messianic sense that the times had been developing in Martí and invigorated his stoic convictions: "Troubles have this much good in them; they strengthen you."

But the breach in love's wall must be built up again. His sudden removal to the United States had placed him in a strange position, without a job or other means of support. Although he had not expected to ask his wife to join him until "after having put down a root in the new country," the harshness of her letters moved him to send for her immediately, and forced him with unexpected urgency to find a means of providing for her. He went from one end of the city to the other, calling at business firms, editorial offices and shops; walking up and down stairs and waiting in anterooms for possible interviews. Penniless, he "fired his last shot on tokens of affection," sending Viondi a hat and a little overcoat for his small son, to protect him against the cold of the voyage.

As for himself, his new friendships protected him to a degree from the tardy snows and the aloof reception he had in offices. And in the enthusiastic comradeship of the Revolutionary Committee in New York, into whose activities he had immediately thrown himself, he found the consolations of hope and activity so necessary to his nature.

Under the presidency of José Francisco Lamadriz, the Committee was desperately trying to further the revolutionary plans of General Calixto García. There was scarcely more news about the state of the revolution in Cuba than what the General had himself brought in October from his quick trip to Jamaica: Almost all of Oriente was in arms. In the central part of the Island, Serafín Sánchez, Emilio Núñez and Francisco Carrillo had risen in revolt, giving the lie to Spanish propaganda that the movement was a "revolt of upstart Negroes."

But the new revolutionists were waiting for their great leaders: General García himself, who had started the movement; and Maceo. . . . Had not both of them agreed in Kingston that the fearless Negro, Maceo, would lead the first expedition and be the vanguard of the first campaign? Why, then, had it been decided at the last moment that General Benítez, who did not have Maceo's following or prestige, should be sent in his place?

At meetings of the Committee the brigadier Pío Rosado defended that decision vehemently, and Roloff [1] supported him in his rough, Russian-bear manner. There were those, however, who remembered, on the quiet, that both these veterans had fallen out with Maceo over certain disastrous episodes in the last war. Meanwhile, rumors were current from Cuba and Jamaica that the omission of Maceo from the plans had disillusioned many on the Island, and that the great Negro leader was biting his lips.

Martí listened, and silently deplored all this. As vice-delegate in Havana and as representative of the Clubs in that province, he had attended the meetings of the Committee ever since his arrival. And he thought—and kept his silence—that this war was being waged rather carelessly, without the needful harmony, organization or maturity. The two headquarters of the movement—Kingston and New York—were too far apart from each other and unconnected; resources were low because the emigrés—impoverished and already tired of contributing in vain to the "Cause"—were asked to contribute too much at one time without having been aroused to do so by adequate explanation and propaganda. Finally, he noted among the organizers themselves a kind of suspecting incoherence, an almost fictitious enthusiasm and professional alarm. Perhaps Máximo Gómez had seen clearly in refusing to support the venture, coming to the conclusion that it could not rely on any support other than that which had already been liquidated at Zanjón. . . .

[1] A Russian Jew who had emigrated to Cuba and distinguished himself bravely in both revolutionary wars.

But hope, even if illusion, was too attractive, and honor too strongly pledged, for Martí to think of withdrawal. The passion for liberty was so strong in Cuba, for those who knew how to measure it, that perhaps it would succeed in overcoming all obstacles. Never before had such an impressive movement been started: There was nothing else to do but to get to work at the task of fanning the fire. And "the General"—García—was confident.

Martí now confirmed by personal knowledge his impression of the indomitable leader who, after a hundred valiant days of holding off the enemy in '74, had shot himself under the chin so as not to fall into the hands of the Spaniards alive. The bullet miraculously was deflected and his life was saved. Zanjón gave him back his freedom and Cubans now saw in Calixto García the leader most appropriate to raise the banner anew, since "he had not signed." They admired his distinguished bearing, his natural air of command, the severity of his face with the scar of the Insurrecto bullet like a lone star on his forehead.

When Martí joined the Committee, García did not consider the new arrival of much importance. Like all veteran leaders, he harbored a certain contempt for civilian helpers, and even more if they were of the oratorical type. But Martí gradually won the General's respect by his reserve, by the realistic aptness of his observations and suggestions, and also by his friendly courtesy to the García family as a frequent guest of the General. Eventually García came to agree with him that public gatherings would be useful in stimulating the spirits of the colony of exiles and win their financial support; he was now convinced that speaking was also a kind of action, and on January 24th, before a heterogeneous Cuban audience that filled Steck Hall, Martí made his first speech in the United States.

The opening phrase, "Duty must be performed simply and naturally," was lost in the noisy murmur of the hall:

People were asking each other who the new speaker was, he was so pale and thin; his forehead seemed swollen in the reflections of the flickering gaslights. Shortly, those in the front rows sat back in their seats and the standees began to pay eager attention. It was the unexpected: a poignant evocation of the war just past, "that wonderful and sudden emergence of a people, apparently servile only a short time before, who made heroic feats a daily event, hunger a banquet, and the extraordinary, commonplace." He drew the contrast between the tame, theorizing, and powerful Cubans "with their Spanish and financial way of thinking," and the people listening to him, emigrants who had preferred lowly work, full of quiet courage, "to the pleasure of raising their homes on corpses still warm. . . ."

Flattered by these remarks, the audience broke into an ovation for the orator who did them such justice. The speech then mounted to heights of vision which the rapt attention given him could hardly reach. In revolutionary meetings they had never heard language so unusual and pregnant as this, passing abruptly from logical reasoning to sculptured detail and lightning metaphor. The beautifully crystalline voice cleared the air, like an electric storm on a humid afternoon, entranced his listeners and left them breathless.

He had been speaking for an hour, and the ecstatic audience did not move or make a sound except at intervals to burst into applause which drowned out the short *bravos* of approval. The faces of the General and the Committee members who presided over the gathering did not hide their astonishment. Nor their uneasiness when Martí, after evaluating all that had happened in Cuba after the truce, dared to touch the Negro question. It was a dangerous issue.

Some of the faces there, at the rear of the hall, were dark faces, faces of Negroes and mulattos, artisans or meek tobacco workers who had experienced in New York the brutish repulsion of the blond Yankee and as well the more subtly expressed disdain of their white compatriots. Even at a patriotic meeting such as this, they were standing at the rear. . . . Their emotion could be seen when the orator declared his faith in "the Negroes and mulattos—for there is no reason to avoid such designations, as plain and natural as any other nouns—" and recalled the example of the Indians who had helped forge the liberty of Latin America. The applause from the back rows checked itself in eagerness to hear the rest of the unusual parallel. Martí continued gravely, raising his voice as if to make himself heard outside the building:

> "And let it be said in passing, from this land conquered by pacific people who rose from their knees in prayer to put their hands to the plow; let it be said from this land of puritan lineage, in order to exonerate the blame that has unjustly been heaped on the people of Latin America, that the monsters who trouble the waters, and not the miserable, thirsty ones who drink them, are to be held accountable for the dangerous backwash of those waters; that the sins of the slave fall wholly and exclusively on the master. That to break earth with the point of a spear is not the same as to break it with the point of a plow."

The argument was too involved and too profound, but its meaning struck home. Momentarily threatened by division because of the racial theme, the interest of the audience united again on the American allusion, on the common resentment. In the United States, the white Cubans, humiliated by the unconcealed arrogance of the Saxon North, all felt "slightly colored." . . . And Martí's American theory gave them for the first time an explanation of the historical inferiority which they had been made to feel so much in their daily lives.

The Cuban and revolutionary purpose in that homage to the masses also became evident. The new revolution had to be a democratic task, a task for all, compounded from "prudence and anger, reason and hunger, honor and thought." It was also the first time the humble had heard themselves specially summoned.

Happy-go-lucky Cubans of the aristocratic and sophisticated type had gone to Steck Hall that night through nostalgic caprice or because they just felt it was the thing to do. Now, some felt caught up by enthusiasm; others were uneasy, anxious to escape that net of persuasion which threatened to carry them away from so many of their prejudices and privileges. And when Martí, gathering up his strength, now almost exhausted by the two-hour oration, announced the decision of faithful Cubans in the new hour of war, hands were nervously locked on knees, or on the backs of the seats ahead. The final oath was almost drowned in the excitement. The audience up front, who succeeded in hearing it, passed it back from mouth to mouth through the multitude as it dispersed in feverish hubbub.

> "Before withdrawing from the pledge to make the homeland free and prosperous, the Arctic and Antarctic seas will become one sea, and a serpent will be born from the egg of an eagle!"

That speech established Martí as one of the New York counsellors of the independence movement, along with Salvador Cisneros Betancourt, Lamadriz, Arnao and other civilian veterans.

The men of the sword began to understand why in the beginning was the Word. It seemed that the movement in the colony had only lacked the unity of spirit and clarity of conviction that Martí succeeded in imbuing them with that night. Unpleasant aftertastes of old dissensions in the

SPANISH VOLUNTEER OFFICER

Committee had maintained a certain division. The humble masses, the colored people who had heard words spoken about "the Maceo danger" had grown rather indifferent to the Cause. But that night a Mexican painter, a small prophetic Indian, approached Martí after the speech and presented him with a card with a sketch of a thundering locomotive followed by a foot traveller waving his little flag in vain, shouting "Danger!"

After that fiery welding, everything seemed firm. Independence showed a stronger pulse in the colony. Donations from the people increased. Martí went with Roloff to see the wealthy emigré, Miguel Cantos. He argued, entreated. Don Miguel rose and throwing his arm around Martí's shoulder, told him: "All right, my son; you will get it all. You will get the ship. You will get arms!"

With that generous gift, and the money Francisco Carrillo sent him from las Villas and from his own pocket, General García was able to sail from Jersey City with twenty-six more expeditionaries on the 17th of April, aboard the schooner *Hattie Haskell.* By decision of the Committee, Martí remained in the United States in charge of providing the necessities of war. Apparently he could better serve Cuba with his speech than with his frail body, impaired by cold, poverty and "the mists of the soul."

Chapter Seventeen

THE "LITTLE WAR"

The true day for my soul dawns in the midst of night. — *Martí:* The Hour, *Oct. 23, 1880*

HIS TEMPERAMENT, governed by the need to serve and to love, had now recovered its balance in political activity. Inaction or a humdrum existence made him melancholy; useful effort made him radiate optimism on all around him. He found now a penetrating meaning to the aggressive Yankee energy, so far removed from the "lazy life and the poetic uselessness of our European countries," and he felt happy at living in a country "where everyone seems his own master."

Whatever impressed him was put down in a notebook in quick sketches which served him also as exercises in English. He had already mastered the "rebellious and beautiful" language to such an extent that Guillermo Collazo, the Cuban artist who also lived at the Mantillas', did not meet with great difficulty in having Martí's comments accepted by the new weekly, *The Hour*, a magazine dedicated "to social interests" and toward making New York resemble Victorian London as much as possible. The editor had stated in the first issue that contributors would not be asked "to write today on electric lighting and tomorrow on Wagner's music" but that each would limit himself to his special field. Since Martí had been in France he was entrusted as a matter of course with art criticism.

He met the challenge with great sensitivity and conscientious thought, his comments imputing "over-delicacy to Fortuny, poverty of invention to Meissonnier, carelessness and lightness to Detaille, and rosy glibness to Bouguereau." Although he confessed to writing "in Spanish with English words," all the warmth of his style went into those articles, melting away the stiffness and sometimes the grammar of the alien tongue. Amidst the circumspect prose of the rest of the magazine the original opinions and romantic outbursts of Martí retained, no matter how much they were edited, the flavor of insurrection. If Whitman read them, his pagan beard must have shaken with delight.

With this and other sporadic jobs of correspondence and translation, he began to get himself out of debt. He was even able to indulge himself in a few of the luxuries and amenities of the well-to-do: "Today I had a dollar and spent it on Japanese tea-cups. My wife is coming." In his notebook there are references to other frailties of his temporary bachelorhood.

Although President Hayes prohibited alcoholic beverages from appearing on his table in Washington and proudly called attention to the stuffed owl that adorned his wife's "cosy corner," cosmopolitanism none the less was fast overcoming all the remnants of puritanism. It had been a year since Edison had invented the electric light, considerably enlivening New York night life. Ladies cultivated elegance in their salons to compensate for the "vulgarity" of their husbands engaged in becoming Naopleons of Industry. The flirt, as a public spectacle, appeared for the first time in the roller-skating rinks, and a Bouguereau was installed in the Hoffman House bar, one of the most popular in New York, a triumph of the nude over all the sermons.

Martí was not insensible of this new-born piquancy in New York society. Since he again felt alive in his devotion to a great cause, all his natural exuberance had been reborn. The ladies who collected paintings and porcelain with a certain domestic fetishism found him—as a foreigner and intellectual—"interesting." And he enjoyed being liked. He went to literary parties, met serious women and their jolly daughters; one of them translated some of his poetry, put flowers in the button-hole of his frock coat and "at a merry and informal affair even crowned me with a bonbon box shaped like a chicken's head."

All in all, what pleased him least in the United States and made him feel like "an inconsolable widower" was the behavior of the women.

"This is the only country," he confided, "of all those I have visited where I have been able to spend a week without feeling a special devotion or deep affection for some woman. . . ." Brought up in the romantic Latin and Creole tradition in which woman should be, according to don Pepe de la Luz, "sun of the home and moon of the world," Martí discovered that women in the United States revolved in their own orbits. As for some, "their self-control, their assurance that they will be respected, their calculated coolness, their scorn for passion, their dry, practical ideas of life, give them a singular boldness and a peculiar frankness in their relations with men."

Others, however, made of their modesty and virtue almost a profession. One morning, the train bringing Martí back from a brief vacation at Cape May was derailed near Philadelphia. One of the jolts threw a woman, well along in years, to the floor. Martí went to help her to her feet, but she protested, shrieking: "Not by the hands! Not by the hands!" Which left him rather puzzled as to what other handles he could use that she would consider more decorous. When recording this incident in his notebook, Martí wondered, gravely: "Could she be an old Puritan?"

With these extremes of boldness and prudery in Yankee femininity, the Cuban preferred to spend long intervals at the boarding house, talking with Carmita Mantilla, a hardy woman who had, nevertheless, the gentleness of the warm countries.

Just as Spring began, his wife arrived. Pepito was a delightful little devil two years old. Each morning, from an adjoining room, one of the other Cuban boarders, young Doctor Eusebio Hernández, heard Martí playing in bed with his son, laughing happily and calling him by the most unusual names: "my little king," "my little steward."

The company of his own family now made "more bearable the bitterness of a truly hard existence" which forced him to employ all his energy "in a world and against a world completely new." With bitter distaste he confided to Viondi: "It is not this which wears me out. The injury comes from the loneliness I felt. I do not feel lonely now, but roots, even after they have been pulled out, leave their impression for a long time in the ground."

But the real root had not yet been torn out, nor would it ever be. Carmen had found her husband attached anew to that hateful abstraction "politics." When Lamadriz went to Key West to stimulate war contributions from Cuban emigrés, who were legion there, Martí had fallen heir to the duties of the presidency of the revolutionary committee. After a grinding day's work, his nights—and his health—were spent on meetings and writing. Carmen, exasperated, sighed. He invoked solemn obligations: self-respect, destiny, country. She invoked others: tranquillity, the future, his son.

Martí listened to her lamentations and sadly understood them. But he could not help living according to his own nature. He wrote Viondi his intention of writing a book some day in which he would examine "that false existence which human conventions superimpose on our real nature, warping it and making it ugly. . . ."

His wife, like many others, believed him to be a visionary. "You, Viondi, know that however imaginative and idealistic

I may be, I have suffered and been chastened enough so that there is no room in my heart for illusions that I do not believe just. The impossible is possible. We madmen are wise." And with sudden, serene intuition he added brusquely: "Although I, my friend, will never be able to shade my house with the branches of the tree I am planting."

In all the colonies of Cuban emigrés Martí sowed the seed, urging them to organize to help the war, magnifying his own faith in it. "We expect such good news from the battlefields . . . that because of a foolish fear that it just might not come to pass, I do not dare tell you about it."

The wonderful news finally came: On May 7th, General Calixto García had landed in Cuba. The New York Committee issued an extensive bulletin informing the emigrés of the event. Martí made it vibrate with the accents of joy he knew to be premature. The presence of the General in Cuba signified "with the triumph it authorizes, the spirit of popular will which bridles the victor."

Strange language. But to Martí it was very important to emphasize the democratic character of the new war: He did not forget that, in the Ten Years War, the excessive authoritarianism of some of the leaders was as disastrous as civilian meddling. The Republic must spring from a military, but democratic, cradle.

Dazzled by this vision and by the ringing phrases with which Martí called them to form "an army of men who work to help an army of men who fight," the emigrés of New York gathered excitedly around their civilian leader. Martí really did not have much news to tell them. He knew only that the General had landed at the Aserradero, near Santiago, with six of his expeditionaries. The high-spirited reports which supposedly were issued right after the landing he could recognize through copies which he had saved when he wrote them a month earlier. But it was said that the

Island was touch and go and, at the time, encouragement was needed; optimism was to him a necessary strategy.

The summer passed, quietly, slowly. Rumors brought from the Island by newer refugees were vague, contradictory, at times very discouraging. Maceo, blockaded in Haiti by the government of that republic, wrote in desperation for funds which could not be sent him since the treasury of the New York Committee was depleted. Martí was on fire with his own impatience, but realizing that those about him needed his stimulus, he kept any doubts or pessimism to himself. The careless and lazy, who always expect the most, had given up when they realized that García's cablegram had not, at the very least, announced the capture of Santiago. Martí disposed of suspicions, explained what was going on, restrained hot-heads.

Little by little, uneasiness began to undermine his own optimism. With his political activity reduced to a secondary plane, he could no longer draw on enthusiasm to protect him against the austerities of existence.

The emptiness of life in New York began to suffocate him. His three long articles published in *The Hour* under the equivocally journalistic title, "Impressions of a Fresh Spaniard" were sophisticatedly frank. He had gathered together and expressed in them many of the observations put down in his notebook. The finished series was a picturesque confession, full of serious apprehensions: The United States was really the hope of the world, but did it possess all the spiritual factors necessary to serve as a solid home for truth, liberty and human dignity? Was not her prodigious energy excessively devoted to the crassest material ends? "When days of poverty come, what wealth, unless it be of the spirit, will be able to help this country in its colossal misfortune?"

The situation in Cuba meanwhile had been growing much worse than Martí imagined even in his moments of most anguished doubt. The prolonged delay of Antonio Maceo, and that of Calixto García himself, who showed no signs of life, kept the rebellion incoherent and leaderless. The Brigadier Benítez, frustrated in his attempt to bring Camagüey to revolt, had been captured by the enemy shortly after his arrival. In the central towns, Emilio Núñez, Serafín Sánchez and Francisco Carrillo defended their areas as best they could. And in Oriente, where the movement had initially made the greatest progress, Maceo's brothers and the gallant Negro, Guillermón, could scarcely repress the discouragement of their troops.

And what of García? Relentlessly pursued by the Spaniards from the very day he landed, prevented from making contact with scattered groups of Insurrectos—who did not even know he had landed—his expeditionaries already decimated by pursuit, hunger and weariness, and he himself sick with fever, he wandered through the hills with only six ragged, barefooted companions. At last, on the first of August, there was nothing left to do but give himself up to one of the flying columns of General Blanco, who notified his government on the 15th: "I have treated him kindly, and am sending him to Spain on the mail packet leaving on the 15th. He seems to me a thorough gentleman and at the same time a very congenial person . . ."

The spark of revolution was smothered. Only the central towns remained to be pacified, and before leaving for Spain, García himself wrote to Carrillo and Núñez urging them to lay down their arms: He believed all had been lost. Carrillo followed his advice. Núñez, in opposition to the proposed peace terms, which he considered "worse than those of Zanjón," resisted fearlessly. However, at last bottled up by the concentration of Spanish troops, he agreed to negotiate on condition that General Blanco would allow him to request the necessary authority to do so from the Revolutionary Committee in New York.

In twenty days the accredited captain returned from the

North with papers signed by Martí, Lamadriz and Pouble. With the official authorization came a letter from Martí in which bitterness at failure was mixed with a clear view of the reasons for it, and a stern integrity of purpose.

> "Men like you and me must desire for our land a radical and solemn redemption imposed, if necessary and possible, today, tomorrow and always, by force, but conceived in magnificent design adequate to rebuild the country we are preparing to destroy . . . Our very honor, our very cause, demand that we abandon the field of armed conflict. We do not deserve to be, nor must we be reputed to be, professional revolutionaries, blind and turbulent spirits . . . capable of sacrificing noble lives to keep alive a cause—*the only honorable one in Cuba*—whose triumph is not now probable."

It was all over. While the Captain-General in the Island declared "the nefarious separatist flag again subdued," the New York Committee was disbanded, publication of *La Independencia* ceased, and the detractors of lost causes were busily engaged in miserable bickerings over reputations.

Over on the other side of the East River, in their simple little home, Martí wrestled in silence with the problems of family life and cares. . . . Above all, he struggled to reach his own conclusions on the devastating failure of the rebellion. It had not solely been for want of leaders, nor had it been only because of the disorganization and incoherence which had seemed obvious to him from the beginning. It was due also to something which he had failed to see at the time: Because the country had not sufficiently *wanted* it. Why fool oneself? What there was in Cuba of enlightened consciousness, of decisive concern, had aligned itself this time—contrary to what had happened in '68—on the side of an expectant and illusory status quo. Those who had the real power of decision were blind. And those who saw—again contrary to '68—did not know how to execute. Cuba was a people exhausted . . . One had to wait.

He could think now about himself and his family again. All through these hectic months only by the greatest effort had he been able "to keep afloat a noble and beautiful bark so battered by its voyage that it is shipping water." His efforts to make a living had been poorly rewarded except for an occasional article which *The Sun* published through the kindness of its editor, Dana, an old friend of Cuban revolutionaries. His home might become a consolation; his little son was now at the delightful age in which children's graces can close the distance between parents aloof from each other. Alone, on the ferry, or in his office, Martí put into verse the exploits of his "little king," the sentry protecting him from despair.

But the enchantments of the new intimacy did not succeed in closing other distances, loosing other constraints. Aloofness pervaded the atmosphere of poverty. Martí's sister Amelia was about to be married and he wrote her tender warnings against the danger of "confusing sexual attraction with the genuine and changeless love which creates a marriage which will not be broken." He added, "Profit from my example how to succeed in this—I cannot be happy, but I know the way for others to be happy." Throughout the letter there was the silence of nostalgia, of intimate frustration.

Carmen guessed, but did not understand, the inner conflict tormenting her husband. It irritated her to see him sunk in endless silences. He did not complain. He experienced even a certain satisfaction in submitting to that hard life as bookkeeper and unknown writer; but he missed his immediate service to an ideal. From the ferryboat that took him home at nightfall to Brooklyn his melancholy gaze wandered over the hazy panorama of the river frozen in stretches and guarded by gray shadows in the distance. And he thought his own life was a great deal like that, a wealth of aspirations turning to ice in the stream of duty, and likewise dominated by fogs and grays.

Leandro Viniegra, purser of the *Alfonso XII*, visited the couple once while his ship was in port in New York. How many memories that good Spaniard whom he had met in a solemn hour of hope recalled: . . . Now the hope was merely a memory; but there was still the predictable future, the great hour for him who knew how to prepare it! . . . After dinner he let himself be carried away by the redeeming vision. For a long time he had not spoken of this. Carmen frowned, kissed the child she held in her arms and asked coldly: "Pepe, and our son?"

On his way back to New York, Viniegra pondered on the obvious lack of harmony in that home where a man and a woman dissembled with tenderness the eternal drama of Woman against Man, the spirit which maintains against the spirit which creates. If only one of the two would give in!

But in one as in the other, Nature willed. Carmen thought of nothing but her home. And Martí was dreaming always of a greater home.

In the winter the predicition that Núñez had made in his letter was fulfilled:

> " . . . I, who will not commit an act of contrition before the Spanish Government, and will calmly watch my wife and child leave my side, departing from Cuba, will strike out for new lands, or remain here. . . ."

Martí decided to strike out for new lands.

Chapter Eighteen

THE LAND OF BOLÍVAR

The story is told that a traveller arrived one day in Caracas at nightfall and, without shaking off the dust of his journey, or inquiring about food or lodging, asked only where he might find Bolívar's statue. And the story goes that the traveller, alone with the tall, fragrant trees of the Plaza, wept before the statue, which seemed to move, like a father at the approach of his son.—Martí.

EVER SINCE he had disembarked at La Guayra, he had been intoxicated with the sense of history. Those very mountains of the Andean range which separated the valley of Caracas from the coast had witnessed the cavalry charges of 1811. That warm lap of the Ávila, where nestled the little, white houses of Venezuela's capital, had felt the first pangs of Hispano-American freedom. He was on holy ground.

And how soon he came to feel it as familiar as his own! Despite its bridges and rivulets and its guardian troop of mountain peaks, how much it reminded him of the other cities of America: Mexico, Puebla, Guatemala, Antigua, even Havana itself. There was the withdrawn and mild atmosphere which Spanish-American cities derive from their colonial tradition and from drawing their sustenance from the countryside beyond the walls: something lordly and parasitical as if they were nourished by the past and by the country round about. He could see this peculiarity clearly now, coming from hectic and crude New York, which did not live on memories but on ambitions and had such an air of self-sufficiency, of indifference to the region lying beyond its river-moats.

The traveller wandered haphazardly about the narrow, moonlit streets. He climbed the slope of the Calvario and entered the silent garden where municipal pruning and trimming struggled in vain against the wild will of the soil. From the Catuche he reached the fragrant gorges through which the Anauco River winds through the city. He gazed at the Cathedral, the Archbishop's palace, the sumptuous Masonic Temple. . . . In a large, central plaza he found a tremendous equestrian statue of the "Illustrious American Regenerator and Pacifier of Venezuela." And in another, much smaller plaza there was another statue, also of Guzmán Blanco—this one pedestrian.

Martí smiled a little wryly and thought of his friend Bolet. In New York this exiled Venezuelan had tried to dissuade him from going to Venezuela and had recounted many times the tragi-comic history of these monuments, not without a shade of repentance, for Bolet himself had been associated with their erection. In 1875, when Guzmán Blanco was the object of hero-worship, it had seemed to Bolet, too, that the leader of the "Blue Revolution" was the providential man, and he even won official honors with a poem to Guzmán Blanco's glory. At the end of the '70's he became convinced how mistaken that deification was and he helped tear down the Caesar's statues that historic day of "the inconoclasts." . . . Sad example, Martí thought, of the fickleness and impatience which all too often lead even the best men in "our America" to believe that a strong man is all that is needed to work out the destiny of a nation. An illusion such as this is dearly paid for. Now the statues were again on their pedestals and Guzmán Blanco, more than ever, master of Venezuela.

From Bolet and other Venezuelans in New York, Martí had brought letters of introduction to persons of note in the country. Carmita Mantilla was a descendent, on her father's side, of one of the Paolis who had fought against Genoa and France for the independence of their native Corsica. The lineage divided itself between Venezuela and Cuba, where the surname, altered to Peoli, had been prominently involved in the so-called conspiracy of the Suns of Bolívar in 1823. Martí often told Carmita in fun that she had inherited her temperament with that libertarian blood. She preferred to give him fond old-wives' tales about her tropic country, the "sun-beloved land" as the poet Baralt had called it in a famous line.

Such recollections considerably aided in counteracting Bolet's advice and in stimulating Martí's old desire to know that country, matrix of South American republics. And a letter from Carmita to her cousin, Merced Smith de Hamilton, distantly related to Guzmán Blanco, had immediately opened to him her gracious home environment, a solace to the pilgrim.

More than ever he needed that kind of atmosphere, now that new winds had separated him from his own home. Could he rebuild it in Venezuela until the hour for serious patriotic decision should strike? The Creole hospitality with which he was received in wealthy homes gave life to such illusions. But the image of Pepito would not leave him, and while Caracas noisily exerted itself in the transitory freedom of the carnival, forgetting the lack of the most vital liberties, Martí in his room studied the picture of his absent boy and dedicated to the small card-photograph a bouquet of violets given to him by a lady. . . . All that night he spent writing his fatherly homesickness in verse as tender as a spring dawn.

Cecilio Acosta received him one morning in his little house "between Velázquez and Santa Rosalía." Through many a laudatory reference, Martí was already well informed about the renowned humanist and jurist and his fruitful work in stimulating education and in molding consciences. Martí went to see him with the reverence of a disciple.

Acosta lived in austere modesty. In the rambling living-room "as bare of furniture as *he* was of vanity" the chapel-like darkness was accentuated by the subdued brilliance of a candle burning before a small triptych Colonial altar with a crucifix in the center. Between the crowded shelves of books there were a few religious prints. . . . After greeting his visitor with a saintly welcome, don Cecilio wrapped himself in his great cloak and made himself comfortable in a monastic armchair. He was a small, slight man with a clean-shaven, sweet face and very high forehead. In that setting there was something of the ascetic about him that surprised and even embarrassed Martí a little. Could that man really be the most eminent writer of Venezuela, the defender of liberty and progress he had been described to be?

Martí had thought the visit would be brief. But he stayed there for two hours. When he went out into the golden noon-day light, within sight of the Ávila, its lavender summit outlined in the frame of a distant street intersection, his spirit was also filled with light. He had felt the substance of sage and saint. He never remembered having met another man who had towered so far above the human level. What vigorous faith was his in talking about America! Only when the conversation touched upon the present Venezuelan situation did a shadow darken the master's face; but it vanished almost at once in the splendor of conviction: "Usurpations are transient dramas. Victory must come in the end to the source of power. . . . The people will triumph. . . ." And not one word against the despot who, as Martí knew, kept him under constant threat and reduced to poverty.

How well Acosta thought of the young Cuban, so gentle

and penetrating in his questions, men of letters in Caracas came to know, little by little. And especially the University students, who frequented the master's house with a ritualistic devotion as well as with an implication of social protest. Acosta subtly indoctrinated them in the theory and practice of liberalism and the young men, as a rule, left him more wary of their dictator.

Guzmán Blanco, who knew all that happened under every Venezuelan roof, was not ignorant of these incitements. But the prestige and wisdom of Acosta imposed even upon him a certain respect. He had tried every means to win Acosta over. Rebuffed, he wished to wound the master's vanity. The Venezuelan Academy of Literature was reorganized without including in it the many-faceted author whose scholarship and vigorous beauty of language had astounded even the academicians of Spain.

A man of no mean education himself, and fond of all luxuries, including that of intellectual discussion, Guzmán Blanco would have liked to have a magnificent Golden Age court with himself as the "Sun-President." He was given to lament that the disturbances of his political life had kept him from the labors of imagination and belles lettres, and he was able to console his faith in himself only in his "extraordinary popularity and in the mission I believe I am fulfilling for Providence, since it has never been my criterion to accept anything as a matter of chance."

This man, filled with political pride, and with theoretical observance of rights, did not therefore dare to use any direct force against Cecilio Acosta for his dignified aloofness. He permitted his own scholarly friends, even the director of the official newspaper, Fausto Teodoro Aldrey, to visit the exalted rebel—whom they might, perhaps, mellow in time. More than once during his visits there, Martí met them and saw displayed all the subtlety of courtier intellectuals. Don

Cecilio, however, sheathed himself in ironies, "like an honorable man who must always tell the truth but not necessarily the whole truth."

At such gatherings the young men of promise also met the Cuban. One of them, in time, was to write his memoir of that "young man of charming and gracious manner, with his gaze luminous and penetrating, and the high, wide forehead of a sage . . . so communicative, frank and attractive that although a recent arrival, he captivated everyone." His conversational gift and lively imagination were in contrast to Acosta's somewhat stammering speech and serenity. Almost always the gathering was a long dialogue between those two archetypes of differing literary traditions: the classical and the romantic-modernistic. "Sobriety, sobriety, sobriety," Acosta advised his followers. But the gentle tide of unusual words in which Martí expressed himself held in it the enchantment of exotic novelty.

The idea of presenting him at a literary forum suggested itself. *La Opinión Nacional*, Aldrey's paper, made the skies ring with bells of praise and so large a crowd jammed the salons of the Club del Comercio, overflowing into the adjacent plaza, that Martí had to speak from a balcony.

Naturally, the speech began with a prose canticle to the beauty of the women of Caracas; it then lingered over the saga of the glories of Venezuelan history, and ended with a passionate hymn to Liberty, who was still awaiting her hour of fulfillment in America. Some of his listeners became uneasy; but Martí turned the reference to his own country. He had just undergone suffering for her sake; for her he lived. The poem of 1810 was still an incomplete epic and he was thinking of helping to write its last stanza.

Ever since General Quesada—Céspedes' brother-in-law—had been in Caracas, in 1871, organizing forums and bull fights as benefits for the Cuban cause, Cuba's problem had found there a friendly sympathy, one through which, often enough, local anxieties concerning liberty found a catharsis. Martí moved the people of Caracas with his evocation of Cuban battles, delineating them with an epic accent, as if he had been describing Bolívar's prowess in Venezuela. The women were enraptured by the madrigals into which he had woven such lyric allusions to flowers and birds of the tropics. And while Señora Smith de Hamilton thanked the orator with profuse admiration, and journalists reporting the event chorused praise of his dynamic erudition as if he were a Michelet suddenly blossoming in America, men who were more strictly concerned with literary values engaged in discussions over this new type of oratory: archaic verbs, newly-coined adjectives, baroque construction.

Martí, also, was satisfied. The following day he wrote to Jugo Ramírez, one of the organizers of the function, acknowledging his gratitude. He also wrote to the director of *La Opinión Nacional.* In this letter, which the paper published, he spoke of his past experiences and his "dreams of future accomplishment" and partially explained them:

> "I have just been defeated on the field of honor. But the loss of one battle is no more than an obligation to win another. I am making myself ready humbly to serve men; to walk, books slung over my shoulder, on the highways of a new life; to enlist as an anonymous soldier in any high-minded and honorable cause and to die for liberty, obscurely and fiercely."

But, for the time being, he was in Venezuela and must earn a living. He might have a chance, perhaps, to teach or to write for the papers. He would really like to start a new magazine. The speech at the Commerce Club had made him a literary sensation; everybody was discussing him. In academic circles his style was criticized as "affected," or "picturesque." These conservatives lived in the tradition of serenity and classic purity of the Bellos and Baralts. With Martí, a new scale of harmonies had come to Venezuela. Someone, without historical deliberation, called it "modernistic."

Naturally the young men were in favor of modernism. A group of youthful literary enthusiasts asked Martí to hold classes in oratory. And so, since the Cuban enjoyed the open-handed pleasure of teaching, he met with the young men several nights a week in the large lecture hall at don Guillermo Tell Villegas' school and initiated them in the mysteries of antithesis and apostrophe. The lectures were more like dramatic improvisations. One of the students, Juvenal Anzola, was to recall, a long time afterward, the session at which the subject was the people of Israel. Martí narrated their history in vivid colors.

> "We thought," wrote Anzola, "that it was impossible to say more beautiful or poetic things, but when the orator imagined himself to be standing on the summit of Mount Nebo with the people of Israel and Moses gazing upon the promised land, his eloquence was new, surprising, and the sublime seemed small before that spirit. . . ."

Generally, the themes were not so remote nor so serene. However much Martí was already aware that certain words —liberty, honor, democracy—spoken in Venezuela, just then, amounted to talking of the gallows in the house of the hanged, he could not always, nor did he always wish to, restrain himself. He was in Venezuela and felt himself constantly visited by those august shades his history lectures convoked. Moreover, he had to impart his beliefs to those youthful consciences struggling for the breath of life in poisoned air. Those youths—Gil Fortoul, Alvarado, Zumeta, Picón Febres, López Méndez, Brito—were the citizens of tomorrow and today was suffocating them. Each night, after classes, the students left with the light of a new horizon shining in their minds.

So enthusiastic were they about the volunteer professor that the directors of the colleges of Santa María and Villegas invited Martí to become a full-fledged member of their faculties. Here was a means of support for the illustrious guest. Literature and French were his subjects now, but not even the well-worn paths of those studies hindered him from continuing to discourse with his students on ideas of liberty.

Although a blind eye was turned on Acosta's activities, Martí was something else again. Official plans did not countenance definite incitation. Guzmán Blanco—the "Illustrious American"—had his own ideas about how Venezuela should be reformed and, in his repertory, liberty was only an intellectual abstraction. The practical world made other demands. A liberal by doctrine and affiliation, Guzmán Blanco had become, through practical politics, a chronic apostate of himself. His entire public career as executive had been a conflict between ideal and reality, between the wish and the deed. Leader of a revolution for liberty, he enthroned the dictatorship of his party and, within it, government "of an absolute sort and very singular." Democratic by principle, he should have desired for Venezuela a popular mandate which could have been passed on legally and peacefully; but always he had held power through the revolution's tactics, and governed with a high hand. A progressive, he was constantly initiating reforms for his successors to live by; but when, by misuse of new rights, the country turned to anarchy, Guzmán Blanco again took personal and absolute control.

To Martí had been given the opportunity to study at first hand an excellent example of the "enlightened despot" engaged in clothing the extremely active body of America in uncomfortable full-dress European attire. At this very time, having recently returned from a trip to Europe, had he not imposed upon Venezuela a new constitution based on the Swiss model? He would like, said Guzmán Blanco in a speech, to convert the presidency into "an office of moral authority only." But, as always, stubborn reality prevented it: from the Colombian frontier a few generals had just entered Venezuela with warlike intentions; Senator Baptista was giving him cause for concern in the Senate, and a newspaperman was stirring up public opinion from Maracaibo. . . . The President, theoretically much against his will, took them all into custody. A few weeks later a frightened peace reigned again in Venezuela and Congress meekly granted to the "Illustrious American" an extension of the extraordinary powers he already possessed.

Martí was not to forget such lessons in American realities. And Guzmán Blanco already had his eye on him. Martí's contacts with Acosta and with the students, his halo as a budding liberator, his insistence on certain dramatic themes, were becoming troublesome. The Caesar would have preferred by far that Martí, like the newspaperman from the Plata who, years before, had visited the country, would make himself heard in some one of the official choirs. But the Cuban, pretending not to understand the hints, had done no more than to write an occasional, seemingly innocent, and random article for *La Opinión Nacional,* and then only after sustained prodding by Fausto Teodoro Aldrey, a generous friend and old-school gentleman.

On the other hand, he kept on frequently visiting Cecilio Acosta, whose health had now become very precarious. Although the master was only fifty years old, he was obviously near the end of his days. Two candles were always lighted at the little altar. The Archbishop frequently went to the head of the bed, sensing the departure of that noble servant of the Church. There was a constant stream of callers: discreet Masons, academicians, students, antique conservatives, secret political rebels. . . . Around that death-bed, at times, there were most embarrassing silences.

How Venezuela was going to miss this great voice now being stilled! The country was so much in need of spiritual coördination, of a common meeting-ground for agreement among men of integrity, that Martí decided to supply that need by publishing a literary, not rhetorical, review; a review in which he could impart, with a foreigner's neutrality, his American perspective. The appearance of the *Revista Venezolana* was announced: It "would decently avoid every domestic passion and question of internal debate."

In the first issue to come out, on July 19th, Martí published a biographical sketch of one of the founders of independence, Miguel Peña. "To honor does honor," the Cuban wrote, and never was eulogy of that fearless patrician, Peña, more opportune than now, when his native city of Valencia was preparing to raise a statue to him. Great celebrations were under way, and Guzmán Blanco himself had undertaken a journey to go there with a large entourage of the palace gentry.

Caracas read, meanwhile, with great pleasure, the glowing but critically just description of Peña's life—a life "which first rose as a mountain and then crumbled down into a plain." Martí, who had devoted much time during these months to readings of the American past, evoked the turbulent, formative period of the Andine republics with superb mastery of facts and vigor of presentation. The figure of Peña moved in his pages in full historical stature—and occasional human pettiness. Martí had drawn a perfect likeness. The somewhat tart prose of his Guatemala period had come to maturity. It was itself rich with the "graphic and daring images" and the "precise and vigorous words" for which he praised Peña.

There was not one single word in his whole sketch about

the "Illustrious American" who was making a pilgrimage to Valencia, speaking and gathering laurels on the way.

On the 8th of July Cecilio Acosta died. Profound—and confusedly timorous—was the mourning of Caracas for the sage who had not known how to bend his knee in flattery to a tyrant. For the second issue of the *Revista*, about to go to press, Martí wrote a majestic biographical sketch of the eminent scholar and citizen. Just as the eulogy of Peña had revealed his enthusiasm for the American of passion and action, his essay on Acosta disclosed his reverence for the American as a thinker. As though each one of these men represented something of his own nature, he put much of himself in his characterization of them. "Every vigorous thinker," he acknowledged, "will surprise himself and will remain captive and tormented by seeing in the work of Acosta his own bold thoughts." Perhaps because of this spiritual relationship his essay on the Venezuelan attained an impressive penetration and subtlety, as though he were writing of himself.

The supreme official censor was keenly aware of that intellectual consanguinity. During some of his stops on the return trip from Valencia, Guzmán Blanco must have squinted darkly at the portrait of his enemy by that elusive pen. What better moment for a secondary measure of internal health? There was no love lost for Martí in Venezuela. He who dared to write that Cecilio Acosta, most subtly disguised of the Iconoclasts, was "one of those who remained viligantly awake when everyone else was lying down on the ground asleep," who hailed the eternal non-conformist, even though it was only an intellectual non-conformity—"that fruitful independence which made him not slave but master"; who exalted in such fashion the man that he, Guzmán Blanco had insisted on relegating to obscurity; that intruder was certainly no less inconvenient than the deceased. And, after all, who was this rebel and praiser of rebels? An adventurer

REGULAR SPANISH CAVALRYMAN

in politics and letters, a foreigner allowing himself the luxury of libertarian attitudes!

The "Illustrious American" came to a decision and carried it out to a finish. He would still continue to be indulgent to Martí if, in the next number of the *Revista*, he showed himself mindful of the glory of Guzmán Blanco, the Regenerator. If not . . . there was a ship sailing for the North that week from La Guayra.

Caracas, July 27, 1881

Señor Fausto Teodoro Aldrey:

My Friend: Tomorrow I leave Venezuela and turn again back to New York. In such haste have I decided upon this trip that I do not have time, before going, to shake the friendly hands this city has extended to me. . . . I have felt the warmth of generous hearts in this land; with deepest poignancy I repay their affection; their fulfillments will be my joy; their hopes and expectancies, my wish; their sorrow, my anguish. When eyes are fixed on high, neither cobbles nor brambles will keep the traveller from his path; vigorous ideals and honest consecration to them are not weakened in a sincere mind by the contradictions of life. I am a son of America: I owe myself to her. And of that America, to whose revelation, purification and urgent maturing I dedicate myself, this land is the cradle. . . . Faithful sons do not deny the cradle of their birth. Let Venezuela tell me how to serve her; she has in me a son . . .

Chapter Nineteen

HARBINGER

He was so immersed in that which was to come that we who live today speak with his words.
Martí: Cecilio Acosta

ALTHOUGH IT HAD LASTED scarcely half a year, his stay in Venezuela had been the final urge in one of the two directions that were to govern the course of his life: the American direction.

To that effect, his destiny had functioned with geometric precision and economy. It had made it possible for him to know three countries of the hispanic continent; Mexico in the north, Guatemala at the center, Venezuela to the south. . . . In the course of this three-fold experience his conception of American reality had been rounded. Mexico initiated him in the sense of continental fraternity. Guatemala taught him the primitive American values: tradition, landscape, the natural man. In Venezuela with its contrast of past and present he found at last the entire tragic dimension of America.

He had had to leave each of these three countries through some personal clash with Authority. This had no effect but to increase his faith in those unhappy peoples, rich in essential endowments, which found themselves subjected to violent swings between anarchy and despotism because public institutions were not adjusted to the interior structure of American reality. They suffered the consequences of having forms imposed on them—cultural, political—which were foreign to their nature and historical stage. . . . America must again come to a full realization of itself in the challenge of new times; must give itself a usable and intelligent culture and liberty. These peoples must march with Bolívar at one side and Spencer on the other. . . .

Martí now saw his duty quite clearly. His task was to fight for the independence of his corner of America, the first step toward its internal freedom. And at the same time, he would assist in the continental task—the work of uniting, stimulating, teaching. He could count on a powerful weapon: the pen. And on a great assortment of samples: the United States.

In the North, by this time, a skin had formed over the deep wound inflicted by the War of Secession. *Dixie*, the war song of the South, was popular in the patriotic repertory of brass bands. An expanding economy had pushed ahead industry, immigration, federal democracy. Napoleons of finance and business were growing enormously rich. It was the era of the roller-skating craze, parting the hair in the middle, souvenir dance programs. With Mark Twain and Bret Harte the vernacular came into its own in serious literature. Superlatives—and grandiose boasting—were the order of the day. Women began to play a more dominant rôle in political and economic life. Blaine, idol of the multitudes, had a clear, economic idea of the imperial mission of the United States. Sentimentality and the "Blue Danube" set the polite emotional tone.

Martí had hardly arrived in New York when he began to write news articles for *La Opinión Nacional*. Aldrey had not wished to lose, through distance, the value of that pen; but, to keep from offending the "Illustrious American," he had charged Martí to sign everything "M. de Z."

The good director forgot that there are natural qualities and styles which reveal themselves. How could the new correspondent be expected to withdraw himself from the challenge of the dramatic event which shortly before his arrival completely held the attention of America? On the 2nd of July, a political fanatic had fired two shots at President Garfield, wounding him gravely. The entire nation lived in suspense. Everybody was talking about political plots and foreign-element conspiracies. Twice, now, in a single generation, a President of the United States had been shot down—a terrifying innovation. Newspapers exploited the anger and sorrowing expectancy of the people. Garfield, "sick man of the nation," continued to hover between life and death. Popular clamor, demanding vengeance, reached even the cell of Guiteau, the assassin.

Martí keenly felt the collective tension. He saw the spectacle of "this country, in appearances lord of all countries on earth, but in reality slave of all the lower passions that disturb and pervert other peoples." And he resolved to teach America by the lessons of that example. Because the United States was "the only nation which has the absolute duty of being great. It is natural for us who inherited storms to live with them. This country inherited calmness and grandeur; it should live with them."

So ended his first letter to *La Opinión*. But his others would offer nothing in the way of admonition. They would be lengthy, dramatic, detailed accounts of each scene of the prolonged presidential drama—the failure of science before the mysterious course of a bullet, the great public funeral and mourning, the sensational trial of Guiteau, the gallows' final seal of vengeance.

Latin-American newspapers had never known such vivid and colorful reporting. In Caracas and in American exchange editorial offices, the readers wondered what dynamic pen could be capable of such racy description. Only a few of Aldrey's friends knew; but the evidential clues to the author's identity worried the editor considerably. Fortunately, with the letters on the Garfield story accounts also arrived from the same correspondent on current events in Spain—the recent elections, the wedding of Infanta Eulalia with the French prince, the struggles between Cánovas and Sagasta. . . . Martí wrote about it all with as much color and wealth of detail as if he had been in the midst of Madrid's newspaper and political circles—thanks to his intimate apprenticeship and profound insights into Spanish affairs.

Often he struck out at what was rotten in Spain or probed the Cuban wound. Lively evaluations broke here and there through the appearance of objectivity. Aldrey became alarmed at various isolated outbursts: "Liberty never dies from the wounds she receives. The dagger that wounds her carries fresh blood to her veins." Was it the Cuban's fault that he did not know how to dissemble? The very style of the articles, intended to be sketchy and factual, erupted at times, when fired by enthusiasm, with sparks and colors readily recognizable in Caracas. It was easier for Aldrey when other letters treated of current events in France, in Italy, in Mexico. . . . From his little room in the Mantilla home—doña Carmita tried to keep the children from making too much noise—Martí displayed miraculous activity as "travelling correspondent."

This was his means of earning a living until he could make other contacts. A good part of the day and night he spent at the table in a sea of newspapers and magazines, filling sheet after sheet of copy-paper with a handwriting made almost illegible by intellectual drive.

At times his endless work was interrupted by some of his Venezuelan friends, brothers in experience—Bolet Peraza, Gutiérrez Coll, and especially Pérez Bonalde, the restless poet who had translated Heine into Spanish and who had himself Heine's sharp and skeptical humor.

Enrique Trujillo brought Martí the latest news from Cuba. Tall, slender, with a short beard which gave his face a smudged appearance, Trujillo was one of the many Polavieja deported from Santiago at the outbreak of the Little War. Having fled from Spain also, he had come to New York to settle, with his whole family. He distinguished himself very quickly among Latin-American emigrés by his

Creole spirit of friendliness, his staunch loyalty to Cuban independence, and his hospitality. His house evolved into a Cuban hotel—where not all the guests paid religiously. In the afternoons Trujillo came to talk over with Martí his political and journalistic projects.

As for revolutionary politics, the correspondent did not pretend to encourage Trujillo's speculations. He did not believe the political opportunity to be at hand. The failure of the last rising was still altogether too recent. Many lesser chiefs were being persecuted or were prisoners in Ceuta or Mahón. The more important ones were scattered throughout other islands of the Antilles and in Central American republics. Spain, inclined to a dilatory kindness through her triumph, was sending to Cuba "crumbs of liberty served on a magnificent platter by a knightly general." In Madrid, Portuondo and other deputies from the overseas possessions were squandering eloquence on behalf of the Islands. Martí thought—and "M. de Z." said so in *La Opinión*—that their diplomatic demands were all but futile. "Honest and healthy politics wants neither ambiguous language nor devious ways. What is urgent should be urgently demanded." But how, when the Island, still "discouraged, disunited and impoverished," was not clear-minded enough to decide what it wanted, could this be done? A country cannot be dragged to liberty; one must wait until the desire for it matures. "Strength comes from waiting. Impulse comes from delay." He would wait.

Meanwhile, his writing of articles was a discipline that obliged him to study and analyze events. His accounts of Spain examined the minute political strategy of Madrid. His extensive reviews of current affairs gave him the chance to understand the history and social complex of the United States, the underlying conditions of her liberty. His observations became increasingly more penetrating, his judgment more sure.

"Ownership: Here is the guarantee of Republics. An impoverished country will always live in tension and revolt. To create ownership is to create supporters of personal independence and the public pride necessary to defend those interests."

In Venezuela and beyond its borders many youths of literary turn were learning in these articles how a great pen managed to express big ideas with natural simplicity, and to make sublime sense out of small every-day occurrences.

Martí had wanted to fill his life with plans and expectations, which is always the best way of waiting. But the innermost emptiness ached at times. With cold weather he had again been maddened by nostalgia for native warmth—country, passion, wife and child. He had written a sheaf of poems to his little boy, and his friends. Pérez Bonalde especially, who was a good critic, found in those short lyrics of classical turn such tender grace that he was persuaded to print them. The book would be entitled *Ismaelillo*, in remembrance of another child of his childhood, long past, but dedicated to Pepito: "Son, driven away by everyone, I take refuge in you. . . . These rivulets have flowed through my heart. May they touch yours!"

The lonely father kept sheltering the hope that Carmen would decide to join him in New York. At one time it seemed that Santa Claus might bring him this Christmas gift. But down there in the large paternal house in Camagüey, amid peace and comfort, Carmen remembered without enthusiasm the cold, gray days of Brooklyn, the meetings which took her husband away from her, the difficult home life. . . . In his account of the Christmas holidays, Martí wrote that "there is a kind of fever in happiness—and in sadness." He had had to find distraction for his homesickness in Trujillo's house, where a group of talkative Cubans celebrated Christmas Eve in typical Oriente fashion. At the Mantillas', Carmita built a fire on the hearth—a real home fire. . . .

It was not a trivial thing that in winter, although his reporting of events was always so impersonal, his news articles lapsed into complaints at the cold and its influence on his frail, Cuban body. Sensations are like indiscreet servants who betray the secrets of sensibility. Such cold transcended the mere flesh, sharpened the needs of the spirit and assumed, in short, a symbolic rôle. Martí was a man who needed warmth. Only in struggles involving love or action did he find his own emotional temperature. The letter he had written Rosario as a youth, that letter so eager for affection, had ended: ". . . and for days I have been so cold."

Again deprived of his natural channel of passion, it was not surprising that he sought in irregular ways for this necessity of his temperament. These were his intense days of nomadic love and lyric poetry. The heart sought its emotional climate and the soul fled from the snow "to the forest of itself."

After the half-day of commercial drudgery at Lyons & Company, an export firm, where he managed to eke out a living "spinning sums and dividing zeros" he wrote the larger portion of his book, *Versos Libres*, poems of lyrical intensity which revealed the tortured solitude of a spirit which, not finding at hand an affinity for its need to love and to serve, "feeds on its own substance," lifting itself to an heroic moral world created by its own imagination.

All of his external contacts at this time in his life had failed him, and this gave his poetic confessions accents of pessimism and even of misanthropy. Deflected from its natural course, his stream of passion had not yet found serenity in following a single path but dissipated itself in the jungles of adventure. Bleak poems were a testimony to the loathing with which the poet always left these episodes of the flesh. His was the conflict, in this erotic aspect, between a strongly emotional nature and an exquisite moral sensibility in which the scruple became law or drama.

The idea of death often visited him in this solitude: But, as always, he was deterred by his stoic evaluation of pain and duty. "Man needs to suffer. When he has no real sorrows he creates them. Sorrows prepare and purify." With this stoicism there was naturally blended a religious emotion. Against the skeptical and even atheistic tendencies of his mind, a sense of dependence and the notion of a future life asserted themselves, and provided the basis for the mystic faith his heroism would need. All his conduct was thus governed by norms and values superior to immediate interests, by a hunger for moral austerity.

But his sensitive tropical flesh, his dramatic need for affection, both lay claim to their own and rebelled against the puritanical temptation that the American ethical atmosphere itself tended to nurse in him.

His *Versos Libres* were still a secret literary achievement. When this "poetry of difficult harmonies" was made public in America, the so-called modernistic movement was already a part of history, but professors of literature would point out 1882—the date of Martí's poems—as that of its inception. Between his sordid commercial tasks, and on the business paper of Lyons & Company, an exiled and obscure Cuban was writing that year, verse new in form and in poetic substance. At a time when worship of neo-classic forms still prevailed in Spain and its literary colonies, Martí was breaking up metres and rhythms to make his poetry seem like "a bristly mane." When the echoes of romantic sentimentality or artificial academic aloofness were still in favor, he unchained the deepest voices and summoned the most vigorous possibilities of poetic idiom. The contemporary and neighboring voice of Whitman inspired him, no doubt, in that broadening of the province of poetry to include everything vital. Poetry was no longer for him either form or attitude, but substance and life.

In those days Oscar Wilde arrived in New York with his studied dress and a sunflower in his lapel. He was the sensation of snob society and a scandal to the newspapers which exploited the tradition of pioneer virility. Martí went to hear him at Chickering Hall. The following day he wrote a serious account of the man and his lecture for *El Almendares* of Havana. With his characteristic lack of humor he gravely considered the finery of the "apostle of elegance" and defended him against Yankee vulgarity. But the aesthetic Epicureanism of Wilde, that "fondness for pleasure rather than the contemplation of beautiful things," was not to his liking, particularly when it concerned literature. Martí, too, was capable of being enamoured of fine pieces of porcelain—in fact his trunk had come back from the South full of native pottery—but writing was not merely something to please the senses, but an instrument for communication, an intellectual weapon.

His articles for *La Opinión* invariably favored instructive themes, concerned with the social temperature or landscape, no matter how much he embellished them with picturesque scenes from American life. Together with a precise, earthy sense, they carried a note of austerity and mysticism. Of Longfellow, who had just died, he praised "that mystic beauty of good men . . . and that yearning for death which makes life beautiful." And when, two months later, Emerson also passed away, Martí felt no sorrow but jealousy, since "when one has lived well, death is a victory." The eulogy of the sage of Concord was proportionate to the size of the man, and as in the biographical sketch of Cecilio Acosta, Martí put into this magnificent essay—generously sent to an obscure Hispano-American newspaper—unselfconscious evidence of his own "angelic tenderness" and "priestly mind."

In the summer of 1882 he was obliged to stop writing for *La Opinión.* Whether it was because Guzmán Blanco had finally discovered the identity of the mysterious journalist or because some other, petty influence had made itself felt on far-away friends, Aldrey's letters made the correspondent aware of a growing coolness. And "fortune," Martí observed, "has indulged me by surrounding me with people who tell me the truth when I need it; but who treat me with unusual tenderness and with a consideration that is a joy to me. . . ." He discontinued his news articles.

Those letters which "had made the rounds of America" and were being put into book form by friendly hands, had created a demand. Martí was invited to contribute to other papers on the Continent. Señor Carlos Carranza, at that time Argentine Consul in New York, interested himself in getting Martí to write for *La Nación,* the great Buenos Aires paper. His initiative was applauded by the Mitres, father and son, who were the newspaper's owners. At that time, Argentina was undergoing the civilizing influence of Alberdi and Sarmiento, and was interested in importing into the Plata the best of the world's culture. *La Nación,* under its distinguished directors, was already a great progressive force, and the elder Mitre, like his friend Sarmiento, did not know of any better founts of learning than those which had made the United States the pride of the new world.

Martí received the letter engaging him, less pleased by the honor itself than by the greater opportunity it gave him to further his ideal. Trujillo, however, considered it a great honor for Cuba, and that very July night he announced the news, which greatly flattered the Cubans he had called together in his house to discuss, with Flor Crombet and Martí, the possibility of a new conspiracy.

Three months later, the Buenos Aires daily published Martí's first article on current events. Mitre the younger wrote him that it had been read "in this country and adjacent ones, with marked interest and it deserves to be widely reprinted." He also expressed satisfaction at having—as he put it in English—"the right man in the right place." But this satisfaction was modified in the same letter by certain admonitions concerning future articles. In his first, Martí had criticized some limitations of Yankee greatness, and the director, after sounding out opinion—"as well as editorial policy"—had decided to cut the harsh criticism "so as not to create a wrong impression that he was opening a campaign of denunciation of the United States." The paper, Mitre added, excusing "the brutality of the word used for the sake of accuracy," was a commodity which had to be geared to its market.

And in the Argentine market, the United States was then in very great favor. Not even the great Sarmiento himself, whose admiration for things American was notorious, had as yet even a glimmer of what the cost of that uncritical acceptance would be. Martí, however, had already heard the birth-cries of imperialism. Still burning in his memory was the boast Senator Hawley had made the year before at an official banquet: "And when we have taken Canada and Mexico and we reign without rivals on the continent, what kind of civilization will we come to have in the future?" The American without a country had answered in *La Opinión Nacional:* "A terrible one, indeed—that of Carthage."

In his answer to Mitre, Martí managed to defer to the editor's judgment without compromising his own freedom to report and to warn:

"Certain it is that I do not believe it to be a good foundation for a country, this exclusive, fanatical and restless devotion to material wealth which disillusions people or develops them in a one-sided manner, giving them at once the characteristics of giants and of children. Certain it is, that in a group of ambitious thinkers there are brewing covetous designs which can neither please nor tranquillize the younger and more generously unquiet countries of our America . . ."

But he would not be one to sit in judgment of the United States because of what "an exclusive group of eagle-screaming nationalists" thought. Nor would he be one to deny its due to the nation "in which, summoned by freedom, all kinds of men and problems have a forum."

"For me," he added, "criticism has never been more than discernment . . . I cherish only a love for the growth—and a horror for the imprisonment—of the human spirit. . . . There is no greater torment than to write against one's soul, or without one."

Chapter Twenty

THE GÓMEZ-MACEO PLAN

On reaching thirty years of age, Martí had succeeded somewhat in coming to terms with his life.

Since he had never thought it "prudent or worth-while" to practice the profession of law in a strange land, he had resigned himself to the slavery of a business office which required him "to leave home on cold, early mornings and to return well-wrapped up in the dark of night." But now, with what he received regularly from *La Nación,* he had somewhat lightened his burden. Appleton's gave him an occasional job of translation, of French or English manuals for the Latin-American market; one such was Jevons' *Logic,* whose rules he deemed "marvelously useless." Finally, his friend Estrázulas, the Uraguayan Consul, a rare spirit and a devotee of painting and frequent vacations, succeeded in having Martí appointed as Vice-consul.

Thanks to these added earnings, when Carmen finally decided to join him, he could offer her the rented luxury of a newly built cottage in Brooklyn, which was growing rapidly now that the Roeblings' great bridge had been placed under construction. The exile could even do more: He sent his mother a regular allowance every month and asked don Mariano to join him in the spring for a little vacation.

These tardy satisfactions gave him great pleasure. He had always regarded his shortcomings as an only son with feelings of guilt, as if he were cheating his family. Now at last it seemed as if all his duties were being fulfilled. In the new home there was a diplomatic peace. Perhaps Carmen was not unaware that under the complicity of separation and disillusionment, another kind of serene and domestic love had been substituted for their cold, reserved affection.

> *Like ivy*
> *This love has crept through my life;*
> *I asked it to let go its hold on me*
> *And it came in through my aching blood*
> *Like ivy weaving in and out the balcony.*[1]

The ivy created shadows and brightness within him. "In me," he wrote his sister Amelia, "there is a murdered one, but I shall not say who the murderer may be." Carmen, too, suffered in silence. Both of them atoned for their error, hushing voices within themselves for the sake of appearances and for the boy who was growing up.

In other respects, Martí led a diligent life, hard-working and methodical. Mornings were spent in writing. In addition to his news chronicles for *La Nación*, he undertook a considerable amount of work for *La America*, a magazine of "Agriculture, Industry, and Commerce" published in New York, to which he contributed practical, informative reports on very factual matters of continental interest. At noon he went to the city, attended to letters and invoices at the Lyons & Company office, and returned to Brooklyn at nightfall. Love and politics had already collected their tribute also. But on Sundays the house was usually filled with Cubans and Carmen had proof that her husband was again travelling the well-worn path of the revolutionary.

About a year earlier Flor Crombet, a fugitive from the Mahón prison, had carried this temptation to New York. Until he came, the emigrés had been absorbed in considering

[1] ¡Como una enredadera
ha trepado este afecto por mi vida!
Díjele que de mí se desasiera,
¡y se entró por mi sangre adolorida
como por el balcón la enredadera!

the failure of the Little War, except in the South, at Key West—almost within sight of Cuba—where the large colony of Cuban tobacco workers had continued to nurse a nostalgic irritation. At such a short distance from the Island from which they were banned, every hope of change in Cuba was as tempting as the tortures of Tantalus. And don José Dolores Poyo, in his newspaper *El Yara,* kept the drums beating.

Crombet found the Separatists in New York extremely skeptical. The Brigadier was a handsome *mestizo* with eyes and complexion which revealed his partially French descent. In his pleasing face only a scar that split his lip recalled the indomitable spirit which had given so many proofs of its valor in the last war. With the impatience that marked the veterans, continually called back by the *manigua,* the Cuban jungle, he did not realize that the time was not yet ripe for rifles and machetes. Through his own eagerness everything now seemed favorable. In Cuba, dissatisfaction became stronger every day; certain tariff and tax "adjustments," imposed just at the time the Island was going through a serious economic crisis, stirred the Cubans and Spaniards alike to protest, so much so that a man of prominence and means from the Peninsula had dared to declare that those laws alone "were a sufficient reason in themselves to cause an insurrectionist movement in Cuba." Natives found themselves systematically barred from an administration now notoriously corrupt. The Liberals, treated like seditious agents ever since they had announced their desire for autonomy, had withdrawn from the fiction of electoral government, and then plundering became wide open. Crombet insisted that the hour for a decisive revolt had arrived.

Martí listened soberly to the persuasive arguments of the Brigadier, around whom the emigrés flocked so proudly. Martí certainly did not need to be prodded. But the need for liberty was one thing, and the will to achieve it, another.

Would the masses this time answer the call of the leaders? And, above all, would the leaders disposed to issue the call get together and organize with the unity and order the enterprise had to have as basic pre-conditions so that it would not again degenerate into just another attempt?

Flor assured him that they would. He had written to Honduras, which was a nest of Separatists. The government of Marco Aurelio Soto—who could use some imported military skills as a precaution against domestic upheavals—had carried his hospitality to the extreme of installing Antonio Maceo, Roloff, the one-eyed Rodríguez, Tomás Estrada Palma and other Cuban veterans in military and administrative positions. Dr Hernandez was superintendent of a hospital. Only Máximo Gómez, a surly Cincinnatus, had preferred so far as he was concerned to go to San Pedro Sula and raise indigo. But "the Old Man," Crombet assured them, was again ready to fight for Cuba; a lot of water had run under the bridge since Zanjón. And don't worry about Maceo; he would jump, as always, at the first blast of the trumpet.

Martí had embraced Crombet at the close of their first session. From that day on, his eyes had a new light in them, and even at home Carmen noticed an unusual vivacity. Flor Crombet, who had to make a trip to Honduras, was the bearer of Martí's letters, one each for Gómez and Maceo, inviting their opinions "on the work recently begun to reorganize the revolutionary forces, to move opinion in Cuba, unanimously and surely, in the direction we are taking, and prepare outside of Cuba . . . for a rapid and brilliant war. . . ."

The year '82 came to an end and half of '83 passed before these promptings, and others that Máximo Gómez received on his own account from Key West and other emigré centers, evoked from those chief leaders—Gómez and Maceo—any favorable response. Steadfast in their devotion to the Cause, the two veterans were nevertheless made wary by the experience of mere passing enthusiasms. Maceo had much to occupy him in Honduras as Commander of Puerto Cortés and Omoa. No less involved by his peaceful agricultural labors, Gómez had answered Martí that he considered the movement premature. It was "very sad but necessary" to let the people who had grown tired in the first struggle learn their lesson through suffering. "Then you will see that when the old movement is amalgamated with the new, the moment will be ripe."

Letters to Honduras became fewer, and enthusiasm dwindled. In New York a patriotic committee headed by the Marqués de Santa Lucía enjoyed scarcely more than a formal existence. An occasional, not always praiseworthy, effort like that of Carlos Agüero, compromised the dignity of the Cause and angered Martí, for whom all agitation had to have the appearance of seriousness in the eyes of Cuba. "If they see us smaller than they expect, it will be as if we were to commit suicide."

So, when Leocadio Bonachea, who had been stirring up the colonies of Jamaica and the South, arrived in New York with plans for a personal invasion of Cuba, and Panchín Varona, later, in the Independence Club, could offer nothing but a few hundred dollars and a disposition equally rash, Martí remained aloof and despairing. That was not the way he dreamed of Cuba's redemption. Without moving the emigrés profoundly beforehand, without acquiring the resources for a full-fledged military campaign, vigorous and sustained; without the support of the accredited leaders; without, in short, winning the respect of Cuba and Spain at the same time, nothing could be attempted which would not be a woeful madness, a way of merely squandering the enthusiasm and faith of the exiles.

Events would not be long delayed which would prove tragically the incompetence of such adventures. But as late as December, 1883, Máximo Gómez could still write peacefully to Maceo about the last harvest, the ailments of his wife Manana, and "the bravado of New York and the Key."

Meanwhile Martí kept up the slow labor of indoctrination, of education. Enraptured, his friends listened to him carefully analyze the conditions of failure and success and outline the great work of the future. He put into it an unusual mixture of the practical and the lyric. When the purser Viniegra, again in New York, went one Sunday to the little house in Brooklyn to say goodbye, the eruption of his Castilian pronunciation of 'z' stirred a fluttering of suspicious glances among the Cubans around Martí. But he put them at ease with a gesture and continued to speak of the future war with Spain. He radiated so much magnetism, showed such hateless fervor, that the purser for a long hour felt himself also an Insurrecto.

Since opportunity for action did not yet seem to be near, Martí concentrated on the only militant program possible: the service of clear-thinking. In the monthly review, *La America*, his articles were more frequent and of an extraordinary variety. He wrote with equal facility on Hispano-American education, in which he advocated "substituting the literary for the scientific spirit," on the benefits of certain fertilizers, or on the ways to make good cheese. He did not have the literary vanity of writing only on brilliant themes; he laboriously spread the range of his attention with the humility of one who only wishes to be helpful. But these articles on practical subjects were studded with prophetic comment and sparks of genius which at times lighted up the matter-of-fact pages with fireworks, as in the one describing the opening of the Brooklyn Bridge—an occasion which also initiated the complacent boast: *The Greatest in the World.*

In all his articles, and especially those he sent to *La Nación*, what impresses one most is the dimension and depth of his

Americanism. While dreaming of the redemption of his little Antillean island, in the cosmopolitan whirl of New York, he never lost sight of the major task of redeeming the whole of America through solidarity and honest culture. He felt one idea in function with the other and he communicated to all his friends, with a contagious enthusiasm, his conviction that America would never be complete nor secure while Cuba was not free.

No more fitting occasion could arise for spreading these ideas than the Centennial of Bolívar, which the Hispano-American colony celebrated on August 24, 1883. The great banquet hall at Delmonico's was decorated with flowers and flags for the dinner which was attended by accredited consuls in New York, and even by a President: Marco Aurelio Soto, host to Cubans in Honduras. After an oratorical tournament in which the Cuban Antonio Zambrana also competed with gallant eloquence, Martí closed with a poignant toast "to free peoples and to those in bondage." That same night, at the official celebration, his majestic eulogy of Bolívar, which brought the audience to its feet cheering, also concluded with a reference to the aching stump of America's amputated limb: "Gentlemen, let him who has a country honor it; and let him who has no country conquer it!"

Those notes were to have far-flung echoes. From that time on, Martí became in New York something more than the living symbol of Cuba, as Trujillo had called him; he was the incarnation of what he himself would sacramentally call "Our America."

At the beginning of 1884, the persuasions to action from exiles in the United States reached Máximo Gómez at his ranch in such increasing numbers as finally to stir him.

The memory of unjust criticism directed at him after Zanjón having faded by now, he was disposed to begin again the fight for Cuba's liberty. But not without imposing his own conditions. In March, one of his trusted agents, Colonel Manuel Aguilera, left for the United States with a message "To the Revolutionary Centers." In this document the General submitted a plan of action to which any movement undertaken must adhere; to wit: an advance increase in Separatist centers; creation of a Governing Board with which the Commander-in-Chief of the revolution could deal; full military powers for the Commander; and, last but not least, the raising beforehand of $200,000 to finance the movement. At the same time he sent this message, Gómez wrote to Maceo, informing him of his decision. The great Negro joined him.

The Independence Club in solemn session approved the conditions laid down by Gómez, which Martí found greatly to his liking. By Aguilera himself they sent the General $200 so that he could come North, and he was secretly advised that a rich Cuban merchant in New York, Félix Govín, was ready to make the $200,000 available for the movement at once.

By the middle of the year the two chiefs were in the States. Crombet and Dr Hernández had come also from Honduras, and while Gómez and Maceo stopped over in New Orleans and Key West to take the pulse of opinion—and to get financial assistance—Crombet and Hernández went on to New York. At the station they were met by Martí and Trujillo, the aged Arnao, Cirilo Pouble, Dr Párraga, Zambrana and other notables of the colony. The Nordic travellers on the platform gazed with amusement at that group of frock-coated immigrants gesticulating as they talked and shamelessly embracing each other.

Conferences began at once. The apartment in Madame Griffou's boarding house, where Crombet and Hernández took lodging, was never free of black tobacco smoke and fiery speech. Nine days later, Gómez and Maceo arrived. A veritable mob of loud-talking, enthusiastic Cubans went to welcome them. Martí saw, for the first time, with deep emotion, those two crusaders who had made the Cuban fields echo with sounds of their battle: Gómez tall, lean, his stiff goatee jutting out below the sides of his drooping mustache; Antonio Maceo, an Ajax carved in ebony, but with manners and speech as soft as velvet. They also went to live at Madame Griffou's—and that good lady was stunned by this new invasion.

In accordance with the conditions laid down by Gómez, the movement began to take shape. The primary question was that of money. When Señor Govín was asked to make good his promise to advance $200,000 for the Cause, he pretended not to know anything about it. When Gómez pinned him down angrily, he begged off, arguing that to lend the promised funds at this time would jeopardize with the Spanish Government the claim he had pending for recovery of property in Cuba which had been confiscated. It soon became obvious that this promise of his had had no other purpose than its usefulness as a threat in dealing with Insular authorities. Govín had been playing with two decks of cards.

Thus the primary, most essential, condition was unfulfilled. How were the enormous expenses for the purchase of weapons and ammunition, and the invasion of the Island, to be met? On taking leave of Bográn, Soto's successor as president of Honduras, Gómez had received $3,000 from him toward the freedom of Cuba, and the exiles at Key West, in their enthusiasm over his arrival, had collected $5,000 more. But this was still hardly a beginning.

Gómez circulated among Cubans of means in New York a leaflet asking for help. There was only one reply—and that, from one of the least wealthy—a donation of fifty dollars. The General was furious. Shaking a fistful of letters in one hand and pulling at his mustache with the other, he walked up and down the room like a caged lion. Maceo tried to tame him down, with that slow and careful drawl of his he had developed in overcoming his tendency to stutter. The others kept quiet, in contrition or anger.

As time went on, Martí deplored the petty and begging slant, the air of improvisation, that the work was assuming under the intensely personal and rather stubborn direction of Gómez. However, he did not want to add his criticism to the difficulties of the moment; he kept on tirelessly recruiting new followers and contributions. In order to give more time to the movement, he resigned—over the natural protests of Carmen—from his profitable position as substitute in the Uruguayan Consulate.

On the 10th of October, anniversary of the Call of Yara, his eloquence in Tammany Hall fired the largest crowd that had ever gathered at any Cuban meeting since the war decade. But not enough money was collected to meet immediate needs. To consolidate all the fund-raising efforts it was decided to found a club, which would innocently be named the Cuban Aid Society, to mask its revolutionary purposes. At the organization meeting, Martí's speech won him the presidency. Other emigré centers established similar societies.

Although the revolutionary treasury was still too low to permit immediate preparation for military action, nothing prevented the beginning of the work of agitation and political organization. Accustomed to the independent habits of the planter, Gómez settled everything without consulting anyone but Maceo, and came to an agreement with him on a system of appointed deputies to Cuban emigré centers outside of the United States—Paris, Kingston, Jamaica, Santo Domingo. . . .

Martí did not approve of some of these time-wasting, dispersive measures. And especially, he disapproved of the way in which they were decided upon, without sufficient deliberation, without consulting all representative opinions. What about the Governing Board that Gómez himself had proposed in his conditions? It was right that the military direction of the war should be entrusted solely to the experienced leaders; but its preparation and organization, its political education of the mind and spirit surely required the spontaneous effort and judgment of all. The profoundly civilian spirit of Martí was alarmed at the dictatorship of the old General. The Revolution was nothing but the seed of the Republic and the Republic must be born free of dictatorship [*caudillisimo*], America's blight. When was it ever possible to recruit hearts, the most important thing to do now, without gentleness and consideration, the outward signs of love? . . . Gómez was autocratic, and his military brusqueness also wounded Martí's sense of civilian values.

One day—about the middle of October—in conference with Martí and Maceo, the General decided that both of them were to go to Mexico to win the Cubans there to the movement. Martí was happy at the thought of returning, with his ideal now on a war footing, to that beloved land. The conference was over. Gómez, who had ordered a bath to be drawn, brusquely started to walk away, towel over his shoulder. Martí, excited, began to suggest things he would do when he reached Mexico. Gómez interrupted him curtly: "Look, Martí: limit yourself to obeying orders; for the rest, General Maceo will do what is to be done." Without saying another word he left the room.

Maceo tried in vain to erase the imprint of those cutting words: " 'the Old Man' considers the Cuban War almost as if it is his exclusive property, and he does not permit anyone to interfere . . ."

Martí took leave of both, then and there. Two days later he wrote Gómez a long letter, respectful but forthright, in which the most vigorous protest was made, not on behalf of his wounded dignity, so much as in the name of the democratic spirit which ought to govern the revolution; in the name of the revolutionary idea itself, which he already saw frustrated by the condition of personal management imposed upon it by General Gómez. He would not lend his aid for the purpose of "changing the present political despotism in Cuba for a personal despotism, a thousand times worse."

Some time later, on the back of that letter, Gómez made a note of the incident, writing: "This man carelessly insults me; if the great friendliness I felt for him were known, it would give an idea how the reading of his judgment has affected me."

With that clash between the military mind and the democratic-civilian spirit, relations between the two patriots remained broken. In full agreement with Maceo, who respected him deeply, Gómez went ahead with all his plans. Martí withdrew, convinced that the movement still lacked the most essential ingredient.

The conspirators divided themselves up among separate commissions. In April Gómez left for Jamaica, where he believed he could successfully gather military equipment. Martí brooded over his disillusionment, invaded by a profound melancholy. He could hardly bring himself to write. To his friend Heraclio de la Guardia he confided:

> . . . "A horror of language has seized me, making me aware, and ashamed of, the uselessness of my existence. The hand, aching to grasp more effective weapons, or for tasks more virile and difficult, rejects the pen as if it were an accusation. The bitterness of my land enters my soul and drives it mad . . ."

However, in spite of everything, he still clung to the hope that Gómez could triumph in his fashion and he took heart on seeing the warriors "burnishing their armor."

Among the exiles his sudden withdrawal from the movement was very badly taken. It had, on the face of it, all the aspects of desertion. In Key West, Martí's name was spoken with sullen scorn. At Clarendon Hall, on June 13th, when the board of directors of the Cuban Aid Society was reconstituted—since Martí had, naturally, resigned its presidency—acrimonious taunts were made about him. Knowing this, Martí published in Trujillo's new paper, *El Avisador Cubano*, a few days later, an invitation "to the Cubans of New York" in which the following words could be read:

> My compatriots are my masters. All my life has been spent, and will continue to be spent, for their benefit. I owe them an accounting for all my acts, even the most personal ones; every man is obliged to honor his own country in his private, as well as in his public, conduct.
>
> On the night of Thursday the 25th, from 7:30 on, I will be at Clarendon Hall to answer whatever charges may be made against me by my fellow countrymen.
>
> José Martí.

That promise of good sport drew a crowd to Clarendon Hall; along with many sincere patriots, not a few of the indifferent who had never before been seen at political meetings. Relaxed, and a little paler even than usual, Martí asked anyone having charges to make to state them frankly. One Señor Rico angrily rose and began to shout an incoherent bill of particulars, "but his tongue," Trujillo noted, "became paralyzed and he was unable to continue." Then Martí put into play all the resources of his eloquence to explain his conduct without belittling glorious reputations or discrediting the revolutionary movement. His speech was at once luminous and subdued. More than by logic, he had to convince by the magnetism of his own integrity, with the obscure magic of words. A great ovation cleared him. The following day Trujillo wrote to Maceo, who was in New Orleans:

"It gave me great satisfaction that in that solemn and magnificent gathering no thought was uttered which might hamper the progressive march of the revolution or give aid and comfort to our enemies by depicting us as divided and hating one another. Nor did I expect anything different from Martí's subtle political and patriotic tactfulness. The only point he made was that a matter of detail had estranged him from the chiefs of the projected movement, but that he was, and always would be, with the Nation."

A few months later, Martí made plain the convictions underlying that speech in a letter to a patriot in Philadelphia declining an invitation from that city to speak at the October 10th celebration. He had concealed his disagreement with Gómez "because it is better to die of wounds than to permit the enemy to see them"; but, he added,

"we Cubans have lived under so many outrages that in me the desire is a madness, and the determination is as hard as rock, to see things in my country guided in such a way that the person of every Cuban is as respected as that of a sacred person; to have it made self-evident that in public affairs there is no greater will than that of the country, and that the country's welfare shall prevail over private interests . . . It is indispensable to the health of the homeland that someone express without vacillation or cowardice the essential principles of thought and method which I have believed to be in peril. . . ."

On his side events were to take care of the justification of these scruples and fears. Difficulties of all sorts continued to

YOUNG SPANISH OFFICER

hinder the plans of Gómez and Maceo, embittering the leaders against each other, weakening the enthusiasm of the exiles. In August, the General was saying publicly that the movement had failed through "unfortunate happenings and obstacles generally always unforeseen, which are never lacking in this kind of undertaking."

But history would confirm—and Gómez himself would admit, later on—that at least errors "of thought and method" which had determined Martí's withdrawal contributed as much to the fiasco as those "unfortunate happenings."

Chapter Twenty-one

THE RESERVES

Patience, in politics, when not carried to the point of exaggeration, is the greatest of talents . . .
Martí: Letter to Ruz, *1887*

WHILE THAT VENTURE was slowly working out its failure, Martí kept to himself in dignified restraint, "determined to lead my life along the path which I find good—where one walks alone and not easily . . ."

The sudden political windstorm had angered Carmen, who left again for Cuba with her son. For a few months Martí's fatherly loneliness was replaced by his affection as a son: don Mariano had come to New York, and the excited way in which Martí walked with him about the great city, listening to his rough and picturesque remarks on American follies, was something to relish. Conversation between father and son often dwelt on the situation in Cuba, and Martí, now noted in the Island as a revolutionary trouble-maker, talked about his dream, taking care not to insult the Hispanism of the former soldier of the King. The old man interrupted him one day, with an amusing forgetfulness of the past: "Go on, go on! Do you think I undertook your education with any idea but that you should be a free man?"

And now the son could well believe him. All his old thirst for tenderness made him see in the "fearless parent the acme and reflection of brave old men." He was quite down-hearted when don Mariano, suffering greatly from the cold, had to return to Cuba in search of warmth for his seventy years.

Other affections consoled him. Manuel Mantilla had died, and his widow, Carmita, spirited and understanding, was always able to calm the havoc of loneliness in Martí's sensitive spirit. Her youngest daughter, María, had inherited her mother's vivacious charm and bright intelligence, and the "rivulets of tenderness" which had never been able to inundate *Ismaelillo* were channeled in her direction. Their home was for Martí a substitute home.

Hardly less intense was the devotion for him in other Cuban homes in New York. He always returned affection "a sea for a river": prompt and thoughtful in his attentions, lavish—on name days and Christmas—with small gifts which he would leave with charming, appropriate messages in verse. If it had not been obvious that he was acting on generous impulse free from all calculation, it might have been thought that he was trying to cultivate good-will.

His formidable journalistic work had by this time made him known throughout all the continent where Spanish was read. The seeds of his thought, started in *La América*, grew into contributions to new papers and magazines, presenting aspects of a whole program of material and vital reforms, conceived with astonishing foresight. There was no Latin-American problem which could escape his far-off study, no local progress that he did not commend, forcing at times a note of encouraging optimism. His letters to *La Nación* were widely commented on and exercised considerable literary influence. At the modernist get-togethers in Buenos Aires, the poet Rubén Darío, on the threshold of fame himself, read aloud many of those "heavy floods of ink" in which were described:

> ". . . a martial Grant and an heroic Sherman . . . ; a literary Brooklyn Bridge equal to the one of steel; a Herculean description of an agricultural fair, vast as the Augean stables; spring seasons filled with flowers, sum-

mer seasons, O yes! Martí's were better than those of Nature herself; Sioux Indians who spoke in Martí's language; snowstorms which made one really feel the cold . . . and a patriarchal Walt Whitman, magical, lyrically majestic, long, long before France became acquainted with the biblical author of *Leaves of Grass*, through Sarrazin . . ."

Graver topics stirred graver men. The great Sarmiento, for one, was not bashful in his admiration of all things Yankee and, established as a critic above reproach, was at times irritated by Martí's "South American, Spanish, Latin conscience." He would prefer to see him more reverent toward North American greatness. But when he read the Cuban's account of the dedication of the Statue of Liberty, he was seduced by that "South American eloquence, austere, capricious, flashing, which blossoms on high above our heads." And he wrote to Paul Groussac, urging him to translate that article into French: "In Spanish there is nothing else like the clarion calls of Martí, and in France herself since Victor Hugo, there has been nothing like this tocsin-tone of resonance."

His pen was never tired. It ran to every theme through its richness, and to every opportunity through his poverty. When *El Latino Americano* asked Adelaida Baralt to write a short novel that would appeal to the colony, and she was unable to overcome her timidity and ended by transferring the task to Martí, he wrote *Amistad Funesta*—which was published under the pen name "Adelaida Ral"—and sent her the royalty check with a note in playful verse.

In *Amistad Funesta* he portrayed a great deal of his own life, and of himself. A little later, Appleton's asked him to translate Hugh Conway's *Called Back*, paying one hundred dollars for his Spanish version [*Misterio*], of which thousands of copies were sold. In it, as in the translation of Helen

Hunt Jackson's famous *Ramona*, Martí achieved the beauty of spontaneity in a prose of gracefully classical turns.

During this time, while the Gómez-Maceo fiasco was running its course, his political attitude was one of detachment, although he was firm in his conviction that the problem of Cuba was approaching its inevitable climax by other and more obscure ways.

His state of mind found expression in a letter of May, 1886 to Ricardo Rodríguez Otero, who, in a recent book, had presumed to detect in Martí a leaning toward the autonomist position. He had not been the only one to entertain this supposition. Martí's language, oral as well as written, defeated itself at times by the very richness of its implications and the subtlety of its incidental remarks. In that letter, Martí explained what he thought.

He would always revere the clear will of his country, although it might be contrary to his own; and he wished the liberal effort success if it could win for Cuba a well-being greater than the catastrophe of a premature war. But war would come at last, as Martos had foreseen, because the Cuban problem was becoming more inflamed every year. Martí would stay in New York so that "despairing Cubans would have arms to shelter them and roads to follow on the day of the explosion."

The hour could not be hurried by wish or caprice. Neither for vainglory nor to "acquire fame for being heroic or as an emancipator" would he try to bring war to Cuba before she gave "obvious signs of desiring it." Meanwhile, advance could only be made through genuine statesmanship, which was a matter of foreseeing, of "knowing the roads to take" and of studying "all the problems and all the factors that are an influence in the fate of a country."

This sketch of realistic politics was rounded out by a brief discussion of principles showing the desirability of respecting the deep roots of the Spaniard in Cuba and on the blindness of the annexationist temptation. One who had lived, as he had, in the North and knew the Yankee character, analyzed its interests and observed in its history and at the present time its "eagle-like" attitudes;

> "one who loves his country with an affection which can only be compared to the way tree roots anchor themselves in the soil, or the difficulty with which they are torn out, does not think complacently, but with mortal anguish, that annexation might become a fact and that perhaps it may be our fate to have a skilful neighbor let us bleed ourselves on his threshold until finally he can take whatever is left in his hostile, selfish and irreverent hands."

After these dramatic words in which the historical suspicion of "Yankee Imperialism" found, so early, a Latin-American voice, the letter ended with a stern judgment that was to govern all his labors: "Our Country requires sacrifices. It is an altar and not a pedestal. One serves her but does not make use of her to serve his own ends."

In Martí himself, patriotic thought and emotion were renewing their vitality through this sacrificial sense. The image of Cuba assumed in his life the importance of a mystic betrothal. He spoke of his Island like a lover, and his praises always ended with a sad smile and a ritual phrase: "That's Cuba for you, isn't it?" When Trujillo's daughter had wished to give him a present she sent him a silk flag. But his own emblem of his Country was more natural and personal: the palm tree. In his office, in his house, he had several landscape sketches of royal palms. At times he would gaze at them almost in an ecstasy of homesickness until it seemed that their fronds were gently rustling.

In February of that year, 1887, don Mariano died in Havana. This was a heavy blow. He confided to Fermín:

> "You do not know how much I came to love him after I came to understand, underneath his rough exterior, the integrity and beauty of his soul. My sorrows, which I thought could not be greater, are so, since I shall never be able to love him as I wanted to and to acknowledge him so that all could see and reward, in the last years of his life, that energetic and proud virtue which I myself did not learn to love until my own integrity was put to the test."

This event seemed to release him still more from personal ties, from the secret bridle of blood. Doña Leonor remained, blind in her affection. . . . But the former soldier of the King had not lived to see an enemy in his son, in whom the obscure desire for a new Country had been born.

Now, more than ever, he stimulated the zeal of those about him and he watched over every Cuban pulse-beat. For a long while after the Gómez-Maceo venture, separatism seemed to decline. The autonomists pushed ahead with their plans and even Santiago de Cuba saluted—in the name of the region "where great endurance and great disobedience were traditional"—the orators who arrived in triumph from Havana to preach "autonomy under Spanish citizenship." Old-time, steadfast Separatists, like Zambrana, more or less openly embraced this policy of gradualism.

Unwavering in his faith, Martí knew that such desertions, temporary or only apparent, were in response to "that natural law which orders sleep as rest from labor and in preparation for it." The government of Spain did not know how to engender lasting confidence. "What are colonies for if not for exploitation?" a Spanish conservative had inquired at a full session of the Cortes; and the Island, in fact, continued to be laden down with taxes and special assessments while barrack-room authoritarianism and administrative thievery flourished like the proverbial green bay tree. In parliament, the sincere and able speeches of deputies from the Antilles were listened to with merely polite admiration, and the more liberal Madrid newspapers constantly kept predicting that Cuba would be lost if her demands were not met. One more year, Martí thought, one more passive legislature ignoring Cuba, and the hopes autonomy had succeeded in raising would vanish. His expectation was grounded on analysis and foresight.

Among the exiles in the United States the ferment of homesickness again produced the fever of impatience. José Dolores Poyo filled the air of Key West with the wrathful cries of *El Yara*. Néstor Leonelo Carbonell and other editors did likewise in Tampa. Emilio Núñez roused the people in Philadelphia. Less closely-knit and more worn-out by old grudges and disappointments, the New York colony was disunited and suspicious. Painfully experienced in local impresarios of patriotism, the humble masses distrusted every would-be leader. Martí understood, nevertheless, that it was precisely in that anonymous mass that the best possibilities existed.

He decided to take advantage of the October 10th anniversary to probe its depths. In agreement with Trujillo, Castro Palomino, Dr Párraga, and other faithful friends, he summoned the Cubans to celebrate the great date appropriately. He took care to see that the invitation, signed by no one, had an impersonal tone: It was not determined men but "popular instinct" that called Cubans to rally, with a foreboding that "days of greater duty may lie ahead."

The Masonic Temple was filled. Tomás Estrada Palma, former president of the Republic-in-arms during the Ten Years War and at present director of a school for Latin-American children in Central Valley, presided over the function. Martí closed the series of speeches with a magnificent oration in which, after vividly recalling the revolt at Yara —"Don't you feel, as I feel, the cold of that sublime dawn?" —after contrasting the memories and longing of the exiles with the abject conditions of life in Cuba, he tempered the passion he had aroused. It was a speech at once eager and sane by a man in whom lyric rapture was always held in check by a very precise sense of political possibility and responsibility. Martí wanted neither to rouse action to a rampage nor to close the legitimate road to it. The plight of Cuba demanded action. It was not, however, a question of waging just another war, but of establishing a republic which would be sound from its very roots.

Those small souls, or souls with a small understanding, who always lie in ambush to trap great intentions, took the form of an anonymous correspondent who sent to the Key West paper a distorted version of the speech. Martí corrected it at once, with his usual foresight. It was extremely important to him that "those who serve Cuba with greater faith and who have never allowed the fire to be extinguished on their altars"—the exiles of Key West—should be able to form a true opinion of what was being done for Cuba.

A few days afterwards he received from the Key itself a spirited letter from a veteran of the first war, General Juan Fernández Ruz, who asked his opinion about practical methods for putting their common hopes into action. The applause of October 10th seemed to buttress the policy of vigilant expectation and simple unity that Martí recommended. In his answer to Ruz he carefully combined encouragement with the reasons which still endorsed a policy of waiting, and he hinted at his desire to talk things over with Ruz in New York.

The General came, full of warlike enthusiasm. To learn his views, Martí called to Trujillo's house all the "natural representatives" of separatism in the city. The fact that the meeting was successful and harmonious was in itself a triumph. After much excited discussion, the bases for initiating revolutionary planning were agreed upon and Martí, Félix Fuentes and Castro Palomino were named to submit a detailed schedule for the practical conduct of the work.

Edited by Martí, that report restored to the revolutionary idea the original civil meaning of 1868 and of Guáimaro. In earlier attempts, calling together the military chiefs had always taken first place, which would give the rising, from its first moment, a dictatorial turn. Martí subordinated military necessity to that "of joining the emigré centers together in one magnificent democratic enterprise" since they were the ones called upon to give material supplies and authority to the war. Besides, the revolution—as Martí wrote at the time to Poyo—could not be a mere military campaign blindly following some renowned chieftain, "but a most complicated problem in politics."

The sword was, without any doubt, indispensable, and Martí, in whom there was no rancor, especially in matters concerning the Nation, wrote to Máximo Gómez, "appealing to his noblest instincts and his clearest understanding." The General answered in a four-line note saying that his sword was at the service of Cuba.

All this opposed rather completely the hopes of General Ruz, who fancied himself commanding at will a warlike improvisation. "The stars," commented Martí in a letter to Emilio Núñez, "are no higher than are the ambition and madness of men." He was adamant: He would not support any relapse into authoritarian, haphazard ventures such as those of four years ago.

Ruz bit the bridle and returned South to evangelize the unwary.

The frustration of this adventure brought to life the memory of Martí's rupture with Gómez and gave rise to jealous intimations that he appeared to want to keep authority in his own hands. Incapable of using tortuous paths to his own service, Martí once more forced himself into a bitter restraint.

In the summer of 1888, a club was founded in Brooklyn —the Independents—with Juan Fraga, an honorable and steadfast patriot, as its president. The Club hoped to start a war chest for the revolution, on its own. Martí, with his always integrating view, suggested that it should obtain the coöperation of other emigré societies. When the question of the use of the funds was discussed—a question altogether academic at that point—the two opposing schools of thought concerning the source of revolutionary authority again clashed. Crombet continued to trust everything to those waging war in the field, and contended that any funds must be placed at the absolute disposal of the military. Martí advocated, as always, civil management and administration. The dispute became overheated and bitter words crossed between the brigadier and the orator. Harmony was reëstablished finally, but the day went to the brigadier. Gold braid was more persuasive than reason.

In *El Avisador*, Trujillo approved of the result, stating that it was only just to grant "to Caesar the things which are Caesar's." He could not have chosen a quotation more ominous to one who with good cause mounted guard against all Caesarism.

The Civil Commission formed the year before had not been dissolved and its members, men of law and letters, knew that the roads of the spirit, if longer, are usually surer. They convoked the celebration of October 10th, which had become a tradition, "without partialities, forgetfulness or mental reservations." Martí, for his part, wished to propose that night "a policy of foresight and love."

Unhappily, petty jealousies were at work in the shadows. When Martí rose to speak, a strategically well-seated group

SPANISH OFFICER

shouted, "Let Armas speak! Let Armas speak! He's a patriot!"

Martí yielded the floor to the man called for. When the latter had discreetly calmed the tumult, Martí again took the floor, facing a public which expected a cataract of boiling invective.

Instead, his was a message of union and harmony; generosity had stifled any natural pride. Without fireworks he defined the nature of the work to be done: There must be an assimilation of "the law of politics with the law of love." And in a vibrant finale which, although he used the democratic plural instead of the singular, scarcely disguised a hurt reference to himself, he declared:

> "We are a brake on future despotism, and the only effective, persevering foe of present despotism. We are the ones who procure what is conceded to others. We are school, whiplash, reality, watch and council. We unite what others divide. We do not die. We are the reserves of the Nation!"

Chapter Twenty-two

CONQUEST

To love is to save, isn't it?
Martí: Desde la cruz

UNFORTUNATELY, the "reserves of the Nation," when that magic voice did not unite them momentarily into a knot of enthusiasm, returned to their customary dispersion. Martí asked himself what method could make permanent the ephemeral conquests of speech.

In his elegy on Torroella, years earlier, he had said: "The only law of authority is love." And now, again, he recognized in love the political criterion. Only he who knew how to love without stint could win others. If until now he had not been able to overcome rancor, jealousy and suspicion, was it not because he had not stripped himself of what remained of personal interests in life; because he had put more faith in reason than in concern for others? . . . To make himself publicly worthy, to win the authority which the military easily preëmpted, he would have to make of himself a pure flame of love.

After arriving at this perception, every act, every one of his words, was to respond to a generous discipline. He was to make constant abnegation credible, and preserve absolute humility in eminence. His life became one of self-purification. He had sent for his mother to come to New York; she, who knew everything in his private life, realized that even his irregular, common-law attachment—concealed only by conventional formalities—even that love, which all knew and respected, had purified itself in its own fire and was no stumbling-block for maternal devotion and tenderness. Her Pepe's life was honest, genuine and simple, like the ring she had made for him from a link of the chain he had worn in prison. And, like the ring, which Pepe never removed, his life bore witness to a sense of self-sacrifice that made her worry.

The official center of that life was now his small office on the fourth floor of 120 Front Street—an old, dingy brick building with iron steps and dark halls, just in from the busy waterfront, below Wall Street. His office, however, was very light and that, for Martí, was always a necessity. The place contained nothing more than a few well-laden bookshelves of white pine—some of which he had built himself—photographs of patriots, writers and don Mariano; some Indian trinkets; the bolt of the chain he had dragged about while in prison, and a map of the West Indies. On tables and shelves lay heaps of papers and magazines. Through the closed window one could hear, muted, the clatter of the city's waterfront traffic over the cobblestone paving, and the whistles and bells of tugs and ships.

That little office was known to all Hispano-Americans in New York. There Martí took care of the business of the Uruguayan consulate (Estrázulas, the Consul, spent most of his time travelling or painting). Martí was, in fact, the supplementary consul of all the other Republics. Two or three times a week he would leave the office to go and meet on shipboard someone sent to him with letters of introduction from Cuba, Honduras, Argentina. Unexpectedly his time would be taken up by a traveller from some hinterland lost in the complex Yankee world; an emigrant in search of work; a cigar-maker on vacation; a Cuban writer coming to get his book published or to have his wife operated on. . . . Often there were North American literati or journalists who liked to listen to Martí's careful, musical English and hear his opinions on Henry James's latest novel or Phillips Brooks's last lecture, or the gypsy art of Carmencita la Coja, who was delighting an enthusiastic public every night at

Niblo's, and who had inspired Martí himself to write a heady poem.

Visitors always found him writing. When he raised his head one saw that the interruption had not taken from his face its customary friendly light. He was then a man of thirty-five. His fine hair had gradually receded until it formed only a thin, dark border about his high, rounded forehead. A black mustache and the down beneath his lower lip framed his smile. His slanted eyes seemed farther apart and more melancholy. He dressed in black; the string tie falling carelessly over the neat shirt bosom was also black. That is the way Norman, the Norwegian painter, saw him on the day he was taken to meet him, and that is the way he wanted to paint him, to prolong the pleasure of listening to Martí's scholarly comments on painting.

From that observation post, Martí noted what went on in Cuba, America and the world. How did he find time to keep up with everything? All who spoke with him were astonished at his up-to-the-minute information, his original perspective. "Conversing with him for a little while," wrote a Venezuelan writer, "taught me more than a year of reading." And the poet Tejera declared that only those who had talked intimately with Martí could know "all the power of fascination which lies in human words."

The secret lay in the way he spoke, but also in his insatiable curiosity, which was an expression of his humility, the focus where interest and disinterestedness joined. Truly, nothing human was alien to him; not even the trousseau of a bride-to-be, or the secret of the marvellous bouillabaise at Madame Taurel's on Hanover Square, where he usually entertained his friends. In writing, no subject was beneath his notice. The details of the Oklahoma boom interested him as much as the noble ideals of Father McGlynn or the sensational heterodoxy of Henry George. He studied Fifth Avenue fashions as closely as Chicago's social drama in which he saw how "the popular republic is being transformed into a republic of classes" and how it also revealed the future dimension of an emerging social force. . . . With all this penetrating insight and aptness of detail he wrote for *La Nación*, or for *El Partido Liberal* of Mexico—whose columns the faithful Mercado had just opened to him—frank articles which were read in suspense and reprinted widely.

Whether a few disgruntled persons liked the idea or not, he was the very incarnation of Cuba in New York. In March, 1889, *The Manufacturer*, a Philadelphia trade journal, published an article "Do We Want Cuba?" in which the advantages and disadvantages of acquiring the Island for the United States were considered. Among the disadvantages it included "the Cuban temperament" which the article characterized as "effeminate, incompetent and lazy," declaring that the Cuban's "lack of virile strength and self-respect is shown by the indolence with which for so long he has submitted to Spanish oppression."

Martí was indignant. He wrote a letter of protest to the *New York Evening Post*, which had reprinted these statements as its own; his protest was as well thought out as it was vigorous and high-minded. He did not confine himself merely to making the proved virtues of the Cuban vividly plain, with his struggle for half a century against despotism, and his right to be respected in a time of suffering by "those who did not want to help us when we were anxious to be rid of tyranny." He met the gratuitous contempt of the article with a stern criticism of United States' politics, and contrasted budding imperialism with the Cuban's will to be free. He trusted that "the nation which had liberty for its cradle and had received, for three centuries, the best blood of free men" would not employ "the power thus amassed to deprive a less fortunate neighbor of its liberty."

The day the *Post* published this strong reply, written in rich and fiery English, Cubans in New York carried their heads higher. The little Front Street office was deluged with letters of congratulation and callers who came to express their gratitude. The leaflet in which Martí included both the affront and the answer travelled from hand to hand, encouraging the disheartened.

But with Rafael Serra, a Cuban Negro who congratulated him for the "flogging of these Yankee bosses" he made it more a point to speak about the society which Serra and other Negro compatriots had just founded: *La Liga.* The League was a society for poor people. Martí had a liking for the poor:

> *With the poor ones of the earth*
> *I wish that my lot may be:*
> *The mountain brook to me is worth*
> *More than the mighty sea.*[1]

Besides, for revolutionary purposes, the strength of the nameless mass had to be relied on. The decisive struggle for Cuba must not be a war of landed classes, as in '68, but a people's war. And more than a third of the people in Cuba were dark-skinned and oppressed. In September, 1886, Martín Morúa Delgado wrote to Maceo that the recent abolition of slavery by Spain could constitute a great threat to independence. "The Negro of Cuba will go with those who know how to treat him. The Spanish element is in Cuba; we are outside. From here it is difficult . . ."

Martí did not know about this letter, but he knew that if it were really difficult to win over the Island Negro from the outside, one could at least win over the Negro exile and thus lay the groundwork of racial harmony for the Republic.

[1] Con los pobres de la tierra
quiero yo mi suerte echar
el arroyo de la sierra
me complace más que el mar.

"That," he wrote to Serra, "is the point from which we must start if we want to go where we must. It is not so much a mere political change as a good, sound, just and equitable social system, without demagogic fawning or arrogance of authority. We must not forget that the greatest sufferings constitute a paramount right to justice, and that the prejudices of men and social inequalities cannot prevail over the equality created by nature. You will see what is in my very soul in respect to these matters when the hour of extremity is at hand."

The hour of extremity was drawing near. The instinct of the leader to unite, aided by a sincere human warmth, was closing the gap. Before suspicion he had a wise way of being seemingly unaware. He had a genius for modesty, and candor, "which is a great force." His guilelessness of nature manifested itself in easy, hearty laughter, an unconcern about conventions—at times even comic—and in a tender affection for children.

The confidence that children had in him, likewise, was indicative: they are good judges. True it was that Martí ingratiated himself with them by every sort of indulgence. As for Carmita's children, that went without saying. They were like his own—and especially pretty little María, of whom it could be said that he saw her born, and who had "the soul of an artist." In the afternoons Martí often took them out, together with the Carrillo children, a lively, noisy parade; they would go to Central Park or to the Eden Musée to see the famous wax figures, and the grown-up friend would improvise educational talks in primer language.

He loved to teach children. Convinced that almost all defects of personality stemmed from education contrary to the laws of nature, or to evil seeds of indoctrinations, he felt a profound respect for the virginity of a child's mind. For lack of *Ismaelillo,* he undertook to teach Carmita's children, showing a marked preference for María.

It was not enough for him. He would have liked for his own, and to instruct in his own way, all the children of America. A wealthy Brazilian, Señor A. D'Acosta Gómez, offered to help satisfy that ambition. Politically-minded Cuban groups in New York were not a little surprised, in the summer of '89, to learn that the noted agitator and untiring propagandist of the Cuban War had just issued a magazine entitled *La Edad de Oro* [The Golden Age], dedicated to the children of America.

When they read the article, "Three Heroes," a concise and thorough eulogy of Bolívar, Hidalgo and San Martín, many of them realized that Martí was still tending his own garden. He was working for the liberty of America through the children—"who are the hope of the world." Moreover, older people themselves could read with profit the simple definition of liberty there given: "The right which every man has to be honorable and to think and speak without hypocrisy," or the maxim that "In the world there must be a certain amount of self-respect just as there must be a certain amount of light. When there are many men without self-respect, there are always others who arrogate to themselves the self-respect of the many. . . ." The first and second issues, and the third, had a goodly share of short stories, fables and other children's delights which the adult pen of *La Nación* wrote without apparent effort.

With the fourth number the magazine came to an end. "An undertaking of the heart and not a mere business enterprise," it lacked, so it was said, the indispensable support from American homes. But the true and unspoken reason was something else: Señor D'Acosta could not conceive of a publication for children without using it to inculcate some of the precepts of Holy Mother Church. And Martí refused, with gentle firmness, to sprinkle the souls of his little readers with theology. When the Brazilian angel made the matter a major issue, *The Golden Age* came to an end.

Not that Martí had become an atheist. On the contrary, the intense spirituality which from childhood had governed him had now reached mystic depths. Obsessed by perception of the Other World, he assured don Luis Baralt that he had seen—really *seen*—the soul taking leave of the body of a dying man, and he had portrayed that experience in *Versos Sencillos*. But, like the American defenders of Father McGlynn, he sought "outside of historic and purely human dogmas that harmony of the religious spirit with the freedom of judgment which is the religious demand of the modern world." The soul, immortality, had nothing to do with the sectarian formulas in which men cloaked their fear of the unknown or their desire for "a land of pity and a noiseless sea." Nor was the bridling of passions to be taught on behalf of the egoism of self-salvation, but rather for the sake of pure human compassion.

He was very disheartened in this regard when his wife insisted, there in Camagüey, on entrusting the education of Pepito to Spanish Jesuits. He was ready to do anything to have the boy with him. And since Carmen would not relinquish her rights to the boy, he would let her come, too—provided that she did not expect to find anything in him but the father of her son. . . .

Carmen decided to come.

Martí went on winning over other estranged hearts in his self-effacing generosity. He kept in touch with a few alert minds in Cuba; he was constantly making speeches and gathering together the emigrés he trusted. "From certain individual states of mind created in Cuba by present conditions," he wrote Emilio Núñez, "there can result . . . a conflict committing us to immediate action." There were short-sighted people to whom these moods of prevision appeared as the gestures of a visionary or an exhibitionist; he was constantly gnawed at by the stewards of local opinion, who felt themselves shunted aside by his growing prestige.

Martí was, however, beginning to understand that such were the wages of an apostolic mission. He had to reconcile a democratic respect and deference with the need for asking adherence to the course he felt called upon to follow, and he countered distrust and sarcasm with a polite objectivity. When he learned that two brothers, professional photographers and Cubans, were slandering him, Martí called on them at their studio.

"I came here to get my picture taken because I hear that you do not wish me well."

The brothers, called "the deuce of clubs" because they were tall and thin and were always seen together, now became part of the revolutionary deck of cards.

Bowed down with his own work, Martí still could find time to help everyone. He sought jobs for the needy, visited the sick, supplied an impoverished artist with a necessary dress coat so that he could attend a social gathering to make sketches. For Gonzalo de Quesada, a young enthusiast publishing his review *La Juventud* with difficulty, he wrote articles at midnight. He procured meeting rooms for *La Liga*, decorated them with palm-tree landscapes, paid the rental on a piano for the first meeting, and made a speech on justice to the dark-skinned men.

He felt souls ripening about him.

In August, 1889, the autonomist deputies, Montoro and Giberga, passed through New York on their way to Cuba, fresh from opening one of their eloquent but futile battles in the Spanish Cortes. Martí called at their hotel to congratulate them. During his conversation with the two fashionably dressed deputies, the emigré with the worn frock coat and shoes obviously in need of repair gathered the impression that autonomist hopes were approaching their crisis. That was all he wanted to know, for the night of October 10th.

On that night, at Hardmann Hall, the usual stalwarts spoke, and the young editor of *La Juventud*, Gonzalo de Quesada, made his début as an orator. He acquitted himself quite well. He even rose to fiery periods which would have sounded like those of Martí if the latter had not followed him immediately as the final speaker.

Trujillo did not exaggerate when he said, the next day, in *El Avisador*, that "the famous Martí, who has won such praise for his countrymen" had run in his speech "the entire gamut of oratorical tones." "He was," Trujillo explained, "by turns eloquent, stern, sarcastic, pithy, stimulating, profound, caustic, but never bitter." But a lady whose Cuban home was for Martí like his own admitted that she was sure people had applauded Pepe without understanding him—because he carried them away.

And, in truth, when printed two days later, the speech made somewhat difficult reading. His approaches to criticism were too richly involved, his examination of the historical background of the current Cuban situation was too subtly profound. It was the meditation in public of a philosopher-statesman serving as an agitator. The immediate response had been a reaction to the fire and magnetism of a born leader.

And, as at other times, he was not free from hostile misrepresentation. Later, in a letter in verse to Néstor Ponce de León, Martí denied having called the annexationists vile. The two final lines of the letter recalled, like a refrain, a phrase of that speech destined to become famous; the Republic would need everyone:

It must with all be founded
For the common good of all!

Chapter Twenty-three

THE EAGLE

During the winter of 1889-90 an event of continental significance took place in the United States: the first Conference of American Nations. After the Cleveland interregnum, Secretary of State Blaine was able, in Harrison's administration, to bring to life the idea he had conceived eight years earlier, under Garfield. Thus, in the presence of America's hopes and Europe's suspicions, a rather feeble child, not yet baptized with the name Pan-Americanism, uttered its first, feeble cry. Chauvinistically jealous, the newspapers of Paris and London labeled the creation a sort of customs union fathered by the United States to exclude Europe from South American markets: the economic counterpart of the political Monroe Doctrine. Washington did not conceal its desire "to cement interests" but, of course, in the name of the most brotherly friendship. And the Latin American countries, some of them without guile and others rather wary, accepted the invitation. Santo Domingo alone refrained from taking a hand in the game.

That winter Martí must have felt as never before for his country, without a voice in the celebrated "concert of the free peoples of America." With the establishment of the republic in Brazil, the Latin American parts of the two continents had now succeeded in eliminating the last vestiges of monarchy. Cuba alone was left, tied to her Bourbon. At the great *fiesta* given by the Cuban colony of New York to honor the memory of the poet Heredia, Martí's speech summarized the travail of Cuba:

> As beautiful as Greece, and like her stretched out in chains, a blot on the world, a prison moated by water, America's hobble.

Had his Island been free, what a voice of warning he could have raised in that Congress, together with his companion and friend, Bolet Peraza, who was representing his Venezuelan people, now liberated! How he would have worked to remove the insolent eagle "clutching in its talons all the flags of America" from the emblematic shield of the Conference! But he had to be content to watch from the outside. In his capacity as Consul of Uruguay he attended the receptions New York held in honor of her illustrious guests, who were already worn out from a tiring tour of the country. The Hispano-American Literary Society could not do less, and at the dinner for them at the Scottish Rite Hall, its president announced "our favorite orator, José Martí."

It was the first really substantial speech heard by those weary pilgrims. The origin and formation of the two Americas were contrasted in two pictures concise and vigorous as etchings, placed in a frame of American faith and hope. The diplomatic discretion the occasion required could not suppress certain notes of prudence and fear. In their great destiny of "levelling off the appetites and hates of the world to a basis of a free peace without wolf-like cupidity or clerical prejudice" how could anyone be afraid that Latin America would prefer

> "to amble along behind any willing shepherd or to go through the world as a beggar so that humiliating wealth should fall into her beggar's bowl? Only the wealth which is created, and the liberty conquered, with one's own hands is lasting and good!"

The numerous letters Martí wrote to *La Nación* on the diplomatic event were studded with such warnings more or less veiled.

Certainly these fears were not in vain. Despite Blaine's official pronouncements which talked of commercial agreements, shipping, communications, arbitration and other apparently innocent matters, one could get a glimpse of the eagle's feathers through the more candid press. "Americans," said the *New York Tribune*, "are obliged to reconquer their commercial supremacy . . . and to exercise a direct and general influence in the affairs of the American continent."

These signs were more ominous in the direction of Cuba. Every day the U.S. press became more concerned with the political destiny of the Island, bestowing unusual importance to the once discredited annexationist idea. Senator Call had introduced a bill in the Senate authorizing the President to open negotiations with the Government of Spain and induce it to consent to the independence of Cuba by means of an indemnity payable by the Island. Less than a month later, that same Senator called Washington's attention to the danger to the United States if the Cuban debt should fall into the hands of German financiers. And in February, when a larger Navy was being discussed, Senator Chandler, formerly Secretary of the Navy, urged the construction of an armada "superior to that of any nation in the Western Hemisphere and to that of the nation which owns the island of Cuba . . ."

The eagle was spreading its wings. Would the attention of the Hispano-Americans be distracted from the flight of the eagle by love-feasts and charming speeches?

It was a winter of anxiety for Martí until he saw confirmed in the deliberations of the Conference "the prudence and courage of our people"; until his fear vanished that the Cuban emigrés would be more solicitous of their Northern stepfather than of the Hispano-American motherland. His anxiety had weakened his fragile health and the doctor "sent him to the mountains."

His poems now had a new accent. Martí was thirty-eight. His life had become increasingly full of distances. He was able to look at the past with a certain emotional perspective. "Perhaps," he had written, years before, "poetry is nothing more than distance." Something inside him warned him that a definite separation was approaching, that the moment had arrived to say farewell to old concerns. The "Simple Verses" he now wrote were largely portrayals of beloved people and of distant episodes: his parents, the siege of Mendive's home, Aragón, his dead sister, Mexico, "the Guatemala girl" . . . Departures: deaths in little. And with it all a few simple parables, some delicate allusions to himself.

When I think as merry
As a carefree young lad,
It's of the gold canary
And the black, black eye it had! [1]

In all these short poems there was the naturalness and informality, the simplicity implied in their title. The romantic was at last free from extravagance. His visions had centered on a premonition of sacrifice. Serenity had come with certainty and detachment. His poetry, like his life, was now pruned of luxury and rhetoric:

Poem, together you and I will die
Or each other justify. [2]

[1] Yo pienso cuando me alegro
como un escolar sencillo
en el canario amarillo
¡que tiene el ojo tan negro!

[2] Verso, o nos condenan juntos
¡o nos salvamos los dos!

The flight of the eagle stimulated Martí's impatience. The United States was altogether too interested in Cuba and "only the liberty conquered with one's own hand is lasting."

And things were going from bad to worse on the Island. After the death of General Salamanca, who was disliked by the conservatives because of his reformist gestures, his successor humbled himself before the loyalist Spanish fury of the Unión Constitucional. The autonomists were exasperated. Their organ, *El País*, published a sensational article entitled, "The Challenge."

> "After twelve years of painful struggle against the combined action of intrigue and violence . . . the Cuban people find themselves in worse condition than in 1878, their spirit hurt by disillusionment, their patience worn out by suffering. . . ."

In the Spanish Congress, Martos, confirming his old fears, advised sailing on a new course at once "if disaster is to be avoided."

But Becerra's suffrage bill—which virtually disfranchised 64,000 Cubans—was still on the agenda, and pilotage, taxes and administrative thievery drove to despair even the tamest among those who had anything to lose. Separatism began to raise its head. Antonio Maceo, who had gone to the Island under pretext of attending to personal matters, was taking his own good time about it; he was holding mysterious interviews and was being fêted by Havana's patriotic young men.

Martí could see already shaping up the danger so much to be feared: that war might surprise Cuba without preparation or bases for support. He had spent eight long years trying to make people see the tragedy of such a situation. In his speech on Heredia his utterances had a tone of epic desperation: "If among living Cubans there are not enough troops for honor's need, what are the conchs of the sea-sands doing that they do not blow their horns to call the ancient Indian dead to wage war anew?" Inertia, suspicion, the dictatorial appetite had prevailed.

Martí's next appeal to the representative New York exiles was stern and austere:

> ". . . we would commit . . . an unforgivable crime before History if we did not unite to see how we can give the independent Cubans of the Island the help they need so urgently . . ."

The only revolutionary organization alive in New York, thanks to the quiet tenacity of Juan Fraga, was the Independence Club founded by one of the men who had two years previously differed scornfully with Martí. But what were personal affronts when compared to the affront to Cuba? Fraga attended the meeting Martí called together, which resulted in an appeal to the masses. Hardmann Hall, a place consecrated by this time for Cubans, was filled on the evening of June 16th. Martí stirred the crowd to enthusiasm. The anemic treasury of the club was fattened by the proceeds of the collection, but the common effort must be organized in a continuing sacrifice. Juan Fraga credited the origin of this idea to Eusebio Hernández in Paris. Martí still felt suspicious resistance around himself; but he was happy at perceiving—in this hour snatched from his sick-bed—a new feeling in the air.

A month later echoes reached New York of the rejoicing in which Oriente had greeted her Maceo. Old soldiers, fiery youths, and even quite a good many autonomists had courted the leader with banquets, picnics, jaunts about the countryside on horseback. Cánovas, however, was not asleep in Spain. He had given Polavieja, ruthless commander of 1879, the top command in the Island; and the first thing the new ruler did was to deport Maceo, Flor Crombet and Amador Guerra.

In the meantime, Martí, lungs "ailing" and the heart "skipping more than it should," had had to go to the pines of the Catskills for a cure. Not through fear of "leaving life," he wrote to a friend in the League, "but because I find myself without strength for the many tasks which our country is about to lay on our shoulders." During this brief interlude he was often to observe, scattered around the foot of the pine trees, the creeping sluggishness of grubs and worms, the dignity of the fat, velvety caterpillars: "The better to understand men, I am studying the insects, which are not so bad as they seem; indeed, they know more than we do." He filled a whole notebook with first-hand observations, drawings, hymns of praise: "to prevent injustice to 'worms.' "

Returning to New York, he discovered that patriotic fervor had grown weary. Maceo had passed through the city and had spoken vaguely about his revolutionary purpose in Santiago and of the "glacial indifference" of the emigré centers. The fact was that they were not informed of the plot Maceo improvised in Oriente. But, even if they had known it, what imprudent enthusiasm—Martí wondered—would have supported a purely local rising run by a single chieftain, inevitably bound to end in failure or a dangerous victory?

His speech on the 10th of October was filled with such reservations. In this profound analysis of Cuban possibilities the idea of "founding" appeared time and again. "Words are superfluous when they do not found, when they do not clarify, when they do not draw to something, when they do not create. For what is thinking if not founding, creating? . . ." This constructive purpose, which did not seek to build a quick and flimsy structure, but rather to build a new society on solid foundations, filled his speech with reality and democratic emphasis. He criticized the proud autonomists who "did not deign to speak to those who go through the world on foot, not realizing that they are more numerous than those who travel on wheels"; and showed that scientific politics can only be "a guiding of the country and its real elements toward that which is possible."

Following that inner pattern, Martí dedicated himself more and more to the humble. He treated the dark-skinned workers of *La Liga* with a mixture of indulgence and respect. He had his María—now an accomplished pianist—make their evening functions more pleasant. He urged his learned white friends to teach classes in various subjects. He went every Thursday after his class in Spanish at the City Night School.

Among the League members, who entertained themselves happily while waiting for him to come, a respectful silence would fall on hearing the quick footsteps and characteristic cough that announced the arrival of their teacher. All wished to be the first to take his books or his frayed astrakhan overcoat. For each one he had a friendly personal greeting. He would seat himself at the table and quietly correct the exercises in composition he had given them. "They felt purposely like committing errors for the mere pleasure of hearing themselves individually corrected," a pupil noted. Since each paper called for precise comment, Trujillo labeled Martí's class "encyclopedic." His Negro pupils listened religiously to the varied dissertations, full of imagination, moral uplift, and, of course, political education.

At times a pupil fearful of having displeased Martí by a somewhat personal question, would write him about this fear. The *Maestro*, as everbody in the League called him, would quickly put such a one at ease.

"... try to keep these fears from creeping in, for I know enough about the anguish of the world to understand all its forms and even its injustices. In things of the soul I must be like the doctor who continues to care for the patient who bites his hand. For if he bites the doctor's hand, is it not because he is ill? Is not discouragement a sickness requiring care? To doubt you, who are a hundred times more generous than I, is more difficult for me than to doubt myself. And I do not doubt myself."

He did not. Nor did the general disillusionment, which retarded his efforts in the great work of his life, cause him to despair. The era was one of bankruptcy of faith. The salt of heroism had lost its savor. In Cuba itself, under the foot of the procounsul, the veteran Ramón Roa—who ten years before on the S.S. *Alfonso XII* had called Martí a "useless Christ"—had just published a depressing book discouraging Cubans against revolution by luridly painting the suffering on the battlefields in the Great Decade. Martí had found an antidote to that reading in the *Episodios* in which Manuel de la Cruz gleaned the epic deeds of the Cubans who had fought the Ten Years War. He wrote him with generous envy: "They have carried off all the glory. There is none left for us who come later."

But he went ahead in blind faith, against all skepticism, with his basic work of unification. Little by little he succeeded in overcoming the weak-willed enthusiasm and the nervous distrust fostered in the emigrés by alien city life. In spite of all appearances, the revolution was under way, "sure and invisible." Bearing out a concept which had not yet become famous, Martí had said, two years before, that "revolution is nothing but one of the forms of evolution." The eight years of agitation and retrenchment, alertness and meetings had not been useless. They had been, for him, a process of intellectual growth and achievement, by-product of the inevitable waiting. And in the masses, a gradual growth of confidence.

He could realize that he was now better liked, more representative, since he had thrown in his lot with the lowly. As one of them he had gradually won affection and respect. The name given him in the League had become general: in New York almost everyone called him "*Maestro*." And this was coincident with the growth of his prestige in the more official Hispano-American colony. The Argentine Republic and Paraguay had both made him their Consul-General. When "the honor of the generous land" came to him he added these "simple verses" to the others in his notebook:

> *I thought of the simple artilleryman*
> *Who is now in the tomb so silent;*
> *I thought of my father, the soldier;*
> *I thought of my father, the worker.*[1]

Uruguay, which he had also continued to serve, substituting for Estrázulas, made him her representative to the Washington International Monetary Conference. Martí ordered out of his office the Washington emissary who came to bribe him to support the silver standard. He delivered before the Conference, in English, a brilliant brief for bimetallism and recalled, in passing, that it is not "the business of the American continent . . . to reëstablish under other methods and names the imperial system by which republics are corrupted and destroyed."

America's watchman did not miss an opportunity. The Hispano-American Literary Society had made him its president and on anniversaries of Latin countries, Martí's evocation of the great figures and events of the past made them live anew as realities. His feeling for "our America" as an integrated whole was crystallized in a magnificent essay, so entitled, published in Mexico's *El Partido Liberal.* It was

[1] Pensé en el pobre artillero
que está en la tumba, callado;
pensé en mi padre, el soldado;
pensé en mi padre, el obrero.

a veritable program for American understanding, urging "the timely study and the unspoken and needed unity of the continental soul."

In these months his private life was rich with emotional events. Doña Leonor returned to Cuba parting from him with a premonition that it was their final leave-taking: "The day I had to say goodbye to her she followed me from one room to another and I fled from her . . ." The arrival of Carmen and his son shortly afterwards partially filled that emptiness. "Simple Verses" confessed:

Heart that bears broken
The sturdy anchor to home
Sails like a ship unbespoken
Lost and doomed to roam.[1]

He would have liked to find the right course again. He was aware that he should present his most intimate flank invulnerable to enemy shafts; that in this, in the eyes of the public, his life had offended. But separations are definitive when other affections intervene. And since Martí was incapable of living a double life or of pretending, his tenderness was completely centered in his son, on his "young gentleman," with an almost painful eagerness. He wanted now to watch over him, guide him, indulge him, to make up for all he had not been able to do in the last few years. Pepito had become a bookworm; he listened to his father, eyes wide open, but somehow aloof. It hurt Martí to see Pepito study him like that. When the boy responded to an affectionate touch, his father felt new life sprouting from dormant roots, and trembled as he thought of the future. . . .

Fate was to decree something else. Carmen—sad and dis-

[1] Corazón que lleve rota
el ancla fiel del hogar,
va como barca perdida
que no sabe adónde va.

mayed—appeared one day at Trujillo's house and begged him to get passage to Cuba for her and young Pepe without the necessary consent of her husband. Trujillo refused. She insisted and was backed by the women of Trujillo's household. He finally gave in. Trujillo found the Spanish Consul quite ready to play that trick on the Cuban "subversive." Without Martí's knowledge Carmen and Pepe sailed away.

When he found out what had happened his anger was like that of a mother animal despoiled of her cub. Between him and Trujillo was generated the terrible bitterness typical of the breaking of great friendships. Martí became gravely ill from his sorrow. Even several weeks later a friend saw him sit up in bed and tremble violently from head to foot, in the presence of Trujillo, with an anger he could not recognize in him—the terrible indignation and rage of the sweet-tempered goaded beyond endurance.

With all tetherings to private past severed in this fashion, his life suddenly coalesced in a burning lightness, like a flame. On the 10th of October, from the Independents' rostrum, his eloquence was truly fiery.

The Spanish Consul protested in a newspaper against his "colleague from the Argentine" showing public hostility to a friendly nation. The following day Martí wired his resignation as Consul to the Argentine Minister in Washington. After a similar, although more personal, incident he resigned the presidency of the Literary Society.

He had burned his bridges.

Chapter Twenty-four

TAMPA AND KEY WEST

ONE OF THOSE fortuitous events now took place, which, coming in crucial moments of Martí's life, gave it its tone of predestination.

On the 16th of October, at the suggestion of Eligio Carbonell, the Ignacio Agramonte Club of Tampa resolved that Martí should be the orator invited to give the main address at the meeting with which the club was to begin a fund-raising campaign dedicated to Cuban liberty. By the irony of circumstance Trujillo was delegated to transmit the invitation to Martí. He did so in a very circumspect letter to his "distinguished compatriot." Martí accepted jubilantly. At the last moment news of a fire sweeping through Tampa almost kept him from going. But Trujillo, with obvious irony, persuaded him that "even the Tampa fire would help make the desire for your visit there even hotter." . . .

Gray and congested cities, the tawny-red countryside of a dying, luxuriant Indian Summer, were left behind. As the train rolled onward towards the South the landscape grew more bland. A more transparent light sifted through the ever-present pines. In the dry gleanings of cotton plantations there still remained a few straggling white cotton-bolls, a few frightened dark faces. . . . Tobacco fields and drying-sheds full of the bronzy-yellow leaves rolled by. The light became golden. A happy excitement within told Martí that he was on his way to the tropics, the road to Cuba. . . . The next afternoon the countryside turned damp and gloomy, the landscape of the sand regions. But there came a moment when the sun broke through a clearing in the woods and spotlighted the delicate, proud elegance of young pines growing straight up among the black trunks of the older, fallen ones. The traveller kept a strong impression of that dramatic glimpse.

The Cubans of the South were calling him. They were new people, modest folk who had not wanted to go too far from the sun of their Island: Cuban tobacco workers, landowners and members of professions who were obliged to flee into exile and, in a strange land, to take up the most menial work. They were folk as open-hearted as children, desperately homesick, and without that hard shell of suspicion which a large city obliges one to grow for armor. And without the evasive shyness of the foreigner, because Tampa and Key West were their own, were almost their own creation, and because there they were in the majority. . . .

How was it Martí had not thought about them before? How was it he had not remembered that these colonies in the far South were like subsidiaries of Cuba, populous and active cells always supporting even the riskiest revolutionary undertakings? . . . He had preferred not to advance himself, not to create hopes he could not yet satisfy. He had had, besides, to overcome that fear of his "seeming guilty now and then of being a monopolist in matters of representation and authority." . . .

Now at last his strong intuition told him that the hour was imminent when his structure of words would begin to take shape on a solid foundation.

He reached Tampa on the 25th, at midnight. Rain was coming down in a torrent. Fifty men or more were huddled together on the station platform at Ibor City, where Martí left the train. Faces white and dark; eager faces; faces merely curious. . . . By the light of lanterns everybody used there at night to watch out for snakes and alligators the small procession sloshed through the sandy streets.

On the following morning Rubiera's Hotel, where Martí

was staying, was invaded at an early hour by the organizing committee: Néstor Leonelo Carbonell and his oldest son, Eligio; Ramón Rivero, a local newspaperman; Andrés Sánchez Iznaga, Cornelio Brito. . . . It was a glorious day. The sun baked the sand of the streets, the few red brick buildings, the small wooden houses isolated on their whitewashed posts. On many of them garlands and little Cuban flags fluttered in the breeze blowing from the Gulf.

A Cuban tobacconist had placed on the map of the United States his name along with that of this Tampa suburb, Ibor City. His factory actually stood in the very center of the Cuban section, where one seldom heard anything but Spanish. Led by Rivero, "reader" in that large establishment, Martí and his companions entered the spacious workshop pungent with the odor of Cuban tobacco leaf. The substitute reader, who was entertaining the workers, stopped speaking. There was a moment of confused silence and then the workmen, almost all of them Cubans, stood up and greeted their visitor with staccato taps of their leaf-folders on the rolling-tables.

Martí knew the reactions of the masses too well not to appreciate that the greeting was one of mere respect. He saw, too, on faces here and there fleeting ironic glances. He understood: These Cuban workers were too familiar with the glow of vain words, the incandescence of fund-raising visitors . . . and no results. He would not be one more to defraud them.

That night, the large banquet room of the Liceo Cubano was filled to capacity. On the walls above the heads of the crowd there was a series of crayon sketches of Cuban notables and a star-studded, tri-color band of bunting. When the curtain rose revealing the group of organizers on the small stage, Martí among them, pale, leaning slightly forward, his hands gripping the back of a chair, the ovation shook the ancient wooden building. The outburst was silenced by Perucho Figueredo's martial hymn which brought the multitude religiously to their feet. Ramón Rivero introduced Martí. González, the stenographer brought from Key West for the occasion, broke the points of three pencils. Martí walked to the front of the stage: "For Cuba in torment the first word . . ."

The speech he made was a model of oratorical tactics. He had to meet the challenges of expectancy, a taste in language formed in the rhetorical school of demagogy, a certain hangover of subtle mistrust, all rather unevenly mixed into the somewhat improvised enthusiasm over his visit—Martí was, after all, the man reputed to have deserted Gómez and Maceo in '84, and later, opposed to Ruz. . . . He had, in short, to mobilize that mass, heterogeneous and rather primitive, not just to join the movement but also to stir them to immediate action; and yet he could not be false to himself or sacrifice his doctrine of "foundation" to revolutionary opportunism.

One by one these problems on which he had meditated during his trip were beautifully resolved in his speech. He quietly acknowledged their cordial reception, which gave him new strength for "the agony of building" and he greeted this spiritual fragment of Cuba in which the "strength of our laboring Country" was being proved. And then he faced at once any possible suspicion by affirming the democratic principle that governed his own life:

> If in things concerning my country I should be given the choice of one good over all others . . . this would be the good I should choose: I should want the cornerstone of our Republic to be the devotion of Cubans to the full dignity of man. . . . Either the Republic has as its foundation the basic character of every one of her sons, his habit of working with his hands and thinking for himself and respecting, as if it were a matter of family honor, the

> unrestricted freedom of others—in short, the passion for man's essential worth—or else the Republic is not worth a single one of the tears of our women nor a solitary drop of a brave man's blood.

Impressed by this austere tone, to which it was not accustomed, the people listened in breathless silence. Martí knew that one makes great progress in convincing others by assuming that they are already convinced, so he spoke of "this glorious night of resurrection," of the "subtle understanding" already reached between Cuba and her emigré children, of an existing "faith determined and methodical." It would seem, listening to him, that the revolution was about to break out. Convinced of this, the audience erupted in thundering applause.

Yes: the revolution was imminent. But it had to be fought with a deep awareness of its purpose. It was not a mere matter of establishing new forms, leaving the "colonial soul" still intact, but a matter of organizing Cuban realities in and for liberty. To cope with this great challenge, which depended for its solution in fusing, through love and respect, the diversities of the social elements in the Island, it was urgent to discard all false fears: the excessive fear of the encroachments of a militarist clique of veterans; fear of the Negro—"the generous Negro, the Negro brother"; fear of the Spaniard, a fear gratuitous also because "we are fighting in Cuba for the liberty of man and there are many Spaniards who love liberty"; and lastly the faint-hearted fear of those Yankee admirers who believed Cubans would lack the ability to live for themselves the liberty they might achieve.

To this array of foolish fears Martí added, perhaps remembering Roa's book:

> the fear of the tribulations of war incited by impure people in the pay of the Spanish government; a fear of

> going barefoot, which is now a very common way of going in Cuba, since, between the thieves and those who help them, no one in Cuba has shoes, except the thieves and their accomplices . . .

This controversial aside, unusually bitter, was to have its consequences, but the audience had no time then to weigh the allusion. Fascinated by that lightning storm of phrases prophesying war and its doom-splendors, and creating the bright image of a free homeland at peace with itself, his listeners waited now for nothing but the call to action, and Martí no longer hesitated:

> Now! Form your ranks! Countries are not created by wishful thinking in the depths of the soul . . . Let us rise so that liberty does not run any risk in its hour of triumph through disorder or indolence or impatience in its preparation. Let us rise for the real Republic. . . . Let us place around the star in the new flag this formula of triumphant love: "With all, for the good of all."

It was as if the call to action had been an order for actual mobilization. The front rows of the audience advanced towards the stage, where Martí found himself choked by embraces. Women, standing on chairs, waved hats, gloves, handkerchiefs . . . People cried, laughed. Shouts of *Viva* multiplied. The racket of the applause drowned out Perucho Figueredo's music, strains reminiscent of Mozart's *Don Giovanni.*

The next day was November 27th, and the twentieth anniversary of the shooting of the medical students. That sacred memory had by now become a symbol of Cuban sorrows and no year seemed so fitting as this one, since it was coincident with Martí's visit, for a memorial gathering.

He spent the day "busy with creating," exploring the opinions of the leaders of the colony on a preliminary revolutionary agreement. Among patriotic organizations existing in Tampa one had particularly interested him for its discipline: the Cuban Patriotic League, founded by Ramón Rivero in 1889, along the lines of the secret political organization which had just been founded in Key West as the Cuban Convention. Although a certain rivalry existed between the two colonies over craftsmanship in cigar-making, their community of interest in patriotic and labor matters sustained a cordial relationship between them through a constant visiting back and forth and coöperation in political initiatives.

Martí did not have to spur the League to action. The idea of gathering all revolutionary groups together in a common cause, using the already existing local organizations as a basis, was met with a jubilant approval accented by pride that Tampa should be doing the pioneering. On the afternoon of the 27th, the agreement was reached and Martí appointed to draft the resolutions.

That night he walked out on the stage of the Liceo, his spirits higher than ever: The dream of his life was taking shape in reality. He felt himself more attuned to raise a chant of optimism than to evoke the tragic image of '71. Perhaps this state of mind was responsible for his speech being so generous-hearted, so lyric in accent, and so serenely fearless in its tender vision of death. He won over to magnanimity even that audience of resentful Cubans in whom bitterness for all the past injustices simmered or boiled. "Crime itself can be redeemed by love." It was "not like Cubans to live like jackals in a cage, milling around their own hate." Those deaths had been the heroic yeast which liberty needed for leavening. What mattered now was to sing "the hymn of life before the not-to-be-forgotten tomb." In the final instant of improvisation a fleeting vision of the countryside in the neighborhood of Tampa came to Martí, and its symbolic usefulness:

> Suddenly the sun broke through a clearing in the woods and there in the dazzling of the unexpected light I saw above the yellowish grass proudly rising from among the black trunks of the fallen trees the flourishing branches of new pines. That is what we are: new pines!

With the pleasure simple people take in natural figures of speech, everyone was repeating that phrase the next day: New pines!

That last day there Martí wanted to devote to further work with the rank and file. He visited the large factories, "holes in the wall," and the homes of the poorest. Dark-skinned Cubans came up to him to shake his hand in reverential gesture, and he in turn patted their shoulders, kissed their ragged children, instinctively knowing the right and affectionate things to say, as if he had known them all his life.

He had noted in Tampa that, probably because of the influence of the Yankee example, there was a certain condescension in the attitude of the white Cubans towards their Negro compatriots. That had to be checked. With great finesse Martí told Cornelio Brito—who because of his intelligence and wealth was outstanding among his race—what *La Liga* was doing in New York, the spirit of fraternity and justice cultivated there. That same afternoon in Brito's house the Tampa League for Instruction was founded, with thirty members. Another link in the chain.

Only a few hours were left to him in that Cuban outpost, and Martí saw sad faces confronting him. Tampa had lived two days of jubilant excitement, greatly surprising the native Americans who were puzzled by such gayety without any apparent reason for it. Now, to bid Martí farewell, the

Cubans went once more to the Liceo, in their Sunday best. It was hot and crowded, there were shouts of *Viva*, and flags were fluttering in the main hall. There were trays of sweets and glasses on the billiard tables. Among the flowers was a large placard reading: "Viva José Martí."

Ramón Rivero, drafted as orator, and Candán, president of the Patriotic League, both gave toasts. So did Cornelio Brito, the Negro leader. A girl, Carmita Carbonell, bashfully presented him with the costly pen and ink stand the Cubans of Tampa gave him as a memento. Martí's voice trembled when he rose to speak: Never had the character of man seemed more beautiful to him nor Cuba more certain of her destiny. His words were full of tenderness, hope, enthusiasm. Successive waves of what seemed like electrical charges swept through the multitude, which finally could not restrain itself and interrupted him with a noisy ovation. Rivero then stepped out of the crowd with paper in hand and, after many strenuous gestures signalling for silence, solemnly read the Resolutions of the Cuban emigrés of Tampa which proclaimed the urgent need for "gathering in one common action, republican and free, all the sincere revolutionary elements" through uniting the local exile groups.

The crowd applauded with only a vague awareness of experiencing an historic moment. Martí then set out for the station, followed by some four thousand people, in the midst of pageantry, music and flags, and took the train for New York. The police followed the procession without the faintest notion of what it was all about.

On his way to New York he remembered that it was exactly twenty years since his vow in Madrid. . . .

In the satisfaction of accomplishment, in the tenderness of gratitude, there was only one small grain of melancholy: To think that there, behind him, so close to Tampa, was the small, barren island of the Key, another honorary fragment of Cuban soil, the most loyal and worthy of the refugee colonies.

How he would have liked to draw to himself the entire South, united in the decisive work! But this leader was also a poet, a man of scruples and almost a fanatic in his respect for spontaneity.

Fortunately, Destiny has its own solutions. Martí had hardly returned when Key West's *El Yara* ran a brief editorial commenting on his visit to Tampa and insinuating that Key West was no less deserving. Martí wrote a letter of thanks to José Dolores Poyo, editor of the paper, and took advantage of the opportunity it offered. No one was so eager as he to "put himself sincerely in the hands of the Key," but would they not think there, on seeing him arrive without any special reason, that he came "because he liked to be in the public eye, or as a self-elected politician, or as an uninvited guest?" By the officiousness of such a visit would they not be afraid that he wanted to impose his own ideas upon the Cubans of Key West—he, "a man of simplicity and tenderness who trembles on thinking that his brothers might fall into the mendacious and authoritarian politics of evil republics?"

The letter—an exceedingly able one—was an invitation to be invited. But the Key had anticipated him. Francisco María González, the stenographer, had gone home full of excitement over the great day in Tampa, and a group of young men—Angel Peláez, Gualterio García and other enthusiasts—had started a drive to "bring Martí." They met reluctance and resistance, especially on the part of the veterans. Fernando Figueredo, who had been with Maceo in Baraguá and was one of the most zealous patriot leaders of the colony, made a wry face. But the boys were not to be stopped. They went from door to door asking for money to pay for Martí's trip. One well-to-do Cuban refused: "I have money to buy rifles, not to pay for speeches!" Others declined to "let themselves be exploited by a busybody."

The little group of pioneers, however, formed into a committee by this time, knew how to mobilize the reserves of confidence and other savings. At the end of two weeks of money-raising, a sufficient sum had been collected. By the eve of Martí's arrival the good Key had recovered its faith, a recovery largely stimulated by the knowledge that Martí had fallen ill during his stay in Tampa: Opportunists are always in good health.

On Christmas Day, 1891, when the small steamer *Olivette*, with Martí, Eligio Carbonell, Candán, Brito and others accompanying him from Tampa standing on deck, was being moored to the dock, a shouting crowd wecomed them with bands and flags. The aged José Francisco Lamadriz stepped forward to greet him who had been his companion in patriotic labors eleven years before, on Calixto García's committee.

"I embrace the old revolution," Martí said in greeting him.

"And I embrace the new revolution," the old man answered.

The two patriots remained in each other's arms in a long moment of poignant silence. One of the Tampans had a happy thought about the new pine reaching its branches to those of the old. The crowd broke into applause and escorted Martí to the Hotel Duval. There a bold youth with courageous self-assurance climbed up on a chair and harangued the crowd. Martí asked for the name of that born orator: Jenaro Hernández. He embraced him, climbed on the improvised rostrum and delivered a beautiful greeting shot through with heroic allusions. His emaciated condition and feverish intensity of appearance seemed to heighten the accents of his speech. Towards the end he became very weak, but when he stepped down from the chair he had already won the crowd.

That same night, remaining on his feet through sheer

will-power, he spoke not once, but three times at the banquet given in his honor; the Cuban gathering had an insatiable appetite for oratory. The effort laid him low with broncho-laryngitis. He wrote to Quesada:

> In bed, very ill. Great worth in the people and many noble hearts. My bedside is the committee-room. Here I am surrounded by a guard of love. But I cannot write, and I shall not leave until all is ready.

From his bed, literally, he drew people together, discussed, listened, planned. Entrusted with congratulating him in the name of the Cuban Convention, a delegation composed of Lamadriz, Poyo and Fernando Figueredo, the three most representative men in the colony, visited him. Martí knew that Figueredo did not like him. He had not been among those to receive him, nor had he attended the banquet. Now he confined himself to carrying out formally the resolution of the Convention. . . . With a certain emphasis, Figueredo himself described the secret activity carried out by that patriotic lodge since its founding by Gerardo Castellanos. He had collected funds, had spurred people to action, was in touch with the old leaders. . . . Martí listened and praised: "Everything is already done here!" he exclaimed tactfully.

Then he brought into action all his powers of persuasion. He explained his fears: the danger of a sudden, almost accidental, haphazard war, one without careful political education; the need to work, not for independence alone, but for the republic of tomorrow; he explained that since hatred was sterile, the war must be, for this reason, idealistic and civilian in origin; that victory would not be feasible without widespread support and sacrifice. . . .

Little by little Figueredo's face mellowed and brightened.

Without disturbing the illusion that "all is done" Martí succeeded in convincing his visitors that almost everything remained to be done. When they left, Figueredo extended both hands to Martí.

Three more days were spent in conversation. Having won good-will for himself, he sowed it among the rest. In Key West there persisted certain dissensions, unpleasant after-tastes of old political feuds between the followers of Aldama and those of Quesada, the two envoys from the Island, a civilian patriot and a general respectively, whose views of organization had clashed at the beginning of the Ten Years War. Martí's sincerity and clear, sacrificial summons to duty healed these rancors and injured prides. Men who had gone for years without speaking to one another now embraced in the sick man's room.

Finally the link was completed. Martí himself wrote the Bases for the Cuban Revolutionary Party—organizing a great chain of local organizations within a functional uniformity. When the plan was finished, he discussed it with Lamadriz, Poyo and Figueredo. He explained, discussed and satisfied objections. He added to it. At last, when the leaders declared their agreement, he exclaimed radiantly: "To work, then!" And he felt well once more.

That night at the meeting held at the San Carlos, the old Cuban club, his hour-long speech did not have the overtones of a faith tortured by waiting and uncertainty so noticeable in all his speeches of the last few years, but an accent of glorious positiveness. The correspondent for *El Porvenir* informed New York that Martí seemed "evangelical" to him.

With committee meetings and public functions, he could scarcely find time for all the informal parties to which he was invited. He paid attention to the poorest people. Cornelio Brito had convinced his friend Ruperto Pedroso, a

Negro saloon-keeper, that it was absolutely necessary to give a luncheon in Martí's honor in his home. Paulina, Pedroso's fearless wife, was not enthusiastic. She was an old-line patriot, a fanatical follower of Gómez and Maceo, men of action. And, moreover, there was no meat at this time at the Key. How could one have a luncheon party without meat? Ruperto suggested that her grandmother's prize kid might be sacrificed. And so, sacrificed it was. Martí found it tender and delicious, but he understood the dramatic antecedents of that capital dish, and Paulina's resentment. When the party was over, he kissed her on the forehead and said to her: "Paulina, you are going to help me a great deal here for Cuba." And Paulina began to laugh and cry at the same time.

That afternoon a Negro boy, bearing a standard and riding a black horse, spontaneously escorted the carriage in which Martí was making a tour of the tobacco factories; the one belonging to Eduardo Gato, the Cuban, gayly decorated to receive him; Soria's, which announced his arrival with an 18-gun salvo and a prolonged military trumpet call; *The Spanish Rose*, where the Spanish manager did not hesitate to embrace the Cuban who was preaching a war without hate. At the urging of tobacco workers he spoke in all the shops. Gato's employees presented him with a silver loving-cup and the women workers with a large cross made of tiny shells.

On the afternoon of the 5th, representatives of the political clubs of Key West and Tampa—Poyo, Teodoro Pérez, Rosendo García and others to a total of twenty-seven—gathered together at the Hotel Duval and discussed fully, under the presidency of Martí, the Tampa Resolutions and the Bases that Martí had drawn up for the Cuban Revolutionary Party. Intending to refer several of these resolutions to the various societies represented, as well as to any others that might wish to join the larger movement, Martí was

SPANISH CAVALRYMAN
ON A TEXAS BRONCHO

charged with the formal drafting of the Statutes thus approved in principle.

Days later he himself, on his return through Tampa, obtained the approval of the Patriotic League. The Cuban Revolutionary Party was born.

Chapter Twenty-five

THE CUBAN REVOLUTIONARY PARTY

A triumph is no more than a duty.
Martí: Letter to Peláez, *1892*

IN NEW YORK, bitterness.

Martí's speeches in Tampa had been printed as handbills by enthusiasts there and had been sent to Havana, where they got under the skin of certain veterans. Ramón Roa, furious, wanted to challenge Martí for the raw reference to his book in his first Tampa speech. His war-time friends dissuaded him, agreeing to send Martí a letter signed by Brigadier-General Enrique Collazo. The letter was published in Havana's *La Lucha* on January 6th. Martí found it in New York on his return.

It was a resentful brief, in harsh language, highlighted by the acids of Roa's literary irony. Collazo noted that he was refraining from starting a discussion of the "pretty solutions" Martí offered in his first speech on Cuba's problem. What the veterans of Zanjón could not take were his references to Roa's book, *A pie y descalzo*.[1] "Is it possible, even after all these years, that exiles can still be frightened by the true relation of trials, struggles and misfortunes which we faced during the Ten Years War?" A cowardly assumption; Martí was insulting this new generation by believing it capable of fearing war because of such an account. This fear could only be explained in one who, hurt by Spain in childhood, was

[1] Barefoot Soldiers.

not courageous enough to take to the savannahs, "valuing his self-love higher than his love for Cuba"; in one who preferred "at a later date to seek office as representative of the Liberal Party in Congress"; in one "who now poses as an apostle and wheedles money out of the exiles by fatuous speeches. . . ." The letter ended with a taunting boast:

> Let us tell you, Señor Martí, that here, face to face with the Government, we keep our character as Cubans and revolutionaries; we have not engaged in any dealings unworthy of, or insulting to, the memories of our forebears; we are today what we were in 1878. . . . If the hour of sacrifice should come again, perhaps we should not be able to shake hands with you in the savannahs of Cuba, because surely you would still be giving lessons in patriotism to exiles, in the shadow of the American flag.

Under Collazo's signature three other veterans indicated their agreement by signing their names.

Confined to bed, exhausted by the feverish days in the South, Martí read and re-read this "unhappy letter." It was a challenge to a man—with all the self-denying integrity the word had always implied for him. "The impassioned are the first-born of the world," he had written at one time, but by passion he had meant love and suffering in the spiritual sense: "There are no conquests more definitive than those of gentleness." . . . One had, naturally, to rise to the occasion, to submit one's self humble and serene to the tribunal of one's own judgment: What did his conscience tell him?

The stream, sweet and bitter, of the past swept through him. He remembered his harassed childhood under the watchful gaze of his father; his impulses to patriotic action checked and guided by Mendive; his pamphleteering rebellion; the horrible experience of prison. . . . Memories of his first exile, poor and sick, in Spain came vividly to mind, and his activity for Cuba at an age usually spent in enjoying one's self. . . . Then, the heavy burden of family obligations in Mexico; the restraint from useless immolation in a lost war; the return to homeland and the sacrifice of everything—everything: certainty of security and worldly honors and even new-born happiness—in his first adult opportunity. Was it accident, or fate, that turned him away from the savannahs in the period of warfare? And from the time of his second exile, twelve years, twelve long years of keeping watch for Cuba by example, by word, by restraint . . . what did they know about the bitter duty of self-restraint? In Greek, doing was called agony; he had done nothing but go through agony twenty years for Cuba, in the hope of her great hour!

On the 10th he wrote to Eligio Carbonell: "I am not unworthy, Eligio, of such great affection as yours. I am not what the letter claims I am, but what you believe me and want me to be." And on the 12th, now calm after the storm, he answered Collazo in a lengthy letter so generously objective in tone, so vigorous in refutation and so free from bitterness that the veteran immediately repented of having provoked it. After political clarifications and polemics in which the opportunity of indicating the founding of the Cuban Revolutionary Party was not lost, he touched on personal phases of the attack with sincere dignity:

> And now, Señor Collazo, what shall I tell you of myself? If my life defends me I can cite nothing that will support me more than that. And if my life accuses me, I shall be able to say nothing in rebuttal. Let my life speak for me. I know it has been useful and meritorious, and I can say this without arrogance because it is every man's duty to work so that his life will be like that.

Public accusations, however, require concrete answers. In a few vigorous phrases Martí vindicated his past:

> Never, Señor Collazo, was I the man you describe. In the first war, although a child, poor and sick, I never failed to do my full patriotic duty; and at times it was a very active duty. Burn the tongue of whoever may have told you I served "the mother country," Señor Collazo. Burn the tongue of anyone who tells you that I in any way served the Liberal Party, or that in the matter of the nomination I did more than listen to those who came in vain to tempt my oratorical vanity. And I shall keep ready for war and if I should be charged to try for independence through peace, I would defer and try that. As for my wheedling the exiles' savings from them, have you not been sufficiently answered by the popular indignation meetings held by the exiles of Tampa and Key West? Have you not been told that in the Key the Cuban women workers themselves made a cross as a gift for me? I think, Señor Collazo, that I have given my country, ever since I first knew the sweetness of her love, as much as a man can give. I believe I have, on many occasions, laid at her feet fortune and honor. I think that I do not lack sufficient courage to die in her defense.

The letter closed with a solemnly provocative gesture. Whether Martí had interpreted Collazo's parting shot as a challenge to a duel, or whether he feared a public inference to that effect, he quietly stooped to pick up the gauntlet. He could not afford to let any doubt prevail concerning his personal valor.

> And now, Señor Collazo, it is fitting that I refer to what you say about "shaking hands in the savannahs." . . . I

live sadly by obscure labor because I renounced, not long ago, for the sake of my country, my most lucrative means of support. My lodgings are cold and scarcely suited to entertaining. But there is no need to wait for the savannahs, Señor Collazo, to shake hands; on the contrary, I shall be pleased to meet you at whatever time and place suits you best.

Fortunately the matter never went further than the duel of letters. After many meetings of protest in support of Martí in the colonies of the South and even in New York, the exiles of the Key decided with good political common sense to send a delegation to Havana; this closed the matter satisfactorily.

For the rest, the incident—which seemed ominous at the start, since it tended to create dissension between the veterans and the new revolutionaries—turned out to be surprisingly beneficial. Martí, up to then hardly more than a name to the Island, now became known throughout Cuba. He stood out, as a visionary, a demagogue, or apostle, depending on one's point of view; in any case, an agitator to be reckoned with. And his clash with Collazo had defined positions.

The protest of revolutionary availability in the Brigadier's letter came at a time when the atmosphere was electric with tensions: Polavieja's reactionary control; the failure of the movement for economic reforms started the year before; the quiet desperation with which the autonomists agreed upon abstention from the elections, while those for union with Spain were cocky over Romero Robledo's appointment as Overseas Minister. Máximo Gómez had written in November from Santo Domingo, where he had retired after working for a time on the Panama Canal, to his old friend and companion in arms, Serafín Sánchez: . . . "now is the time or never, and there is no time to lose." And he charged

Sánchez to get in touch secretly with Martí in New York. It was the beginning of a reconciliation. . . . Martí promised to keep the General informed of what was going on.

But it was necessary to create the political conditions necessary for war well in advance, to perfect the civil mechanism which would guarantee authority, restraint and support for the undertaking. . . . Martí lost no time in organizing New York. As always, the big city was his problem. Old contempts, "resentful reservations" and "jealousies of leadership" were embedded in the Cuban colony there. In *El Porvenir* Enrique Trujillo, Cuban and journalist above all else, had published a report of the southern visit. On the 17th of February, at Hardmann Hall, Martí could give a more lively and extended version. On that trip he had had his first real contact with the Cuban mass. And he had found the soul of his people beautiful.

> What I have to say before my voice is stilled and my heart ceases to beat in this world is that my country possesses all the qualities necessary for the winning and maintenance of liberty.

His account of his trip was full of an epic optimism which could reach and move even the exiles of a great city. He stirred them with his pride, his confidence, even with the overtones of personal satisfaction pervading his words no matter how hard he tried to subordinate his own achievement.

Now they would no longer scorn him. That night the crowd left the meeting of *Los Independientes* not with a flash-fire patriotism as of old, but with a burning determination. *Vivas* for Martí were more plentiful than they had ever been. He was surrounded by the good and the poor, almost all of them newcomers, sensitive to new words.

Clubs were established which in a few days notified the

Key by telegram of their acceptance of the Bases and Statutes of the Party. *Los Independientes* followed suit. Only Trujillo believed that all this was being done too quickly and without sufficient discussion; that the Key wanted to impose itself on other exile centers, and Martí on everybody: "I shall keep still and keep working," was Martí's answer to *Porvenir's* remarks.

Trujillo's attacks increased, and since it was not practical for the Party to go along without a favorable press, Martí agreed to start a new paper, particularly since the League had been wanting for some time to establish one of its own. *Patria,* as it was named, first appeared on March 14th, the expenses of that first issue being met by the tobacco workers of New York. Martí's name did not appear as editor, nor was it declared to be the organ of the Revolutionary Party. But it published in full the Bases—"which this newspaper respects and upholds," and an article which needed no signature.

This essay, entitled "Our Ideas" was, in fact, the basic program of the revolution and its instrumental war. All of the sensitivity for the human and democratic in Martí's political thought, his sense of "wing" and "root," his vision of a Republic "with all and for all," were condensed in those six compact columns of prose. Both the Spaniard who loved justice and the down-trodden Negro found his word of love there. To gather forces together and to keep faith with an already historic thought, the Manifesto emphasized that the cause of Cuba was also that of Puerto Rico. The Antilles, Martí was shortly to say in *Patria,* "must stand together or together they will disappear from the annals of free peoples."

So it was not strange that he entrusted the responsibility for editing *Patria* to a Puerto Rican who, ever since his arrival in New York two years before, had impressed Martí by the frankness and vigor of his writing. Sotero Figueroa, who was a mulatto, had immediately won an influential position in the League through his literary talents, a fact Martí did not overlook.

He picked his other assistants with the same care. Gonzalo de Quesada had just arrived from Argentina, where Sáenz Peña had taken him as his secretary after the American Conference. He had returned with considerable prestige and the designation as Argentinian Consul in Philadelphia, a post he had shortly resigned, following Martí's sensational example. In that youth with flowing hair, gentle eyes and exaggerated mustache, Martí saw his spiritual double and he made him Secretary of the Party.

Estrada Palma, great civilian saint of the Ten Years period, was the elder statesman, conveniently located near by at his school in Central Valley. Benjamín Guerra, a respected and thriving tobacco merchant, took charge of the funds.

"Good men," wrote Martí in *Patria*, "can now be taken in by the armful." He did not note that he had performed beforehand the miracle of inspiring confidence through which men's goodness could be exercised. To the leaders in the South he wrote letters constantly, letters filled with basic ideas, with "roots" as he put it, and above all with the root of his tenderness. With delicate tact he played on every string of response—self-respect, love of home, love of country. He saw to it that no feelings were hurt. Towards Figueredo, still slightly aloof because of Collazo's letter, he was particularly affectionate. When he learned that a Key West patriot was resentful through some petty jealousy, he wrote to Peláez:

> Seek him out without flattery or fear. Do not give him any reason—for there isn't any—to think himself ignored by us. Attend to this immediately and do your best. Ask some favor of him . . .

He mixed spirit and speed with his affection and diplomacy. He did not give enthusiasm a chance to cool off. "What doesn't go forward, goes backward." He was afraid that extended discussion and formalities would delay the official constitution of the Party, which was to follow ratification of the Bases and Statutes by all the clubs. This fear, no doubt united with that element of compulsive absorption characteristic of every authentic leader, gave to Marti's organizing a decidedly personal and expeditious character.

At last, on April 8th, the clubs of the South, New York and Philadelphia simultaneously elected Martí as delegate, an office calling for yearly election, and in which the Statutes invested the general management of the Party. Benjamín Guerra was elected treasurer. Two days later, on the anniversary of the Constituent Assembly of Guáimaro, the Party and its framework of representatives and local member councils were formally proclaimed in their respective constituencies.

Martí collapsed from overwork. From his bed he dictated his official message of acceptance. "I shall confirm it," he wrote Poyo, "by completing the cleansing of my life, if it is not already free from all thought or fault which could hamper my absolute service to my country."

It was necessary, of course, for him now to make himself more invulnerable than ever. He was in a position of authority and "the tall tree invites the throwing of stones." Petty intrigues bubbled around him. Dissent about some minor Antillean celebration more or less touched off a disagreeable incident in the Literary Society. *El Porvenir* continued its opposition, denying that the Partido Revolucionario had any reason to exist as such, labelling its organization as forced, and accusing Martí—without naming him—of exercising a civilian dictatorship. *Patria* did not answer. But in the face of that "resolutely hostile and disturbing" attitude, the Advisory Body of New York, over which Juan Fraga presided, decided publicly to disavow Trujillo's newspaper.

From Havana, where there was official alarm over the progress of the exile organization, the Government mobilized spies and stool-pigeons and spread the insidious rumor that Martí, for his own gain, had robbed emigrés of their savings. The delegate might have revealed that only lately he had just had occasion to throw out of his office a campaign worker for Blaine who had come to propose financial backing in exchange for four thousand Cuban votes in Florida. Martí limited himself to private comment:

> It is a pity that I may not say . . . that my derby hat cost me two dollars on the Bowery and I've already had it for six months. . . . I dread malice, but my answer is in my heart and there it sweetens the bitterness. . . .

Chapter Twenty-six

THE "OLD MAN"

If he were not generous he would be useless . . .
—Martí

REVOLUTIONARY ACTION must comprise three principal undertakings: to extend and consolidate the Party, adding new elements to it and winning recognition for it inside and outside of Cuba; to raise funds for war, and to organize its military contingents.

As soon as he was elected Delegate, Martí applied himself to this triple task with impatient activity, but at the same time with an exact sense of its possibilities.

> I would like to be lightning and cover it all; every duty; let others reap the glory . . . But the heights are not scaled in one leap. The first step is our solid unity. Then let us start to climb without waiting for more of an agreement than is possible; wars are not an ivory-tower study, nor like the created pages of a novel. . . .

Tampa, Key West and New York were already working. In Chicago and Philadelphia, new local clubs were organized. Martí wrote incessantly to them and to other less populous Cuban centers, putting into his letters, as if they were meant to be read in public, the eloquence he was unable to take to them in person. He was greatly concerned that the revolution be the fruit of a collective will and not of an individual inspiration; yet at the same time he had to reconcile with that democratic spirit the executive authority necessary for speedy and coherent action. He advised the Advisory Councils in tactics, and to avoid hurting anyone's feelings he was extremely considerate and watchful in his speech. His communications abroad, where it was more difficult to impose the flexible, but sound, organization needed by the Party, were so explanatory in detail and so mindful of local spirit that they commanded enthusiastic respect. By May the chain was almost complete and the understanding perfect.

The principal function of the clubs was to feed the revolutionary treasury. In that regard, Martí circulated detailed instructions. He left to local discretion the manner of collection. Each club was to withold one half of what it collected, thus accumulating its own war fund; the other half would be sent to the Delegate for expenses of preparatory action. It did not matter to him that this second destination of the funds might lend itself to villainous insinuations. The poverty of the Delegate could be seen in his celluloid cuffs, and he knew that calumny is one of the rewards of authority. As for *Los Independientes*, always so jealous of their old leadership, he confined himself to reassuring them that "the work of action which now engaged him is of the greatest necessity and delicacy and is real war work."

Martí would say no more. The naturally communicative man had suddenly learned the discipline of rigorous silence, of a discretion impenetrable to all curiosity and all doubt. Secretly he gathered supplies for war while *Patria* kept emigré centers at white heat by preaching principles and examples from which the note of hate was absent. "Keep the paper on a high level, free from petty allusions," Martí urged Quesada from the South, where he had returned to put the rest of Florida "on a war footing."

He travelled in the company of Poyo, Roloff and Serafín Sánchez for a week through towns which had large Cuban groups. Jacksonville, St. Petersburg, Thomasville, St. Augustine, Ocala, competed as strenuously as they could with

Tampa and Key West. The enthusiasm and willingness to sacrifice that Martí was able to evoke were incredible. Even liberal Spaniards and "cold" North Americans were won over. Blond farmers and merchants applauded his lecture in English on the Cuban ideal when he spoke one night in the principal theatre in Ocala. Since appearances were important on that occasion, Martí had been forced to borrow a frock coat from one of his countrymen; his own was too nearly worn out from age and hard use to be worn in the presence of "strangers."

In the Key, where he was received with a proud affection, he reached an agreement with veteran leaders who lived there to have them sign a public pledge of enlistment. His purpose was to stir up an invincible revolutionary momentum before Spain could thoroughly prepare to resist it. Answering to a thorough-going concept of the revolution, which Calixto García alone, before him, had had, Martí wanted the new war to break out simultaneously throughout the whole Island as an expression of unanimous will. His democratic zeal and republican foresight made him reject the imposition implied in a war without internal coöperation.

It was necessary, therefore, to organize the latent forces in Cuba for revolt. A difficult task, since separatist groups there were confused and dispersed, connections being kept only in the eastern part of the Island. In Havana there were a great many tame wiseacres who held the idea of revolution to be madness. One of them, on a visit to New York, tried to convince Martí that there was nothing in the Island atmosphere to indicate the threatening storm he was imagining. Martí answered: "But you are talking to me about the air, and I am talking to you about the soil."

Martí had spaded deep in it. He had profited from the contacts he had established with the Cuban Convention at the Key; he had got in touch with his old comrade-conspirator in Havana, Juan Gualberto Gómez; he had obtained from veterans in all the clubs intelligence on revolutionary conditions in their own bailiwicks; he had taken a census of leaders and soldiers known to be available in and out of the Island. Armed with this information, he profited from his trip to the South by arranging in Key West for the dispatch of a secret agent to Cuba.

The man chosen was Gerado Castellanos, one of the founders of the Convention. Since Castellanos was in the tobacco business, he could travel throughout the perilous western part of the Island without arousing suspicion. He was intelligent, conscientious, and combined in himself "the enthusiasm for noble ideas and an expert, unswayable knowledge of human nature." The instruction sheet which Martí gave him was a model of organizational strategy:

> Explain the greatness, the breadth and the energy of the Party. . . . Find out for me all the revolutionary elements in Las Villas [the Central Region], and the men and the local opinions which have to be reckoned with. Arrange for me . . . so that in every region there will be a nucleus in harmony, and in touch, with nuclei in other regions and all of them in regular communication—secured by *them* to avoid risks—with the Delegate . . .

He especially charged Castellanos to insist on the character of the new revolutionary politics—its refusal to exploit hatred of the Spaniard or the autonomist, its discretion towards the United States, its democratic integrity and completeness.

> And above all, Gerardo, lasso and corral for me any *talker's* revolution, one without enough reality and revolutionary strength, without good will and moderation and justice enough to start the war and finish it. . . .

Martí was greatly concerned about this. He was not the only one creating a following. In Las Villas a local leader was making ambiguous progress, somewhat under the secret protection of double-dealing autonomists. Other leaders with higher motives were recruiting supporters by invoking the name of Máximo Gómez. One of them, Luis Lagomasino, had arrived at the Key three months before, firing the enthusiasm of the veterans for an uprising to take place August 25th. Martí arrived in time to smother that premature impetuousness. With Castellanos he sent orders postponing any rising until further notice: "Insist, without anger, heart to heart, the danger of entering into that reckless and aimless revolution suddenly announced."

Martí was not unaware of the fact that these threats of unruliness stemmed from the old suspicion of the veterans and were nourished by the lack of an ostensible military leader in the movement. As soon as the more sanguine older men were out of the reach of his words and his personal charm there arose in them again the nostalgia for a *caudillo* —a chieftain. As soon as he had come back to the North, Serafín Sánchez urged him to come to an agreement with Gómez. Martí had been promising and delaying.

No one realized better than he the necessity of utilizing military prestige as soon as possible, bringing into the movement the most outstanding military leaders. The memory of his old clash with Gómez had now lost all bitterness; there was left only the distillation of experience. Martí knew that Gómez was the indispensable man because of his experience and influence. But he wanted, before inviting him, to set up all the civil checks which could prevent a falling into the errors of '84. And he could not violate his conscience as authorized representative of the Revolutionary Party: It was the latter's privilege and duty to select its military chief.

In his letter of June 29th, distributed to all Advisory Councils, asking that military men be polled on the matter, one seemed to detect a note of personal civilian regret, something like his renunciation of a glorious leadership.

> "It is," he said, "the hour in which duty commands the dearest dreams or the most romantic personal aspirations be sacrificed to the unification of our efforts. A sincere patriot must forego everything for Cuba—even the glory of falling in battle, defending her against her enemy . . ."

While the referendum—of which Martí could predict the result—was being taken, complications of various sorts kept him in a state of tense watchfulness and subtle activity.

The most dangerous was Spain's diplomatic moves against the Party. For several years Spanish consuls in the United States had had orders to watch Martí and they had grown weary of informing Madrid and Havana that they were upsetting themselves over a mere rabble-rouser. But now his speeches were being translated into action. War funds were being collected, arms were being purchased; in certain localities spying had revealed even Cuban military training maneuvers. Spain denounced these activities to Washington, and tried to rouse the press of the country against the Revolutionary Party. The press in general was favorable towards the Cubans, or indifferent about the cause; not so the State Department. Official symptoms of control at once made themselves felt. Washington needed unmistakable evidence before acting. Correspondence between the delegation and the clubs was opened; Martí, *Patria*, and the Front Street office were being watched.

"Mounted on lightning," Martí got wind of the enemy; he conferred, tied up loose ends, warded off attack. He warned the clubs over and over again to hide all evidence of warlike preparations. In the meantime he mobilized numerous friends—and they were no mean ones—in New York newspaperdom, particularly the aging Dana of the *Sun*, above whose building, forty years before, the banner of Narciso López had waved. The right of Cubans to peaceful propaganda was stoutly maintained by the newspapers. Martí prepared statements in English for readers of the United States, and in Spanish for the Island. And *Patria,* whose every issue was an indoctrinating essay, clarified and informed without let-up.

This incessant work obliged him to "multiply himself," to keep tirelessly on the go, and to spend many hours at his Front Street office, dictating so much that at times three secretaries were kept busy. After his evening class in Spanish —which was now just about his only source of income, because he had had to cut down his work for periodicals very considerably—dawn would find him still writing letters to his local lieutenants, letters full of drive and explanation, in which the similarity of subject matter did not prevent each one from being warmly individual and taking into account the particular psychological make-up of each recipient. Rarely did these letters close without some kindly allusion to his correspondent's wife or child, since Martí instinctively knew that in the hour of sacrifice much would be demanded of such beloved hostages to fortune; his letters also were apt to close with some very personal expression of concern or tenderness, rather than the conventional generality that one might expect.

Only the constant tension sustained him, defying his health, which was daily growing worse. Now and then a deep sigh, almost a moan, would escape from him. "I am like the old man in the French tale, very dashing in the salon while his rouge and his court dress bucked him up, but only a dried husk when homeward bound in his carriage with his make-up gone."

By the the middle of August the poll of the exile centers had decided in favor of Gómez as military chief. Martí, who, from the start, had decided to go to see the old leader himself, was delayed in the North by complications. Serafín Sánchez and Figueredo, suspicious of his attitude, wrote urging him to communicate with "the Old Man." Sánchez had just received a letter from Gómez indicating respect and admiration for Martí, but no liking.

> "Few know Martí as I do; it may be he does not know himself as well. Martí is all Cuban heart; he must concede that I adjudge his purity of motive immaculate; he could go to fight in the fields of Cuba for the redemption of his country with as much gallantry as the Luaces and the Agramontes—Martí is all this; but he lacks self-denial and he is inexplicable. He will never forgive you for what he may call your disdain which, in fact, is nothing more than a difference of opinion, and he will never be able to march in the same line with you, believing himself superior . . ."

It was evident the "Old Man" still resented the clash of '84. Presumably Serafín Sánchez passed on to Martí the pleasing part of this estimate. Martí answered: "Concerning Gómez, from whom I expect only great things, I am going to talk with the man himself to see how he can adapt his circumstances to public convenience and how he can organize without delay and without alarm." His answer to Figueredo's entreaties was more intimate:

> Why do you talk to me, Fernando, about efforts and sacrifices concerning Gómez? You know, don't you—although it may seem very awkward for me to say so—that in me there is not one particle of egoism or presumption, or of self-concern or self-aggrandizement; that death is my pillow and Cuba my only dream, and that my only concern is to smooth her difficulties and serve her? . . . I see myself at the gateway to my country, with my arms

> open, calling men to me and guarding the pass from danger. But only thus do I see myself, confident that I shall be felled to the earth by the very ones I have helped to save. But I shall smile then as I do now. And in this spirit, confident that the brave old man will come to know and understand before long, I shall go, with the firm honesty that he already knows in me, to see the glorious Gómez. I shall thus open a track of affection and those coming after me will have to travel the same road. . . .

He left for Santo Domingo. On the 11th of September, his spirit revelling in the landscape of palms that reminded him so poignantly of his own land, he arrived at the Gómez farm in the outskirts of Montecristi.

The meeting of the two patriots—which Martí himself was to describe in a memorable article—was of a simple greatness. Leading his horse by the halter "like one who has no right to be on horseback in the presence of his betters," Martí approached the dwelling house. The General came out to receive him and opened his arms. "In his very soul he could feel his eyes, scrutinizing and tender . . . and the old man again embraced the traveller in a long silence." Immediately the household was roused and coffee served—"strong coffee and a glass of good Beltran rum."

> "The first conversation was welcome rest for the soul, with that rare clarity which comes to men from the pleasure in doing good work. In the high-ceilinged room dimly lit by candles the first broad outlines of fatherland and liberty seemed like splashes of light."

Martí was given the General's own bed to sleep in. In the morning they exchanged views "on the trials of the past and the obligations of the future, on the fading causes of past defeat and the better arrangement and present elements of triumph. . . . There was no word which might make a son ashamed of his father, nor empty phrase nor any looking askance nor any suggestion of hateful ambition which might have tarnished the love, as deep as blood in the veins or the marrow in the bones, with which General Gómez had vowed himself to Cuba." From his hammock the Old Man carefully sized up Martí. He did not see in him now the desire for superiority or the rancor which he spoke of in his letter to Serafín.

Conversations continued for three days. When they had agreed on a course of action, Gómez accompanied Martí to Santiago de los Caballeros, and only there the Delegate, now certain, wrote for History his official letter to the military chief, inviting him "without fear of refusal, to undertake this new task although I have no other remuneration to offer you than the pleasure of sacrifice and the probable ingratitude of men." The General answered in military fashion: "From this moment you can count on my services."

With his mind greatly unburdened, Martí crossed the savannahs and hills on the way to the Dominican capital. He travelled full of the thought that love is a great cement for unity. To Henríquez y Carvajal, the great Dominican, who extended to Martí the honors of his city, he wrote in farewell: "To my way of thinking, if a people has the capacity to love, it is saved."

In Haiti he gauged the enthusiasm of its small Cuban colony and left it ready for action. He went to the neighboring island of Jamaica; there, too, he preached an eager patience. The 10th of October was "a spiritual rapture." Even the women and children, intoxicated by his speech, established revolutionary assistance clubs.

Antonio Maceo's wife and mother were living there, near Kingston. That other great military leader of the Ten Years War was now managing an agricultural colony in Costa Rica. He was just as distant emotionally. Martí had not wished to write him before interviewing Gómez. Now was

Grover Flint

A "SUPPLY TRAIN" FOR THE CUBAN ARMY

the right time to prepare his conquest through the social means of showing his interest in Maceo's family. The Delegate visited the two women, and his open-hearted tenderness overcame their surprised reserve. Mariana Grajales was eighty-five years of age but, on speaking of Cuba, her eyes still sparkled with the fire with which in '68 she sent her sons off to war, one by one. Martí listened to her, strongly moved. For a long time she held his hand between hers.

A few weeks later, on the night the clubs met in New York to hear Martí's account of his trip, there was in the atmosphere of the Hall a new emotion of respect. A year had passed since he had resigned his consular offices, an ostensible sacrifice of his material well-being for the cause of Cuba. Now he had just shown that he was capable of the most difficult sacrifice: the surrender of pride. At the banquet given for him someone toasted: "José Martí, the good man" and José María Vargas Vila,[1] a Colombian youth who had come to New York to campaign against the petty tyrants of America, emptied a cornucopia of metaphors in praise of the Cuban.

Patria gave a detailed account of Martí's trip in unsigned articles which could not, however, conceal the pen that wrote them, nor a certain simple and profound satisfaction of historic pride.

[1] Later a famous novelist.

Chapter Twenty-seven

PURNIO AND LAJAS

THE AGREEMENT of Montecristi clearly defined the fields of activity. On the one hand, civilian direction under Martí for all the preliminary work of coördination and preparation; on the other, the military leadership of Gómez for the hour of battle. Even before Martí's visit the old warrior had understood the need for this separation: "Among ourselves," he wrote Serafín Sánchez, "there prevail disagreements and even discord, and we could not very well act, disorganized as we are, as organizers."

To complete the phase of enlistment of the highest officers, Martí needed only to be sure of Maceo and to determine what part the Island was to play. On February 9, 1893, Maceo wrote to Ángel Guerra, who had just arrived in Costa Rica, in a rather angry mood:

> "I have not seen Martí lately nor have I received any letter from him inviting me to take part in his work of reorganization, a matter which, considering my natural disposition and lack of aptitudes for that sort of thing, I have not thought necessary; but if it is true that he has declared he is counting on me to wage war, no one is entitled to doubt it, because I do not believe that in such essential matters it is necessary to consult my wishes already sufficiently known in this regard by friends and strangers."

Martí was counting, in fact, on the bravery of the revered General as much as on his intelligence. For very obvious political reasons, Maceo could not be given the top military command—since the Spanish government could then attribute the rising as a Negro rebellion. But at the time that letter was written, Martí's first letter, in which he spoke of the new duties and his visit in Kingston with Maceo's wife and mother, was already on the way to Costa Rica.

In the meantime, Gerardo Castellanos had again been to Cuba and back. He had performed his first mission with such subtle brilliance and carefulness that Martí had immediately sent him on a similar mission to the eastern provinces. On his return, Castellanos did not tell about isolated disappointments; he did not tell, for example, about the separatist intellectual who laughed at him over Martí's credentials, pretending he did not understand the language. He assured Martí only that he had found the will to revolution in every section, and that he had made commitments with every genuine separatist on the Island, from Juan Gualberto in Havana to Guillermón in Santiago. Martí was quick to make use of these contacts.

Having completed the weaving of the net, it was now essential to speed up the accumulation of supplies for war. The revolution needed money. In Key West, Teodoro Pérez suggested a lottery. Martí, bowing to the practical, overcame his repugnance to this means

> "which will no doubt be rejected in our organized Homeland because of the weakness it creates in the character of man to rely on a source of well-being other than his own effort."

Sacrifice must be made a habit; the systematic continuity of emigré contributions must be maintained. Since people tire of giving more quickly than of anything else, he frequently visited the various colonies to stimulate their enthusiasm for war. At night he might go to sleep as a guest of the Carrillos in Bath Beach; and his hosts on awakening would find that he had taken a train for Philadelphia, Chicago . . . or Ocala, Florida, near which was Martí City, founded by a hundred or more Cubans in his honor.

On each trip his language and his personal tact were called upon again to overcome the saturation of local effort and to combat intrigues. It was not all patriotic unity around him. The Spanish Embassy and the Island Government had planted agents in all the colonies who busily plotted subtle treacheries among the exiles.

One day when Martí entered a factory in Tampa with Ramón Rivero, the workers remained seated and silent, contrary to custom. A muttered "Here comes the bandit" was heard. Paulina Pedroso, who had crossed the street behind Martí, jumped up on the rostrum:

> "Gentleman: If any of you is afraid to give his money or go to the savannahs to fight, let him give me his pants and I'll give him my petticoat!"

The building shook with laughter and applause. Martí embraced her and from the "reader's" tiny rostrum he spoke straight to their hearts. When he had finished, the skeptical glances had vanished. Faces were flushed with excitement and enthusiasm. That afternoon there was trouble in the factory with "traitors."

On one occasion mercenary enmity became more treacherous and determined. Since there was too much activity at Rubiera's inn, Martí had chosen, on one of his visits, to stay at a small, isolated house on the same street. Two Cubans among the many who constantly sought to assist him —one white and one colored—offered to serve him at his refuge. After much pleading, Martí accepted them as helpers. One afternoon he happened to be alone in the house and, worn out by speeches and travel, he helped himself to a small glass of *coca de Mariani* wine, which he ordinarily took in such case. On touching the glass to his lips he found the taste peculiar. With instant intuition he spat out the little he had sipped.

When Dr Barbarrosa—who in Tampa watched over the Maestro's health—arrived to visit him, he found Martí sunk in an armchair, his face thoughtful and sad. Anxious to have his suspicion disproved, Martí told the doctor what had just happened. Barbarrosa smelled the liquor, tasted it with caution and frowned.

"Yes, I think so . . . acid. Let me have it analyzed."

While the doctor was stowing the bottle away in the inside pocket of his frock coat, Martí took him by the arm and, gazing at him intently, said: "About this, my friend, if it is true, not one single word!"

But secrets are sometimes revealed by the very discretion taken to hide them. Dr Barbarrosa's unexplained insistence that Martí move immediately and the fact that the two "helpers" had suddenly disappeared, stirred Paulina's intuition. She arrived at the house in Martí's absence and swept out with all El Maestro's possessions, astonished at finding more books than clothes in his suitcase. Martí found himself installed at once in the home of the Negro couple.

From that moment the little house opposite Martínez Ibor's factory became a place of jubilee. Ruperto affixed a flagpole to the gable of the house and whenever Martí was at home the flag of the budding Republic fluttered from it. Evenings, the Cubans formed groups in the street to watch El Maestro through the windows. The highest windows, those of Martí's room, remained lighted until late at night; at times, in the silence, the scratching of his pen could be heard. Anyone attempting to enter the room would have found Ruperto lying in the hall, across the doorway.

After dark, late one afternoon, one of the missing assistants —the white—appeared at the house. He came trembling, repentant. Ruperto sprang to rush at him. Martí held him back and, throwing his arm about the visitor, closed himself in the room with him. After some time the fellow left, eyes reddened, his head held higher. When he had gone, Ruperto reproached Martí for his confidence.

"That man," Martí answered, "will be one of the first to fire shots in Cuba."

(This prediction was fulfilled. Two years later, both of those men were members of one of the first expeditions. The one Martí had embraced won a major's rank in the field.)

In *Patria,* Martí's first article after the trip during which he almost drank the cup of treachery was to proclaim that the fortress of the Cuban ideal did not have "one crevice through which a single criminal might pass." The spirit of construction, he added, "prevails over the spirit of destruction, which, by human law, always blocks the road."

He had succeeded in arranging for the tobacco workers to contribute one day's earnings each week—a matter of about two dollars and a half per man. On "Cuba's Day" they doubled the contribution. By this and other less continuous means he was successful in raising organizational expenses and in providing a fund of twelve thousand dollars. A little more and he would be able to acquire military stores for the initial expeditions, which did not have to be numerous nor in force: What was necessary "is that the first assault force on the Island must be invincible."

Thus, in March 1893, he writes to his well-to-do friends —Eduardo Gato, Carlos Recio, Manuel Barranco, Teodoro Pérez—considering "the era of preparation closed," and inviting them to be decisively generous. Martí's plan was "to fall on Cuba with the hot weather." Public opinion in the Island was at a critical juncture. December had produced in Spain the final replacement of Cánovas by Sagasta; and the Overseas Ministry was given to a liberal of new stamp, Antonio Maura, to whom the desire for a generous solution of the

Cuban problem had been attributed. This hope now brought the autonomists out of their retirement, but not without stating with some defiance, at their first meeting, the alternatives: autonomy or independence.

Martí accurately judged how far the Spanish concessions would go, since they were fundamentally limited by the competition between Peninsular and Cuban interests. But he was afraid that the new illusion might rein in the revolutionary spirit now stirring in the heart of the Island, or that, paradoxically, it would make the spirit of rebellion a runaway. The Spaniards did everything possible to provoke a semblance of rebellion which, nipped in the bud, would make the propaganda of the Revolutionary Party, which had become more and more respected in Cuba, seem ridiculous. It was even noised about that Martí was going to launch an expedition, headed by himself, against the Island. The Delegate denied such stories, reiterating the Party's solemn obligation before conscience and history "not thoughtlessly to precipitate a war in Cuba . . . nor to rush the country to ill-timed and uncoördinated activity."

Nevertheless, three weeks later events seemed to give him the lie. Cables from Madrid and Havana stated that in the vicinity of Holguín at a place named Purnio, a revolutionary movement had broken out, headed by the Sartorius brothers, obliging the captain-general, Rodríguez Arias, to declare the province of Santiago de Cuba in a state of siege.

Feeling among the exiles ran tremendously high. Martí, who had just been unanimously reëlected Delegate and was then in the South, was surprised by the turn of events. The Key was a delirium of warlike enthusiasm. At Teodoro Pérez's house, a large scarf whereon the names "Sartorius-Martí" were intertwined was displayed between Cuban flags.

Only Martí kept calm. Vexed by this beginning, about which he was not consulted, he was ready nevertheless to assist it if it showed sufficient strength. But from Cuba he was warned that the rising was not important and that it was even questionable in its political intentions. Within a few days after taking the field Manuel and Ricardo Sartorius, with about thirty men, asked for an amnesty. Havana recovered its frivolous tranquillity and was making ready to receive the Princess Eulalia with great pomp. . . . From his sickbed at the Key, Martí then issued his "Purnio Declaration."

"A vigorous censor of every partial and incomplete rebellion," the Revolutionary Party offered Cuba "what it had prepared for the Revolution: The Country will decide if, having this opportunity to be free, she will reject it and continue to be enslaved."

Enthusiasm died down. At the Key, Martí could encourage the disappointed and was able to raise ten thosuand dollars for the real war as a result of the incident. But New York was another story. There, the feeling of ridicule found consolation in acrimony. There were some who insisted on imputing to Martí the responsibility for the frustrated uprising. Had he not been in touch with the Sartorius brothers for some time?

To erase this sullen impression Martí called a meeting at Hardmann Hall. Gonzalo de Quesada arrived that night with the new Consul General of Colombia, the Nicaraguan Rubén Darío, a poet who was already achieving Hispanic fame. Martí stepped forward to meet him with only one word: "Son!" And he had him seated in the presidential chair. His sad, Indian idol face lighted up when Martí introduced into the austere and polemic preamble of his speech a very beautiful allusion to Nicaragua's musical poet. One day Darío was to recall:

> "The applause was enthusiastic. Martí took advantage of the instant to justify and defend himself against the clever accusations and, since he had already won over the audi-

ence and delivered on that occasion one of the most beautiful speeches of his life, his success was complete, and that audience, previously hostile, applauded him long and loudly."

On leaving that night with Darío, El Maestro was greeted by a Negro workman who handed him "a small memento"—a silver pencil case.

"See," said Martí, "the humble are the ones who most realize what I endure and contend with in struggling for the liberty of my country."

They went on to Carmita's house where she prepared chocolate for them. The great poet was to remember:

"There I listened to his conversation for a long time. Never have I met, even in Castelar, so admirable a conversationalist. He was gracious and friendly, endowed with a prodigious memory, and agile and quick to quote, to recollect, to give facts, and to create pictures. I spent unforgettable moments with him; then I took my leave. He had to go to Tampa that same night for the purpose of arranging I know not what vital matters of organization . . ."

Martí actually did not absent himself for long from his base of operations, his principal source of "purses and souls." But since Maceo was not a prolific letter-writer and it was not wise to confide certain matters to letters, he undertook a trip to Costa Rica at the end of May.

His principal objective was a matter of delicacy. When the plan of '84 failed, relations between Gómez and Maceo became strained. A certain reticence in Maceo's letters permitted the inference that he was not in accord with the choice of the Dominican as Commander-in-Chief. Martí would have to use every ounce of tact. Before he left for Costa Rica he notified Maceo of his coming and praised his María highly—"the most prudent and zealous guardian that your good fortune was ever able to give you." And he added, "Now I shall again see one of the women who have most moved my heart: your mother."

On passing through Santo Domingo he visited Gómez at "La Reforma" and suggested the general outline of the invasion, which he had been developing, in such a way that it appeared to be the General's own. . . . The Old Man gazed at him steadily through his glasses, brusquely brushed his mustache with the back of his hand and uttered grunts of approval.

Martí went on towards the Gulf. From the ship, by letter, he kept watch over, and guided, Sotero, Quesada, Guerra.

In Costa Rica, the twofold admiration for the writer and the patriot brought him a fervent welcome. Political exiles from almost all of the South American countries were there in numbers: "pamphleteers," orators, political leaders, literati. Martí delivered a lecture in the Lawyers' Society, embodying for those men a romantic combination of poet and leader. In the lecture a concept was emphasized which Martí had never greatly discussed in the North: The cause of Cuba was not an isolated cause; it was the cause of all America. He urged that Cuba and Puerto Rico be free so that they could strengthen

> "the security, independence and definitive character of the Hispano-American family on the continent where English-speaking neighbors covet the key to the Antilles, and with it to lock the whole of the North to the Isthmus and to push later with all this weight towards the South. If our America wants liberty, let her help free Cuba and Puerto Rico."

Costa Rican lawyers must have found these views rather fantastic. Maceo, who hated the United States, agreed with Martí. The rest of the Cubans listened with rapture to their orator.

Costa Rica was filled with Cubans at the time. When Maceo had settled in the country, after his brush with Polavieja, the Government had granted him lands and funds to establish a colony on the Atlantic coast. Needless to say, Maceo filled it with Cubans. The Spanish Government protested that it was dangerously close to Cuba and the colony had to be moved to Nicoy on the Pacific. But Maceo's prestige in the country grew as a result of the incident. Now, with his brothers José and Tomás, with Flor Crombet, Cebreco, Duverger and fifty other veterans, the inactive military chieftain was the nightmare of the Spanish colony, which constantly spied on him.

Martí did not have to resort to oratory to stir those warriors; all he had to do was to indicate a definite course of action without wounding the over-sensitive feelings of the great colored general. Biting his mustache, Maceo listened to Martí's thoughts about the traditional leadership of Gómez, about the "recent election by his former companions," about brotherhood in glory. . . .

At the end of a week Martí sailed for New York. He informed Gómez that Maceo had accepted "the part of the task that you believe natural for him" . . . An expedition would leave Costa Rica with the Nicoy settlers. They would supply men and munitions; the Party, a ship and money. Moreover, Maceo had obligated himself to prepare the organization of Oriente, where he enjoyed high prestige, to bring it in line with the rest of the Island.

With the intelligence arriving from Cuba to give assurances of unanimous readiness in "the country," the Delegate found a new obstacle. Maura, of the Spanish Overseas Ministry, had presented a reform bill to the Cortes, proposing provincial representation for Cuba with powers of administration and petition. It was not by any means a lavish grant of liberties and even under the cloak of the projected reform Romero Robledo's very burdensome taxes and a crushing tributary budget were kept intact. But Maura's plan represented at least the present abandonment of the old principle of "assimilation" and again the hopes of the timid and the evolutionary glowed in the Island.

Martí believed with conviction that the plan would never be realized. "You do not know the Spaniards," he answered Maceo and Crombet, who, spurred on by Trujillo, had written to investigate his reaction to this news. On the other hand he did not want to give time for the empty promises to demoralize the independence movement all over again. So he speeded up the conspiracy as much as he possibly could. Vacationists returning to Havana told about a thin, nervously energetic man in a black suit and worn shoes who ran up and down the stairs of the New York Elevated like a squirrel, carrying a bundle of papers, always, under his arm, at times reading even on the sidewalk. They spoke of his intent gaze, his high cheek bones almost ready to pierce the skin of his lean face, his livid coloring. "Martí is a madman," some of them declared.

But the madman knew what he was doing. He would hold interviews in a hotel lobby with munitions salesmen. He would then go to another hotel to meet with recent arrivals from Oriente—Castillo Duany and Portuondo, or with Dr Pedro Betancourt, spokesman for Matanzas. He would pass by Barranco's house to pick up the latest letter in code from Juan Gualberto. On the composing table in the *Patria* printing office he corrected proofs of the next issue, adding perhaps some concise, cautionary item. If it were Saturday, he himself would help Quesada, Sotero, Figueroa and Iznaga to wrap papers and carry the bundles to the post-office. A hurried look at his watch would remind him of a secret interview on the East River with a broker for maritime equipment, or to take the ferry for a train to Central Valley for a conference with Estrada Palma. . . . Sometimes he stopped for a moment to take stock and sighed aloud. "To act is always to suffer," he wrote Poyo. To act is agony.

His letters to those aides became every day more charged with the immediacy of action. In July, *El Yara* indiscreetly published a private circular in which the Delegate had stated: "Everything is done which should at this time be done. Everything which should be settled, is settled." Now it depended only upon what General Gómez decided in the way of military action. Martí had taken great care that the Old Man—whose irritability he knew—should not feel his jurisdiction infringed upon in matters strictly military. This considerateness delayed action. Gómez "does not seem to be abreast of the true situation on the Island."

In the autumn unfavorable circumstances developed. A financial panic in the United States affected the tobacco industry of the South to such an extent that many firms closed their factories, depriving a large number of Cubans of a means of livelihood. The Spanish Consul took advantage of the situation to demoralize them, offering to repatriate the unemployed gratis: so many workers less at the Key! The exiles of Tampa answered him in a vigorous manifesto. Martí went there to help, not without first going to Señora de Baralt to ask what would be appropriate to take as a gift to the little daughter of a tobacco worker.

Poverty "put on its last smile" to receive him. Martí knew that want was causing discord to grow between white and colored Cubans, and the first thing he did on reaching Tampa was to walk with Paulina Pedroso arm-in-arm through the streets of the city. He encouraged and united them again and returned to New York.

In the first days of November word reached New York

that another rising had taken place in Cuba, at Lajas and Ranchuelo. Warned by the experience of Purnio, the emigrés restrained themselves. As a precaution Martí warned Gómez by cable. The newspaper *Cuba* of Tampa published a telegram of warning and caution from the Delegate which, due to errors made in the telegraph office, could be interpreted as though the Party endorsed the action.

The only definite fact to be learned was that the rising appeared to be led by a minor military leader from Las Villas: Federico de Zayas, whose impatience Martí had restrained a month earlier, obtaining his "formal promise not to start a revolt until he received definite orders." Martí did not know that part of their correspondence had been intercepted by Insular authorities, but he suspected that de Zayas, Esquerra and his companions had been the victims of a false order. It was promptly learned that the new fire had been quenched with blood.

Patria declared that the Party had seen "with indignant silence" those trusted and generous men taken by the net of the "assimilationists." But *El Porvenir*, in an article entitled "The Temple of Janus" insinuated that the Delegate himself kept two exits ready, depending on whether the initiatives on the Island prospered or not. . . . Martí swallowed the bitter pill. He knew his own truth. And he knew that "from the isolation of truth one emerges into respect in due season."

A few weeks later the latest number of *Hojas Literarias* [Literary Pages] better known as "fire-brand sheets" arrived from Havana. In it Manuel Sanguily pointed out that the reformists and autonomists themselves "and perhaps those who are neither one nor the other" attributed the abortive rising at Lajas "to intrigues of the reactionaries designed to hinder the Maura reforms"—which the Union Constitucional considered a "wretched project."

In the "Cave of Covadonga"—as Serafín nicknamed a certain bookshop in New York where the backbiting gossips met—defamation of El Maestro went on for a long time. But the emigré masses were with him. When he returned from a trip to the colonies in the South unharmed by plots, his joy was not of the kind one finds in little agitators, but that of a statesman who has gotten the feel of his substance, the soul of a nation.

> "There is in me now such pride for my country that I cannot describe it to you, lest it seem like flattery. For her honor I live; I would die of her dishonor. What does it matter if, like the mason, we see on our working clothes some splashes of lime or mud? We, like the mason, on taking off our working clothes can say: We have built something!"

Chapter Twenty-eight

THE FERNANDINA PLAN

THE CHRISTMAS HOLIDAYS seemed to be decisive. With proofs of the Island's impatience, Gómez hurried to put his shoulder to the work of organizing the expedition which he himself was to lead with his people from Santo Domingo. At the year's end a secret agent brought Martí, for his distribution, military orders for preparedness.

But 1894 was born under ominous signs. When tobacco factories at the Key, closed by the financial panic, reopened, a great many of the workers found themselves replaced by Spaniards imported from the Island, their transportation provided free by the Spanish Government, their entry a violation of the immigration laws. The community called a strike. The manufacturers threatened to move the industry to Tampa, which would have made Key West a ghost town. To ward off this danger, the local authorities and business men, at a meeting where the Cubans were denounced as anarchists, decided to bring in more Spanish cigar-makers from Havana.

Naturally, the controversy assumed political aspects. The Cubans were for reviving the old "Big Stick" organization,[1] whose members years before had religiously gone to the dock, each armed with a cudgel for the Spanish "ducks" who dared to set foot on shore at the Key. But this time the strikebreakers were brought in under the protection of guns, and two Cubans who picketed in protest at their entry were jailed. Martín Herrera, founder of the San Carlos Club, indignantly proposed a general exodus of the colony. An appeal was made by telegraph to Martí, who was then in

[1] *La Tranca.*

Tampa. He decided to rush to the Key and summoned Horatio Rubens, a young New York lawyer with whom he had become friendly at City College in New York.

Rubens persuaded Martí not to go to Key West. He must not expose himself in such a way that advantage would be taken of the circumstances to discredit the cause he represented—or worse. Martí had doubted, understood, and kept away. But now in New York he did everything in his power to help the victimized Cubans.

For the revolution the situation at the Key was a calamity. More than eight hundred Cubans were stranded without means of support. Contributions to the patriot cause from Key West were out of the question; the tiny margin of savings was pitifully inadequate to take care of local need. And this, at the moment of greatest economic urgency! While Rubens was making efforts to repair the damage, appealing to Samuel Gompers, head of the cigar-makers union, and taking legal steps to have the Spanish strikebreakers returned, Martí drew some strength from weakness. Indignant at the "Caesar-like and rapacious nature" growing stronger in the United States with luxury and economic conquest, he felt that lamentation and criticism were unavailing; he profited from the adverse situation to point out that since Cubans had no security even in the land of liberty, they ought more than ever to create a free land for themselves. Let that be their New Year's resolution!

In Cuba, the situation was equally difficult and confused. Although the risings at Purnio and Lajas were being cited to show how little revolutionary appetite there was, the Government was very far from being at ease. Scenting danger, it incited discord, harassed separatists to the point of arming themselves, and even arrested Guillermón Moncada in Oriente. Martí saw that it had become necessary to "fall on the Island before the Government could fall on the revolution."

He set in motion the amalgamation of the war funds accumulated in the several clubs. He arranged for the enlistment of military contingents. He checked final agreements with the provincial leaders and with Juan Gualberto in Havana. He worked out techniques for smuggling arms, using a thousand stratagems. To frustrate the espionage of Spanish agents he had to use extreme precaution, creating a public impression that the revoluition was something for a vague future, and cloaking feverish movement with apparent inactivity.

Early in May one of Madrid's blunders—of the sort Martí could always count on—ended the vacillating attitudes in Cuba. In the course of a factional fight within Sagasta's cabinet, Maura was ousted from the Overseas Ministry and supplanted by the assimilationist Becerra, which meant the end of the heralded reforms. In Cuba those favoring status quo breathed freely again. The autonomist liberals protested loudly and the Government countered in violent fashion. Disappointment and disgust were apparent throughout the Island. Martí smiled. "Repression will touch off the explosion." What was Gómez waiting for?

With the caution of an old warrior, the General wanted to be certain of his positions and forces. It was very important for him to know, before invading, what would be the attitude of Camagüey, where the Marqués de Santa Lucía, who was representing it, seemed undecided. Also, the cause had just had an inexplicable set-back in Puerto Principe with the seizure of smuggled weapons which Enrique Loynaz—taking advantage of his position as secretary of the street railways—had brought in in a shipment of rolling stock, by arrangement with Martí. Loynaz had barely been able to escape to New York, miraculously enough. This episode reflected on the quality of the conspirators in that central city, through whose indolence the contraband was discovered; but Martí could not permit himself to express his disappointment and anger. "The failure," he wrote, "will at least serve to show the Island and the emigrés the reality of the work."

From Costa Rica Maceo—more impetuous in temperament than Gómez—was urging haste, although he set conditions. And Betancourt from Matanzas. And Carrillo from Santa Clara. And others from Oriente and Havana. . . . As the center of this nervous system, Martí received stimuli from all; in turn he goaded the parsimonious, curbed blind impetuosity, cleared up suspicions. His correspondence revealed the anguished haste and the tremendous energy of those months. The need for saying much quickly lent to his writing a style of dramatic compression. Tense phrases, taut as a bow-string, tried to communicate his own precision to the rest, and at the same time not reveal too much. He appealed more than ever to faith.

He did not allow for a moment the means of action to becloud the great ends of the republican ideal. When the highwayman, Manuel García—who, making good his title as "King of the fields of Cuba," was keeping the authorities of the Island in check—offered to contribute ten thousand dollars to the revolutionary treasury, Martí declined the offer. The Republic, he insisted, must be born clean from the roots. And as for talk about future white or future Negro supremacy, the struggle was for greater human dignity in Cuba, not to create a national, a racial or a class consciousness. "Political parties are nothing if they are not the expression of social conditions."

In these days of continuous self-denial, in which he was beset by the double-dealings of jealousy, cowardice and egotism, the presence of his boyhood friend, Fermín Valdés Domínguez, was a great consolation. Martí did not have to ask him to take him on faith. With Fermín he could be understood without words. And when Fermín went to Key West to await the great hour, he became Martí's spiritual deputy. There he was to receive Martí's more intimate revelations:

> "there is not a nerve in me that is not a harp-string of sorrow: I cannot move my arms from so much typing and moving and packing . . . and what hard work it is to be intelligent and sincere—and to be energetic and good-tempered—and to be all this in solitude and sorrow! I think I have only seen Carmita once since you went away."

But when sorrow overflowed its bounds, he curbed it stoically.

> "Undeserved pain is sweet. It tightens the throat a little, but sheds light within. . . . Steel yourself by doing good, which is now for us the only way to live: to serve, watch and forgive."

In April General Gómez had come North "to check over everything personally" and to decide final details which could not be confided to paper. Accompanying him was his son, Panchito, a resolute young man in whom Martí sensed the stuff of heroes.

In the eyes of enthusiastic exiles, the visible unity of these two men, the war-seasoned Máximo Gómez, the "Old Chinaman" as he was fondly called, scanty of word and uncomfortable in stiff collar and frock coat, and Martí, tense, nervously active, talkative—was an indication that the hour was at hand. Martí had told Fermín that one of the objects of the reunion was "to remove the last obstacles yesterday's revolution might oppose against today's." And it was not a difficult task so far as Gómez was concerned. The Old Man was a big child and Martí had learned how to find the tenderness in him behind the gruff mask.

One afternoon he took Gómez to Barnum's great circus, and that same night they worked out the general plan of the invasion.

> "Here is the principal feature," Gómez noted in his diary. "When the decisive moment arrives, a nameless ship will arrive at a known destination on this Island, cautiously chosen, to pick me up, and at least two hundred others, Cubans and Dominicans, and carry us to the lands we propose to set free."

But this "principal feature" was not all. Serafín Sánchez and Roloff would also lead an expedition from the coast of Florida. For both tasks men were ready, arms purchased and two ships chartered. Since Gómez was to land in the south of Camagüey, there remained the problem of Oriente, whose contingents were to be increased by the forces of Maceo, Flor Crombet and their people, coming from Costa Rica.

This phase of the campaign was the only thing remaining to be settled in detail. Relations between Maceo and Gómez were still rather too formal. And what the former's plans of attack were had to be determined. In Central Valley it was decided that Martí should go himself to confer with him. Panchito Gómez was to go along as living testimony of the solidarity of the old and new pines.

The trip might also serve, perhaps, to raise new funds for the revolution. Money was needed above all. Although Rubens had succeeded in having Washington order the return of the imported workers to Cuba, the Key West feud had ended sourly, with an exodus of Cubans to Tampa; confusion in the industry had left the plan for war-chest collections badly weakened. Martí had to knock once more at the doors of the rich before leaving for Central America. His letters drummed out persuasion with an accent so dramatic it would have seemed extreme if it had not been so profoundly sincere—and if later events had not tested it and proved Martí was right.

> "I am going to die, if indeed, any life worth mentioning still remains to me. They will kill me with bullets or with some evil deed. But I still have the pleasure of knowing that men like you have loved me. I do not know how to say goodbye to you. Help me now as if you were never to see me again."

Lately his old sense of death had become intensified in an insistent feeling of its imminence. But to his mother he wrote, none the less:

> "My life is like that of a glowing carbon filament that burns to light the darkness. I feel that my struggle will never cease. The private man is dead and beyond all resurrection; for that, a real home is essential; therein is the only human happiness or the root of all happiness, and it is an impossibility for me. But the vigilant and compassionate man still lives in me, like a skeleton come forth from the grave; and I know that he can expect nothing but combat and sorrows in the struggles between men, in which it is necessary to take part to console them and to help them better themselves. Death or solitude will be my only reward."

At the beginning of July Martí was on the way back. He had stayed just a few hours in Panama, in San José de Costa Rica, in Jamaica, leaving new clubs behind him to fatten the treasury, and having defined the strategy of Maceo and his men.

There was no rest for him. He took advantage of the interval between his report to Gómez and the latter's completion of plans for a quick trip to Mexico. He had always believed he could obtain assistance there, where he had so many friends. And, besides, these trips afield kept the Spanish spies guessing; they watched him like a hawk.

What a feeling of youth renewed he had when he saw old places, old friends, again: Manuel Mercado, Peón y Contreras, Justo Sierra . . . celebrities now! *El Universal* greeted him generously: "He no longer belongs to Cuba; he belongs to America." Justo Sierra who, in the shadow of Porfirio Díaz, had lost his old fieriness, tried to persuade him to stay in Mexico and devote himself to literature. Martí answered him in such a way that the illustrious Mexican hugged him excitedly and said, "Go, go make Cuba free!"

In the "shadowy groves" of Chapultepec which long ago had seen his romantic walks and talks with Rosario, new writers such as Gutiérrez Najéra and Urbina listened to him enraptured. The Indian poet wrote: "I was astonished to find in him at times a Christlike silhouette. His attitudes were like those of the Sermon on the Mount." . . . On the eve of his departure from Vera Cruz, Peón y Contreras went to find him at an old convent beneath whose arches he had hypnotized his Cuban listeners with a talk both epic and mystic.

The final months of 1894 had, indeed, something of a *Via Dolorosa* about them. When he thought everything was ready and that there was nothing left but "to proceed," unexpected difficulties arose. Maceo, who wanted to mobilize his entire colony of Nicoy, with definite guarantees, asked for more money than could be supplied from the slim treasury. From a money standpoint the trip to Mexico had not been very profitable, and the Delegation now had to provide for the simultaneous distribution of weapons throughout the whole of Cuba. Couldn't Maceo manage to get along with the same amount Gómez had had to work with? How could anyone say that he needed more when he had less to prepare? . . . And again Martí's requests to the rich were poignant:

> "I need every moment to synchronize the work from outside with that within the country. Will I have to throw myself out into these streets, worn out and sick unto death, selling by my desperate begging our secret hour, when you through this great favor can furnish me the means to meet every demand with ease and to cloak my movements with secrecy and serenity? I have lived like an unhappy dog, but I do not complain for myself, since I began this work of salvation; and you who see it all, who know it all, who love Cuba, who see me suffer, will you give me these moments—perhaps the last of my life—of glory and breath, or will you leave me alone in sorrow and responsibility, surrounded by men who have already done everything they possibly can, crawling and begging, in order to save your Motherland, praying in vain, scratching the ground like a dog for a bone?"

The recipient of this letter, Eduardo Gato, complained only of the overwrought tone of the request. His donation arrived just in time; they were already becoming restless in Cuba and certain isolated rash adventures jeopardized the plan. At last, it seemed that the assault on the Island would be possible about the middle of October.

Fearful of his own enthusiasm, Martí abstained from the patriotic anniversary celebration. He was "filled with the great hour," filled with new pleasure and anguish. In the Carrillo home, in New York, one of the girls found him forlornly sitting in the living-room, his overcoat thrown over his shoulder in characteristic fashion, with empty sleeves dangling. The girl was frightened on seeing his wide-open, staring eyes. . . . He spent one of those last nights at the home of a friend and his friend was awakened in the morning by Martí's wild sobbing:

"War! War! How much necessary sorrow we have to bring to Cuba!"

Gómez's final orders took their time. With the delay, doubt again raised its ugly mask. Martí bore in silence the blame for the General's caution. His own friends in the South reproached him for the delay which was consuming Martí himself. Protests arrived from the Island. Slander was rampant in New York. He suffered and kept silent: "Although they rush to devour my entrails I shall pull them out in my fist triumphant." He knew that he was spied upon. The Island Government had gone to the trouble of establishing an entire family in a New York house so that, through attentions and feigned friendship, they might gain his confidence. But Carmita shielded him, watched over him and decoyed the decoys. She had been his most confidential collaborator all along; the most faithful, since she had given him encouragement when everyone else denied it to him; the most generous, because she sacrificed herself without reward and in spite of an anguishing foreboding. . . .

In his anxious vigil, Martí finished his plan to the last detail. As soon as Gomez's orders would arrive, three ships, the *Amadis*, the *Lagonda* and the *Baracoa*, were to sail from the little port of Fernandina in Florida, where he had ably arranged everything with a local lumber dealer, Mr Borden. To his own docks and in cars exclusively chartered, the weapons were to be shipped, listed as agricultural implements . . . Everything was ready. Even a partial mobilization rehearsal had been held. Trembling, Martí waited like a stage-director for the curtain to rise.

But again clouds darkened this dawn of history. Cables from Costa Rica arrived on November 12, informing him that Maceo had been gravely wounded in a fight provoked by Spaniards at a theatre exit. A few days later, in Madrid,

Abarzuza took the Overseas Ministry, with the Government creating the impression that Maura's discarded reforms would immediately be reinstated. "The promise of fear," commented Martí in *Patria.* But that promise was dangerous, and Enrique Collazo arrived almost at once from Cuba to tell Martí that the Havana underground could wait no longer: they were all of them in danger of being taken.

After the bitter clash of 1892, Martí and Collazo had exchanged letters of political friendship. It was one of fate's ironies that now the veteran of the unforgettable letter should be the one to come to Martí. His arrival in Philadelphia coincided with that of Loynaz del Castillo, expelled from Costa Rica for having shot and killed one of Maceo's assailants in the theatre scuffle. Loynaz was witness to the meeting between Martí and Collazo at the Philadelphia station.

"Martí, no one has attacked you with greater rudeness than I, nor with greater injustice . . . but now, no one loves nor admires you more than I . . ."

"Why, Collazo, what are you talking about? There are so many things we must do! You are just in time for dinner. . . ."

At last, in the first days of December, General José María [*Mayía*] Rodríguez brought in person authorization from Gómez to synchronize with Martí and Collazo—the latter as representative of the Western zone of the Island—the final instructions for the invasion and rising. The Delegates decided to arrange with Havana for the earliest date in January. The Revolution would be born with the New Year. Martí breathed more easily. "We have had to endure a great deal, but at last we are rewarded."

More than ever his energy was now condensed and distributed in electric activity. With scarcely any food but sandwiches and Mariani wine, or sleep other than that caught on trains, he worked out arrangements for the final details. Of the three ships under charter, the *Amadis* would have to leave first to pick up Maceo and his men in Costa Rica. To clear the owners, ship brokers and the crew, Martí had to resort to fiction: The ship was going to Costa Rica to pick up workers for manganese mines being developed in Eastern Cuba by a certain Mr. Mantell. Mr. Mantell's son (Manuel Mantilla, Carmita's first-born) would sail with them to give the fiction substance. Weapons would be the cargo, crated under the label of tools. And there would be money and revolvers to "make reason prevail" at the last minute when the *Amadis* was close enough to Cuba to permit Maceo and his men to reach the coast in a boat which would be ready for that purpose . . . The other two ships would sail, chartered under similar pretexts. The Revolution was too poor to purchase them outright, too poor for complete truthfulness.

And did it have to be a Cuban, and no less a Cuban than a Colonel of the Ten Years War, to wrangle over commissions and raise difficulties at this decisive moment? . . . Fernando López de Queralta was the trusted man Serafín Sánchez and Roloff selected to settle with Martí the details of the expedition, and to lead it. At the last minute Queralta refused to go under false clearances and insisted that he was able to procure a ship, as he had already done for the Honduran Marco Aurelio Soto, with warlike intent clearly declared.

Martí opposed this new idea and stated all his objections. But to the end he refused to be inflexible, to try to dominate. Queralta took him to confer "secretly" with his ship broker with whom, he said, he had already talked the matter over. The office was crowded and noisy, and Martí found himself introduced as Mr. Mantell—the same name Manuel Mantilla had used when chartering the *Lagonda* from the same broker for "commercial" purposes!

Immediately he realized the danger: the secret was out! The broker, confused, scrutinized him. Martí took advantage of the fellow's dullness and with extreme agility parried his inferences. Having saved a critical moment, he left with Queralta and angrily forced him to stick to the original plan.

In those fifteen minutes he had drunk the brine of suspicion, of his own feigning, of imminent failure. His companions knew nothing, would know nothing, of what had happened. All his secrecy had not been enough.

That evening, *Mayía*, Collazo, Queralta and Loynaz waited to have dinner with him at the Hotel Marten. On arriving, Martí hung up his coat spattered with snow, and sighed deeply. He lighted another lamp at the table and, after seating himself, sighed again.

"You know, Martí," *Mayía* said affectionately, "I do not like to hear you sigh this way. A man at the head of a people must always show himself strong. As for me," he added with the vanity of an old soldier, "they broke my kneecap in the past war and set it without medical aid and no one can say he heard a single complaint!"

"I know, General," Martí answered, "and that is one of the claims you have to love from Cubans." He paused and added, emphasizing the verbs and accenting the *s*'s in his peculiar way, "But a sigh is not a complaint nor is it weakness. . . . Haven't you been in Yucatán? Well, there are in Yucatán certain subterranean and brackish rivers; at intervals the earth opens and one can hear the noise of the river through the crevasses as it flows with its bitter waters to the sea. They are called *cenotes*. Well, that's what my sighs are!"

On the 25th, the *Amadis* sailed. The other ships were ready. Martí was able to spend Christmas Eve with his beloved ones at the Carrillo home. He arrived late and jokingly noted that he was the thirteenth at the table. The dinner was not a happy one.

And suddenly, catastrophe!

On January 10th, in New York, where he was attending to last-minute shipments of military stores, Martí was thunderstruck by a telegram announcing that the three ships with all their cargo had been seized by the United States Government. The *Lagonda* and the *Amadis* were now in Fernandina; the *Baracoa* had been stopped on her way down from Boston.

Martí rushed to Fernandina. He could not show himself because the small port was swarming with Federal agents, police and spies. His arrest would be the final blow. He discovered that Manuel Mantilla had succeeded in avoiding the primary danger of a search. Horatio Rubens, called to emergency action, filed an appeal against the Federal order. Desperate, Martí summoned Collazo, *Mayía* and Queralta to Jacksonville.

They met that night in a room at the Travellers' Hotel, where he had registered under an assumed name. Enrique Loynaz and Tomás Collazo were with him. Livid, a wild look in his eyes, he walked up and down the small room like a madman. Every little while he stopped, and lifting his arms sobbed: "I am not to blame! I am not to blame!" On seeing *Mayía* come in with a frown on his face, he threw himself into his arms.

This was the sudden, inconceivable failure of three years of strenuous work, and all that was feminine in his nature came to the surface in that instant. The visible depth of his sorrow stayed the reproaches that Collazo and Rodríguez had stored up for two months against his secret activity. Now, before that man who wept they had nothing but respect.

When Queralta and Rubens appeared in the room, the consolation of the other friends had restored him to sombre tranquillity. Everything had not been lost. Rubens hoped to save the embargoed weapons. Queralta brought the last

$1500 in the treasury and a message from his mother-in-law offering to advance the necessary bond money. But Martí was still overwhelmed. He paced the room incessantly, thinking out loud. What will the General think? What will they say in Cuba? Would they see at least that all of it, all that work they had done for three years, so many assurances and promises, had not been a farce? Though the work was tremendous, he had wanted to entrust vital matters to no one, in order to give the least possible opportunity for indiscretion. He had preferred to have himself considered as authoritative, self-centered, ambitious. . . . Only Mantilla, who was like a son to him, had known all his secret plans—and Queralta.

Queralta! . . . Now, at once, he saw clearly the twisted tangent of cowardice, or of betrayal! in all its details. That dispute of Queralta's over commissions at a time for sacrifices. Queralta's insistence upon his own methods. That matter of taking him under the cloak of "secrecy and previous agreement" to brokers who already knew the plan under another aspect and who were the very representatives—only Queralta knew this!—of the owner of one of the ships. But if that suspicion could be overcome, there were certain later careless oversights of the Colonel himself: the shipment of arms for which he was responsible shipped, not by the specific chartered freight car, nor with bills of lading directed to the docks reserved by Borden, but shipped publicly and with the cartridge cases poorly sealed and marked "Military Goods." . . . Wasn't it more than chance that one of them should have opened right in the Cortlandt Street Station, where any spy even slightly observant could see it? But how could he have possibly suspected a man of the Ten Years War whom these good men, Serafín Sánchez and Roloff, had sent to him without any reservation?

With all the bitterness of failure he had to drink this poison, too, at the last minute. He thought he had made an invulnerable shield of his faith. He had been wounded under the shield.

For a long while he remained in deep silence, with his chin sunk on his chest. Finally he lifted his face, filled with a new light. He would triumphantly hold his entrails in his fist.

Chapter Twenty-nine

"CUBA LIBRE"

EVADING THE VIGILANCE of the secret police who had searched for him in every Cuban home in Jacksonville, Martí and his companions succeeded in escaping to New York.

He hid himself at first at Quesada's. Every friendly attention consoled him there, and especially reports of the reactions to the calamity in the South and in New York. The general reaction had been astonishment. And in the United States, exhilarating astonishment.

Only a few intimate co-workers had been in on the secret of Martí's work. The mass of emigrés knew nothing beyond the vague generalities released by the Delegate and *Patria* aiming to have them regarded as substantial information. Due to such generalization there were always those who lost no chance to insinuate that Martí's only revolutionary work consisted of making speeches and asking for money. But now, in the dramatic light of disaster, the exiles discovered that Martí, with a few pennies and courage, had succeeded in achieving something so positive and so obviously difficult as to charter three ships and load them with weapons. Had it not been frustrated by disclosure, his invasion plan would have resulted in a formidable achievement: He would have set revolution free simultaneously throughout the whole Island with an irresistible momentum. The exile centers, which had so many times known deception, now recovered an awareness of their own power and possibilities. A sudden blaze of faith brighter than ever was kindled by the fiasco.

On the Island the surprise was just as great. Not even the people "in the know" had themselves suspected preparations of such magnitude. A fantasy of Martí as a "mere poet," a madman and a visionary, had been painstakingly cultivated. The Government itself had hardly seen in his campaign at first anything but an exploitation of workmen's savings. This unexpected evidence of strength alarmed the Spanish, but it still could not overcome their chronic conviction that Cubans were incapable of anything practical . . . They saw the smoke of the fire now and began to try to put out the blaze.

The predicament of the revolutionaries in Cuba was extremely dangerous. A prompt decision was necessary. Martí's first thought was to "release the Island from the obligation of coördinating its movements with those from outside, which must not cease." The possibility of an immediate joining of forces from outside with those from within having vanished, he let the Island forces decide whether, "extinguishing all fires visible," they preferred to wait for such a union or whether they would rather take to the savannahs at once. As for him, he pledged himself to open "new ways and a new effort."

This letter to Juan Gualberto was dated January 17th. Six days later, in a house on Trocadero Street in Havana, it was agreed to recommend a rising at the earliest possible date. While this resolution was being considered in Havana, Martí was writing to Maceo: "Neither you nor I will lose a man's time in complaining." What was important now was to strike while the iron was hot, to reach Cuba, no matter how. Martí offered to send him $2,000 to provide a sailing ship and arms. Maceo needed more; he expected much more, to mobilize his colony with certain assurances, but, wrote Martí, "isn't this the hour? Isn't this your spirit? . . . Aren't you the man capable of real greatness?"

Once the agreement reached at Trocadero Street was

known in New York, Martí recalled Collazo from Tampa. And on January 29th, after they both had come together with *Mayía* Rodríguez and Gonzalo de Quesada at Quesada's, Martí carefully outlined the situation. By dawn they had solemnly agreed to authorize the uprising for "the second fortnight in February and not before," leaving it to Juan Gualberto and the others in Occidente to set the actual date in agreement with the rest of the Island.

They could not wait in New York to receive decisions. Martí wanted to go immediately to confer with Gómez, to whom he had already sent a cable: "Business impossible. Wait for me." The S.S. *Atlas* was sailing the next day for Haiti.

His last hours in New York were feverish. In the revolutionary arsenal there remained sufficient military stores for three expeditions; but money was lacking. Quesada, his "spiritual son," left for the South to make an effort to collect a few hundred dollars for Juan Gualberto and Gómez. He carried letters from Martí asking a sympathizer "to pledge for your country's sake the roof that covers you"; asking the Pedrosos to sell their little house if necessary: "Don't ask questions of me. A man like me does not speak this language without reasons."

He knew he would pay them with a free country. Even in those dark moments his faith did not abandon—or even fail—him. Tampa and Key West responded with more than five thousand dollars. He had failed in one material undertaking; but the great work, the decisive work, the union of all Cubans in one single will and doctrine, had been achieved. Awareness of this restored to him his great serenity.

He left instructions with Benjamín Guerra to send Maceo the two thousand dollars as soon as he revealed his decision. Martí had received a letter from him at the last minute by which he could see that Maceo and Flor Crombet were at odds. One more thorn for him; he had just written to his faithful Serra: "Whether I am here or there, act as if I would always be watching. Do not grow weary of defending or of loving. Do not tire of loving."

He had a foreboding of the definitive nature of his trip and went to say goodbye to all of the friends who had shown him tenderness in his years of exile. The weather was very cold. He departed from the Baralts "into the frozen morning like an arrow." He had forgotten his overcoat, leaving it behind in the living-room.

With *Mayía*, Collazo and Manuel Mantilla he reached Montecristi in Santo Domingo on the 6th of February. General Gómez, brooding over Martí's mysterious and alarming cable, received them with question-marks all over his face. While Martí explained the Fernandina affair to him in minute detail, the Old Man kept fingering his white mustache, erupting frequently in muffled growls of rage. The situation greatly upset him. To attack the Island like this, in an act of desperation, was a thing madmen or children would do. But Martí understood the resiliency in that spring-steel will; Gómez ended by saying that he would go to Cuba in a row-boat if necessary.

Gómez had kept intact the money Martí had sent him. It was not enough, however, to mobilize all his people. The General remembered "Lilis," [1] now President of Santo Domingo, who in 1886 had retained possession of funds for the Cuban cause, and who now was aiding it secretly although passing for a thorough friend of Spain. *Mayía* left for the capital of the Republic while Gómez and Martí sought ways of arranging embarkation through Samaná.

These negotiations obliged them to travel through the interior of the island on horseback, carefully avoiding the eager espionage of Spanish agents. Contact with this most inner heartland of the Antilles somewhat dissipated Martí's

[1] Nickname given to President Heureaux of Santo Domingo.

melancholy. On the various stops along the road he wrote his impressions in a notebook, dedicating them to his "daughters"—Carmita Mantilla's girls. They were fugitive comments, but written in his most distilled prose and with that earthy tang, raw and fresh, found in men and things inland. With new vigor Nature taught him her age-old lesson. And the palm trees:

> In the sugar fields I felt with a son's love the wonder of the eloquent serenity of the glowing night and the palms grouped as if resting one against the other, and the stars shining on their crests. It was like a perfect and sudden cleanness, and the revelation of the universal nature of man. . . .

About the middle of February the news came that Juan Gualberto, replying to the order for the rising sent by Quesada from the Key, had cabled: "Drafts accepted," which meant "Ready."

But the Island—or at least its leaders—would not start the revolution without definite guarantees from outside. From Costa Rica more letters from Maceo had come, "complaining and still angry." Gómez himself, who now saw the impossibility of adequate forces for an assault on the Island, felt "the natural misgivings of a realist upon entering an undertaking so great." But the certainty that Serafín Sánchez and Roloff would be able to succeed in launching their expedition decided him. This would be enough for a beginning, provided that afterwards reënforcements from the North could be maintained.

There was only one man who could be depended on for this: Martí. Only his word, his tenacity, his self-denial, were capable of keeping the fires of generous enthusiasm kindled among the exiles. But Martí objected most strenuously. He had already counted on going to Cuba with Gómez.

He felt the irresistible call of his country, so near at hand. And there was, inside, the scar of the old wound inflicted by Collazo, who was now one of his companions in this critical hour, the taunt which in days gone by described him as a mere man of words; it still rankled. He knew intuitively that a people "does not accept without a certain disdain and coldness the services of one who preaches the necessity of dying and does not begin by risking his own life." Finally, he believed that his presence was just as necessary in Cuba as it was outside.

On February 25th, *Mayía* arrived from Santo Domingo City. He brought $2,000 from Lilis. And the news that on the day before, revolution had broken out in Cuba! Martí was possessed by a solemn rapture: "We have done it; it still seems like a dream." Although *Mayía's* tidings were vague and scanty, they permitted a suspicion that the war had not started with all the necessary impetus. The leaders, meeting in military council, reached a formal agreement that Martí should leave for the United States immediately. Would he set an example of indiscipline and self-will in this hour of greatest sacrifice? Martí bent his head and submitted.

That same afternoon the mail brought letters and newspapers from New York. Martí devoured them. He broke into Gómez's room, changed completely in mood, and handed him a copy of *Patria*. "Read this!"

The General asked him to read it aloud, so Martí read the news item in which *Patria* made public a telegram from Quesada to Figueredo, confirming the outbreak of the Revolution and stating that Martí, Gómez and Collazo were already in Cuba—news which, the paper said, had been received with overwhelming joy.

"I'm going!" Martí declared, radiant. And his attitude was so determined that no attempt was made now to dissuade him. When the Generals agreed, his happiness was like that of a child.

By mail, Martí kept directing the Revolution until the last moment.

The Maceo problem was serious. His last cable showed him as "decided" on sailing—provided $6,000 were sent to him for the expedition. Where would they get this amount? Could he not do with the $2,000 offered? Flor Crombet assured them from Panama that he could arrange, with even a smaller sum, for an adequate expedition. The moment did not allow too much time for coaxing, but Maceo was indispensable. Martí ordered Benjamín Guerra to hurry the delivery of money to Flor in Colón. To Maceo he wrote as delicately as possible:

> ". . . I decide that you and I leave to Flor Crombet the responsibility of attending to the expedition from there, within the means available, because if he can arrange with the sum in hand to have all of you sail from where you are, neither you nor I must deprive Cuba of the service he can render. And he will place under your orders the work which you again inform me you cannot perform in San José without a sum that is impossible. . . ."

The letter ended touching to the quick both self-respect and love of country:

> "Your patriotism, which overcomes bullets, will not allow itself to be overcome by our poverty—by our poverty, sufficient for our duty. Cuba is at war, General. When that is said, the picture is changed. For you, it is, and I know it. Let Flor, who has everything at hand, arrange things as best he can. Can the slightest obstruction come from you? From you, and Cuba at war? Such poison will not enter my heart."

Gómez supported Martí's entreaties. On the 21st, reliable news of the revolt was received; the hour was now one "of pure action." One must start out "from wherever he was, and however he could." At the same time Martí made this difficult decision, he sent to all emigré centers long, urgent letters full of guidance and doctrine. With the minute instructions he would like to send Quesada and Guerra, his two tireless associates in the Delegation, something of his own substance: "my driving and affectionate soul, my strength to entreat and unite, my sense of, and respect for, reality." He reminded the clubs in his last letters of the doctrine of the new war:

> Let the tenor of our words be, especially in public matters, not the useless clamor of fierce vengeance, which does not enter our hearts, but the honest weariness of an oppressed people who hope, through their emancipation from a government convicted of uselessness and malevolence, for a Government of their own which is capable and worthy. Let them see in us constructive Americanism and not empty bitterness. This is our war; this is the Republic we are creating.

Such was the spirit of the doctrine which was set forth in the historic Manifesto of Montecristi, signed by Martí and Gómez, March 25, 1895. More than a declaration of war, it was the outline of the Republican Constitution. In those moments in which he found himself "at the threshold of a great duty," Martí emphasized the founder's purpose and the far-reaching meaning which his words always held. It was apparent that he wanted to build indestructible foundations for the country he was setting free.

The letter he wrote Federico Henríquez y Carvajal, of Santo Domingo, associated that historical intention with a personal emotion:

I called forth war: With it my responsibility begins instead of coming to an end. For me the Country will never be a triumph, but agony and duty. Blood is now blazing. The present task is to give respect and human and lovable meaning to sacrifice, to wage a sensible and undefeatable war; if it commands me, in harmony with my only wish, to stay in it, I stay; if it commands me, against my soul, to go far from those who die as I would know how to die, I shall also have that kind of courage. . . . I shall raise the world. But my only wish would be to affix myself there, to the last tree-trunk, to the last fighter: to die in silence. For me it is now time.

To his mother, as if he wished to express what was by now a definite foreboding, he wrote: "In the anguish of your love you bewail the sacrifice of my life; and why was I born to you with a life that loves sacrifice? . . ."

Curiously enough, in ending this letter, so intimate, he signed it "J. Martí" just as he did his love letters to Rosario in his youth. . . .

Their proposed embarkation by way of Samaná having been frustrated, Gómez and Martí went through untold efforts to leave the island. They chartered a sailing ship in Montecristi; but at the last minute the crew drew back from the dangerous adventure: The coasts of Cuba were under strictest watch, and the prospect of being sent to the bottom of the sea or to the Ceuta prison in Africa was not pleasant to think about. Finally, they found a captain who agreed to take them in his own schooner provided they purchased it and paid him a large bonus besides.

General Gómez and Martí embarked with the Brigadier Francisco Borrero, Colonel Ángel Guerra, César Salas and the Dominican Negro, Marcos del Rosario. Collazo, *Mayía* and Manuel Mantilla had returned to the North on different missions. On reaching Inagua the captain of the schooner went ashore. Shortly afterwards a port officer arrived to investigate the vessel, suspecting it of carrying arms. The captain returned later to announce that all of the crew had deserted. . . . The man's behavior aroused suspicion. In the afternoon another search, more zealous than the first one, was made. It was impossible to conceal the weapons Martí had acquired with so much effort weeks before at Cape Haitien. Martí resorted to his friendly diplomacy and "won the sportsmanship" of the customs inspectors. Then he went ashore to find sailors, but he had no luck.

The situation was touch and go. If the faithless master denounced them or succeeded in sighting a Spanish gunboat, they were lost. Rising to meet the danger, Martí managed to recover from the captain the sum of money paid him for the voyage and dismissed him. But how was he to proceed without a crew?

Luckily, that afternoon a German fruit ship on the way to Cape Haitien stopped at Inagua. Thanks to the assistance of the Haitian consul they were able to get the captain—for $1,000 and other severe conditions—to agree to take them as passengers and to put them off in a boat when passing Cuba on his return voyage.

From his hiding place on the ship Martí wrote to Manana, the General's aged wife: "We are sewn to one another, Father and I, with only one heart." He comforted the abandoned wife: "The world brands us, and whether man or woman one cannot go against the brand the world puts on us." And remembering the tender and constant gaze of Gómez's daughter in Montecristi, "Tell Clemencia for me that in the spot where life is most vulnerable I wear for armor a blue band . . ." the loving memento she gave him the night of his departure.

On the 10th the fruit ship returned to Inagua. The next

day it weighed anchor and at five in the afternoon they could already make out the mountains in the south of Cuba. Martí was unable to speak.

The ship approached to within three miles of the coast. The night was dark and stormy and the captain himself hesitated to send them out into the fury of that wind and sea. But Gómez commanded: "To land." The ship's boat, with six men on board, was launched and the swell hurled it against the ship's hull. The wake made by the ship in suddenly pulling away almost capsized them. Gómez manned the rudder; Borrero acted as lookout; the others rowed desperately, with Martí at bow stroke. A heavy sea tore the rudder from the General's hand. They used an oar as tiller to keep from drifting, but the squall became stronger in the darkness and they lost their course.

They went through a long quarter-hour of despair, when everything seemed lost. Suddenly they thought they saw the blinking of small, far-away lights and they began to row towards them with new strength. The heavy rainstorm was abating. At last the moon came out and Gómez pulled out his watch: it was a few minutes past ten o'clock. Almost unexpectedly they heard the keel scraping against rocks in the bed of the sandy beach. There was a muted shout of joy in the night. Guerra, Salas and Marcos pushed the boat ashore until it grounded on the small beach which lay like a soft carpet before a steep, rough cliff. Gómez jumped ashore, knelt and kissed the ground. The good Marcos, assuming some white "witchcraft" was involved, followed his example, adding gestures of his own from some African rite. Martí, erect, gazed at the new-born stars.

They spent a good part of the night walking inland, cutting brambles and vines, by-passing marshes. "In spite of the heavy pack he was carrying," Gómez was to write in his diary, "I was able to see how radiant with pride and satisfaction Martí was because he was able to hold his own in all this with five rugged men . . ." They halted to rest on a little hillock. Gómez looked at his pocket compass. The palm trees were nodding gently. From the savannah was heard solemnly and at intervals the hissing call of the *sijú.* Martí trembled with excitement: "Let's go on, let's go on!"

They came down into a valley and noted the smell of woodsmoke, the cry of a rooster . . . a small village. Friendly people? Thoroughly tired, they stretched out on the ground to wait for the dawn. Finally they decided to knock on the door of a shack. Friendly people! The country family, somewhat suspicious at first, and then generous with attentions and coffee, informed them that the place was called El Cajobal and where they landed, Playitas.

They could no longer risk going on by themselves. A youngster guided them to a near-by cave at the edge of a clearing. There, for a few hours, they slept while waiting for an answer to the message Gómez had sent by the same guide to an old officer of the Ten Years War who lived near by. From the mouth of "the temple"—as Gómez named the cave with his faculty for colorful phrases—Martí contemplated in ecstasy the play of morning light on the wet and dark greens of the landscape.

The scout returned so late that they were unable to start on their way again until the next morning. They forded rivers, climbed steep banks, cut through thick underbrush. Martí and Gómez competed in helping each other, Martí relieving the General of his reed-covered canteen and later passing it to the guide who was rested; the Old Man taking Martí's rifle from him and carrying it with his own. "We pull one another up the steep inclines. We fall down laughing."

Late in the day they ran into Ruenes' small encampment; he leaped up with joy and amazement. The "Old Chinaman" and "Dr Martí" really there in their midst! The fifty scat-

Grover Flint

CUBAN PATRIOT SOLDIER WITH IMPROVISED RAINCOAT OF GREEN ROYAL PALM BARK

tered soldiers, some with no weapons but their rustic *machetes*, gazed at Martí with curiosity. There were among them an Asturian and a Biscayan. The Negroes smiled happily when Martí threw his arm about their shoulders in brotherly greeting. They brought him water with honey, roasted bananas, a few bitter oranges—the precious gifts of the savannah. Ruenes and the officers called Martí "President," which made him blush a little.

On the 14th, General Gómez summoned the rest of the leaders to a meeting in the depths of a glen, signalling Martí to keep away. He thought they were going to decide on some war measure without him and he was hurt. But shortly he saw Ángel Guerra running towards him, grinning from ear to ear. At the meeting of officers it had been decided, on the motion of "the Old Man," not only to recognize Martí as Delegate of the Cuban Revolutionary Party, but also to confer on him the rank of Major General of the Army of Liberation. . . . "With an embrace," he wrote, "they brought my life up to the level of their veterans' glory." The letters in which he confided this to Mantilla, Quesada and Guerra—letters written "in the shade of a palm grove" and "on a kind of table made of palm wood, held up by four crotches"—also told of his profound emotion at finding himself at last in "Cuba Libre," as the Insurgents called the territory they occupied.

> "My happiness is very great. . . . I can say that I have finally arrived at my full maturity. . . . Not until today have I felt myself to be a man. I have lived in shame, dragging the chain of my country all my life. The divine clarity of the soul lightens my body; this rest and well-being explain the faithfulness and joy with which men offer themselves to sacrifice."

Chapter Thirty

DOS RÍOS

For me it is now time.
—Martí

THROUGH FÉLIX RUENES they had received the great news: A few days earlier than they, and after similar adventures, Maceo, Flor Crombet, Cebreco and twenty other companions had succeeded in landing near Duaba from an English schooner they had chartered in the Bahamas. According to Ruenes' information, the expeditionaries had scarcely landed when they dared to fight the Spanish garrison at Baracoa, defeating it and then heading inland towards the south. "Now they go ahead," wrote Martí, "and we proceed on foot; we will meet in time to articulate our plans for the first blows and give form and meaning to the war."

Leaving Ruenes in his zone, Gómez and Martí advanced with about thirty men, "very closely followed now by Spanish troops." Near Guantánamo, they heard the first shots of the war, and in two hours' time they ran into the forces of José Maceo, Antonio's brother, who had just fought a successful action in Arroyo Hondo. The brave, tall mulatto, who had always been very devoted to Martí, lifted him up in his arms as if he were a child. They listened to José's account, epic in its simplicity, of the dispersion of Antonio and his companions, leaving José alone to wander through the Baracoa mountains, hunted like a wild beast until he had succeeded in joining the Guantánamo forces.

That night Martí kept watch until dawn, caring for the wounded "without anything but the knowledge of how the human body is formed and having brought with him the miracle of iodine. And affection, which is also a miracle."

Another march through thick jungles and stony passes. On the 25th, in Filipinas, they received news that Masó, one of the Oriente leaders, was near by and that Antonio Maceo, his men reorganized, was operating in the Santiago area. Martí signed, with Gómez, military dispatches of greater substance and style than had ever been written in any encampment. José Maceo said of him: "He leaves happiness and the will to fight wherever he goes." In his private letters he described himself as enjoying the natural and heroic surroundings, declining the title of President, which everyone gave him, harboring a certain internal sense of grace which seemed to him a sufficient reward. "I feel pure and light; there is within me something like the peace of a child." He was anxious to get into battle. Faced with bloody incidents he steeled himself against his own tenderness. News of Flor Crombet's death brought him great grief, but he communicated the news of it with spartan sobriety: "Flor is dead: he fell from a bullet wound in his chest . . ."

These private letters and the one he wrote the *New York Herald* on May 2nd, on the state and purpose of the war, reflected an intense faith in the Revolution upon which Martínez Campos was about to fall with the biggest and best-equipped army ever sent by Europe to America.

During the first days of May they succeeded in joining Antonio Maceo's three thousand men in Carahueca. From a tobacco drying-shed that dominated the valley, Martí spoke to the turbulent and motley crowd which roasted in the sunlight and applauded him with frenzy. He was sad at not having been able to save from strict military justice, severely ordered by Gómez, a soldier convicted of rape. On the 5th, all forces pitched camp at Mejorana, almost at the gates of Santiago.

At this meeting of the three supreme leaders the course of the war was to be decided. And other, more personal matters, as well, had to be decided. Antonio Maceo's last letter showed him to be irritated at Martí. His anger dated from the time Martí had entrusted to Crombet the expedition from Costa Rica, even though charging him to place it under Maceo's orders once it was organized. . . . Perhaps this detail was not known by the General, jealous of his prestige and rank. The circumstance of his being on poor terms with Flor at that time embittered his spirit even more deeply, stirring the old dregs of '84.

What happened that morning at the meeting? The officers who, at a distance, were guarding the corner of the old sugar factory where the three leaders were conferring on the grass, were able to perceive an occasional brusque gesture by Maceo, his voice pitched higher than usual; the paternally authoritative and at last cutting voice of the "Old Man," after which the conversation calmed down; Martí's even and firm voice.

Later it became known that Martí had been chosen there as supreme chief of the Revolution; Gómez as Commander-in-Chief, while Antonio Maceo was named Chief of Oriente. The latter had argued that his troops were almost disarmed and that Martí should, without delay, go to the United States to speed war supplies and reënforcements; Martí had replied that he would not do so without at least having entered once or twice into actual combat. . . .

As for strategy, Maceo was of the opinion that the invasion of Occidente could not be achieved until a government had been established and the revolutionary forces somewhat realigned. Gómez, on the other hand, held that the Revolution, whose outbreak had been suppressed in Occidente, was "at a standstill" and what he considered most pressing was to stir the whole Island into revolt immediately, before Martínez Campos could get the 22,000 men he awaited as reënforcements from Spain. Martí supported Gómez and thus the decision was made.

The following day, while Maceo left to renew operations in the most vulnerable parts of Oriente, thus diverting the attention of the enemy, Gómez and Martí marched in the opposite direction to join Masó's forces near Manzanillo.

On May 12th they camped at Dos Ríos, where the Contramaestre adds its waters to the wide Cauto River. Fertilized by the generous waters of the Sierra Maestra, which festoon the southeastern coast, the valley bed there is richly verdant. Amid cedars and shrubs, the slender forces of Gómez bivouacked a few days, waiting for Masó. On the 17th, the General was notified that an enemy column was coming up the highway to reënforce a detachment of Spanish troops. Gómez went out to lay in ambush for them.

Martí's old ailment had been irritated by the continuous marches; now with a swelling of the groin which prevented him from moving or even arming himself, he had to remain in Bija's encampment. There, on the night of the 18th, by candle light, he wrote a letter to Manuel Mercado, his faithful Mexican friend, in which he openly revealed his political testament:

> " . . . I am now, every day, in danger of giving my life for my country, and my duty—inasmuch as I realize it and have the spirit to fulfill it—is to prevent, by the independence of Cuba, the United States from extending itself through the Antilles and with that added momentum taking over our American lands. What I have done up to now, and what I shall do, is towards this end. It has had to be done in silence and indirection because there are things which, to be achieved, must be hidden; and should they be shown for what they are, they would raise

difficulties too powerful to overcome. . . . I have lived inside the monster and know its insides—and my weapon is only the slingshot of David."

That letter, in which Martí also declared his resolve to go "to the center of the Island to lay down before the Revolution I have raised the authority given to me by the emigrés," was interrupted by the arrival of Bartolomé Masó and his men. The Manzanillo leader preferred to pitch his camp in Vuelta Grande on the other side of the Contramaestre and about a league from Dos Ríos. Martí went with him after sending word to Gómez.

On the morning of the 19th, Gómez also arrived, tired of waiting uselessly to ambush with his forty men the reported enemy column commanded by Colonel Ximénez de Sandoval. The enthusiasm of the now united forces—about 340 cavalrymen in all—in the presence of the chief leaders of the Revolution was indescribable. Gómez addressed them in his vigorous and concise language. Then Masó. Finally Martí rode forward. The sunlight bathed his pallid face and lighted his hair like a halo. "His voice," observed a witness, "smooth and melodious at the start of his speech became thunderous, like the sound of a hurricane." When he finished, the troops, fired with passion, broke into *vivas* for the "President of the Republic."

At the council of the leaders, Masó supported the motion that Martí return immediately to the United States. After luncheon, two soldiers of the advance guard Gómez had stationed on the Contramaestre brought news that there was gunfire near Dos Ríos. Gómez understood that the Spanish column had followed his trail. He did not know that Ximénez de Sandoval had captured one of the scouts he had sent out that morning in search of provisions, and that, later, the scout Chacón, sent by Martí on a similar mission, had also been taken and questioned. The Commander-in-Chief decided to advance towards the column and to await it at the Dos Ríos ranch where his cavalry could maneuver freely. "Mount!"

The troops, still excited by the speeches, hurled themselves towards the Contramaestre with such dash that for a moment Gómez thought it would be another Palo Seco.[1] The fording of the river, however, obliged the cavalry to break formation. On the other side of the river, after clambering up the bank, they fell on a small advance guard of Spaniards and dispatched them by machete, while on the gallop. Gómez observed that the column had anticipated him and had already formed its lines into squares on the small plain between the woods and patches of farmland.

He ordered Martí to stay with Masó with the rear-guard while Borrero and he advanced right and left, respectively, to encircle the enemy. When the troops were thus disposed and violent gunfire had already begun, Martí asked the young Ángel de la Guardia, one of Masó's aides, for a revolver and persuaded him, notwithstanding orders, to go with him to the front.

Epic rapture? Inexperience? Eagerness for his hour? Alone, they rode at a gallop through the smoke. On emerging in a lane of stumps and second-growth brush, flanked by tall trees on either side, they were met by a surprise volley of shots. Ángel de la Guardia fell beneath his wounded horse. On raising himself, half-blinded by the blow and the smoke, he saw Martí stretched out on the ground, a few paces away, breast and jaw stained with blood. The youth tried to carry him but could not. As soon as he ran towards his own lines to get help, the Spanish vanguard advanced under the increased fire of its own musketry.

Borrero's cavalry was hindered in maneuvering between the river and the steep bank that bordered it. Gómez tried

[1] A celebrated Cuban victory in the Ten Years War.

without success to break the strong Spanish positions. On withdrawing to organize a new charge he received the fateful news and hurled himself alone in the direction Ángel de la Guardia pointed out. He was stopped by the fierce fire of the enemy, who fell back with their prize.

While the Cubans gathered to attempt a rescue, Ximénez de Sandoval examined, unbelieving, the body which had been brought to him and which the scout Oliva assured him was that of Martí. The identification was further confirmed by a captain who had seen Martí months before in Santo Domingo. And by the scout Chacón. Under the blue, bloodstained jacket, papers left no room for doubt.

"The pupils of his eyes," Sandoval wrote, "seemed blue."

The efforts of Máximo Gómez to retake Martí's body were as hopeless as they were bold. The Spanish column, larger in number and ably officered, could protect its withdrawal by employing the natural defenses of the terrain. A bog forced Gómez to retrace his steps and when he arrived at the hovel which Sandoval had just left he was informed that the column was going on to Remanganaguas by forced march to bury Martí.

That night in the Revolutionary encampment at Las Vueltas "there was no reason to sound curfew." The light of the bivouac fires glittered on the wet cheeks of the "Old Chinaman." Someone then coined for posterity the title of veneration: "The Apostle."

In the middle of the Spanish column which had been obliged earlier to pitch camp because of a torrential downpour, the body of Martí was lowered from the guide's mule and left all night under the black sky . . . The palm trees could not be seen, but in the darkness the crickets hissed their implacable call.

On the following afternoon he was buried in the village cemetery, with its wire fences and wooden crosses, in a shallow grave. Sandoval was in a hurry to taste his victory.

When he was almost in Santiago, where he had sent the news, he received orders to return to Remanganaguas and bring Martí's body to the city, so as to remove all doubt in Havana . . . and in Florida and New York, where emigrés would soon be trying desperately to deny the news.

Badly embalmed, in a coffin made of crude boards and placed on a stretcher, Martí's body reached Santiago on May 27th. The column, which had been several times fired upon en route, opened a road for itself in the city through stern and silent crowds. After formal identification the coffin was taken to the cemetery, escorted by a large body of troops. There, Colonel Ximénez de Sandoval inquired as to whether any of the civilians present wished to speak. After a long silence he pronounced a few brief words himself:

> "Gentlemen: When *hidalgos* like ourselves wage war, hate and rancor vanish. No one inspired by humane sentiments should see in these lifeless remains an enemy. . . . Spanish soldiers fight until they die; but they treat the vanquished with consideration, and the dead with honor."

On the same day, in New York, Mariá Mantilla received the letter Martí had written to her weeks before, telling her he carried her picture over his heart as a shield against bullets.

EPILOGUE

EPILOGUE

THE SACRIFICE at Dos Ríos whipped the revolution into raging flame, like a kernel of resin dropped into a brazier, and Cuba was pervaded, as with a fragrance, by an almost mystic heroism. In vain did the Spanish Government force itself to concede the autonomy which it had been denying its colony for more than half a century; and in vain was the Island deluged with soldiers to face the new will for absolute independence. In the autumn of 1895, Gómez and Maceo, contemptuous of the *trochas*, or chains of forts, which were expected to contain the revolution in the East, smashed across Camagüey to wage the spectacular invasion of the rest of the Island. After putting the Spaniards to rout a hundred times, the fearless Antonio Maceo fell in battle, but his troops were at the gateway of Havana.

The Madrid government, with military actions checkmated, decided to snuff out the rebellion by terror and starvation, herding into the cities the outlying country populations which were, in the vast majority, friendly to the insurrectos. This measure, cruelly carried out, produced untold misery and served only, in Cuba, to win more devotees for the cause of independence, and outside Cuba—especially in the United States—to excite equally a condemnation of Spain and an admiration for the Cubans who were struggling for their freedom.

Considering North American interests in the Island menaced by the hostile attitude of the "integristas"—the Spanish and pro-Spanish factions—Washington ordered the armored battleship *Maine* to Cuba as a preventive, defensive measure. On the 15th of February, 1898, a mysterious explosion blew the *Maine* to pieces in the harbor of Havana. A great wave of indignation swept over the United States, and diplomatic tension, which had long existed between Madrid and Washington, now became hourly more taut. When Spain was willing to concede, it was too late. On April 20, 1898, the Congress of the United States passed a joint resolution declaring "that the people of the Island of Cuba are and of right ought to be independent." This amounted to a declaration of war, and war, indeed, followed like a bolt of lightning. Three months later the Spanish army yielded to the combined forces of Americans and Cubans in Santiago de Cuba, and on the 12th of August a treaty of peace was signed in Paris which declared Cuba, Puerto Rico and the Philippines independent of Spain.

Such unforeseen events could not do other than stir up in patriotic Cubans mixed feelings of jubilation and fear. For almost half a century they had been struggling for their liberty in the realm of ideas, by conspiracy, and in exile. Uncountable Cubans had died in prison or on the gallows; even more numerous were those who had seen their fortunes and prospects ruined, their families decimated or scattered to the winds. For ten long years—from '68 to '78—they had fought in the field. Though defeated, they knew that independence was a matter of time. This second war, begun in '95, evoked by Martí, had begun under better auspices; the incident of the *Maine* had added to the Cuban strength the weight of the United States. Cubans could not doubt the generous intention with which this last-minute aid was given, but what deflections might not be forced under the pressure of other, less noble, interests? And in what proportion was the generosity of the powerful to be blended with respect for the free determination of the weak, small neighbor? With the Spanish power ended in the Island, the military occupation by the United States, over the protests of patriotic Cubans, appeared to throw over the destiny of Cuba the shadows which Martí had with foreseeing earnestness wished to ward off. On May 20th, 1902, almost exactly seven years after the tragedy of Dos Ríos, the Republic for which there had been so much sacrifice was inaugurated; but the rejoicing over this realization of long-cherished hopes was dampened by the Washington imposition of the Platt Amendment, which potentially swaddled the constitution of the new nation and limited its sovereignty under the guise of protection.

Martí's ideal did not consent to mutilations or compromises. It continued to live and to give sustenance to new Cuban generations. Within the United States, also, working in favor of this ideal was the self-respect of a people who always have wanted to live up to their own greatness. In 1934, after civil strife and a vigorous upsurge of nationalistic feeling, the Platt Amendment was set aside. Cuba, now the sole mistress of her own responsibility and free will, has continued to advance, ever since, in the laborious apprenticeship of democracy, under the inspiration of Martí's ideas. Seldom has the personality and work of a man been so consubstantial with the will of a whole people.

While Cuba adheres with growing intensity to the cult of "The Apostle"—as all Cubans call Martí—the America of Iberian backgrounds has come to know more thoroughly his work as a writer, thinker and seer. It recognizes in Martí one of its highest and purest voices—the voice of a teacher for whom political liberty was only the social prerequisite for a freedom more profound: The freedom of the spirit, the sovereignty of a man in his own conscience, and the sovereignty of peoples in their own culture to live a life of moral and material independence in which they can be true to themselves and to the spirit of their own genius.